ACT
Verbal Prep Course

NATHAN
STANDRIDGE

* ACT is a registered trademark of ACT, Inc., which was not involved in the production of, and does not endorse, this book.

Additional educational titles from Nova Press (available at novapress.net):
- **ACT Math Prep Course** (402 pages)
  ACT Science Prep Course (364 pages)
- **SAT Prep Course** (628 pages)
  SAT Math Prep Course (480 pages)
  SAT Critical Reading and Writing Prep Course (350 pages)
- **GRE Prep Course** (624 pages)
  GRE Math Prep Course (528 pages)
- **GMAT Prep Course** (624 pages)
  GMAT Math Prep Course (528 pages)
  GMAT Data Sufficiency Prep Course (422 pages)
  Full Potential GMAT Sentence Correction Intensive (372 pages)
- **Master The LSAT** (560 pages, includes 2 official LSAT exams)
  Ace The LSAT Logic Games (504 pages)
- **The MCAT Physics Book** (444 pages)
  The MCAT Biology Book (416 pages)
  The MCAT Chemistry Book (428 pages)
- **Scoring Strategies for the TOEFL® iBT:** (800 pages, includes audio CD)
  Speaking and Writing Strategies for the TOEFL® iBT: (394 pages, includes audio CD)
  500 Words, Phrases, and Idioms for the TOEFL® iBT: (238 pages, includes audio CD)
  Practice Tests for the TOEFL® iBT: (292 pages, includes audio CD)
  Business Idioms in America: (220 pages)
  Americanize Your Language and Emotionalize Your Speech! (210 pages)
- **Postal Exam Book** (276 pages)
- **Law School Basics:** A Preview of Law School and Legal Reasoning (224 pages)
- **Vocabulary 4000:** The 4000 Words Essential for an Educated Vocabulary (160 pages)

Copyright © 2016 by Nova Press
Previous editions: 2015, 2014, 2013, 2012
All rights reserved.

Duplication, distribution, or data base storage of any part of this work is prohibited without prior written approval from the publisher.

ISBN-10: 1–889057–66–5
ISBN-13: 978-1–889057–66–8

ACT is a registered trademark of ACT Inc., which was not involved in the production of, and does not endorse, this book.

P. O. Box: 692023
West Hollywood, CA 90069

Phone: 1-310-275-3513
E-mail: info@novapress.net
Website: www.novapress.net

ABOUT THIS BOOK

If you don't have a pencil in your hand, get one now! Don't just read this book—write on it, study it, scrutinize it! In short, for the next four weeks, this book should be a part of your life. When you have finished the book, it should be marked-up, dog-eared, tattered and torn.

Although the ACT is a difficult test, it is a *very* learnable test. This is not to say that the ACT is beatable. There is no bag of tricks that will show you how to master it overnight. You probably have already realized this. Some books, nevertheless, offer inside stuff or tricks which they claim will enable you to beat the test. These include declaring that answer-choices B, C, or D are more likely to be correct than choices A or E. This tactic, like most of its type, does not work. The only reason it's offered is to give students the feeling that he or she is getting the inside scoop on the test.

The truth is the ACT cannot be beaten. But it can be mastered—through hard work, analytical thought, and by training yourself to think like a test writer. Many of the exercises in this book are designed to prompt you to think like a test writer.

The ACT verbal section is not easy—nor is this book. To improve your ACT verbal score, you must be willing to work; if you study hard and master the techniques in this book, your score will improve— significantly.

This book will introduce you to numerous analytic techniques that will help you immensely, not only on the ACT but in college as well. For this reason, studying for the ACT can be a rewarding and satisfying experience.

To insure that you perform at your expected level on the actual ACT, you need to develop a level of skill that is greater than what is tested on the ACT. Hence, about 10% of the problems in this book are harder than actual ACT problems.

Although the quick-fix method is not offered in this book, about 10% of the material presented here is dedicated to studying how the questions are constructed. Knowing how the problems are written and how the test writers think will give you useful insight into the problems and make them less mysterious. Moreover, familiarity with the ACT's structure will help reduce your anxiety. The more you know about this test, the less anxious you will be the day you take it.

CONTENTS

	ORIENTATION	7
Part One:	ENGLISH TEST	9
Part Two:	READING TEST	93
Part Three:	WRITING TEST	159
Part Four:	VOCABULARY	203

ORIENTATION

The Verbal Section[*] contains three parts: English Test, Reading Test, and Writing Test.

English Test

The English Test is 45 minutes long and consists of 75 multiple-choice questions. The test is designed to measure your ability to revise and edit a piece of writing. Two categories of questions appear on the test:

- **Usage/Mechanics**
    Punctuation
    Basic grammar
    Sentence structure

- **Rhetorical Skills**
    General writing style
    Organization

These subsections have their own scores: The Usage/Mechanics score is based on 40 questions, and the Rhetorical Skills score is based on 35 questions.

The English Test is always the first test given.

Reading Test

The Reading Test is 35 minutes long and consists of 40 multiple-choice questions. It's too late now to pretend that you can't read, so strap on your reading hat and get ready to read about the following subjects:

Humanities: This passage can be about music, dance, theater, art, architecture, language, ethics, literary criticism, and even philosophy.
Social Studies: The social studies passage can include sociology, anthropology, history, geography, psychology, political science, and economics.
Natural Sciences: The natural science passage can cover chemistry, biology, physics, and other physical sciences.
Prose Fiction: The fiction passage can be taken from a novel or a short story; however, don't expect to have read the passage before.

---

[*] The ACT does use the term Verbal Section. They view and grade each of the three parts of the Verbal Section separately. We are using the term Verbal Section to conveniently distinguish these sections from the Math and Science sections.

Writing Test

The Writing Test is 40 minutes long and consists of one prompt from which to write an essay. Although the Writing Test is optional, three-quarters of colleges and universities require this section of the ACT, so it might be in your best interest to take it.

The Writing Test is always the last test given.

Skipping and Guessing

Some questions on the ACT are rather hard. And since it is a time-pressured test, you may not be able to answer every question.

Often students become obsessed with a particular problem and waste valuable time trying to solve it. To get a top score, learn to cut your losses and move on. All questions are worth the same number of points, regardless of their difficulty.

There is no penalty for guessing on the ACT. So, if you skip a question or do not finish a section in time, be sure to at least mark an answer for good measure.

Check Your Work

Throughout this book, you will come across sections titled "Check Your Work." These sections are designed to shed light on tips that can help you master the ACT, so pay special attention when you see them.

Part One
ENGLISH TEST

- **INTRODUCTION**

- **PUNCTUATION**
  Commas
  Semicolons
  Colons
  Dashes
  Apostrophes
  Sentence Fragments
  Run-On Sentences

- **GRAMMAR**
  Pronouns
  Subject-Verb Agreement
  Modifiers
  Parallelism
  Verb Tense
  Diction

- **RHETORIC**
  Style
  Structure

Introduction

The English Test portion of the ACT consists of 75 multiple-choice questions and tests standard written English. The test is designed to measure your ability to revise and edit a piece of writing. Remember those composition classes you took freshmen year? When you knew how to use the subjunctive and actually cared about the differences between adjectives and adverbs? If not, the following chapter will give you an in depth refresh.

Two categories of questions appear on the English Test:

- **Usage/Mechanics**
    Punctuation
    Basic grammar
    Sentence structure

- **Rhetorical Skills**
    General writing style
    Organization

Don't worry if your grammar and punctuation is a little rusty. Just read the following section carefully, and you'll master the English Test in no time.

Punctuation

In this section, we will discuss the most commonly used punctuation marks: commas, semicolons, colons, dashes, apostrophes, and quotation marks. We will also discuss using punctuation to correct run-on sentences and sentence fragments.

Commas

When talking, we separate our ideas by pausing between them. In writing, these pauses are represented by punctuation marks. The shortest of these pauses is indicated by the comma – the most frequently used mark of punctuation in the English language.

Even though commas float around in just about every sentence, it is possible to obtain order in the midst of all this comma chaos. If you can remember a few standard rules, you'll be placing commas in their proper place in no time.

- **Rule 1** – Use a comma to separate words, phrases, or clauses in a series.

    Example:
    Will you pick up some <u>hotdogs, chips, and drinks</u> for the party tonight?

When you have three or more items in a series, the final comma before the conjunction (*and, or, nor*) is optional.

    I made the bed, swept the floor, and vacuumed the carpet.

However, you should never use a comma after the conjunction in the series.

    Incorrect:
    I made the bed, swept the floor, vacuumed the carpet, and, cleaned the bathroom.

- **Rule 2** – Use a comma to separate two or more adjectives that precede and modify the same noun.

    Example:
    It seemed like a crime to disturb the <u>beautiful, serene lake.</u>

However, when the final adjective is so closely related to the noun that the words form a single expression, no comma is necessary before the final adjective.

Before you watch TV, I want you to clean the <u>dirty, grimy kitchen sink</u>.

Don't use a comma between the final adjective and its noun.

When are we going to surf that <u>secret, beautiful</u> beach you used to talk about?

✓ <u>Check your work</u>
Look through your work for any series of words, phrases or clauses. If there are two or more of these elements, place a comma after all but the last one.

Example (without punctuation):
He thought taking a road trip would <u>help him feel rejuvenated allow him to work through his feelings</u> and <u>provide him with some much needed solitude</u>.

In the sentence above, there are three modifying clauses. Each clause modifies the verbal phrase *taking a road trip,* which is acting as the object of the sentence. Once these clauses are identified, a comma should be placed after each except for the last:

He thought taking a road trip would <u>help him feel rejuvenated, allow him to work through his feelings, and provide him some much needed solitude</u>.

Lets try some adjectives:

She looked longingly through the window at the <u>lovely elegant pearl necklace</u>.

First, identify the list of words: *lovely*, *elegant*, and *pearl* modify *necklace*. Now confirm that each adjective equally modifies the noun *necklace*. To do this, insert the word *and* in between each adjective:

She looked longingly through the window at the <u>lovely *and* elegant *and* pearl necklace</u>.

Clearly, the sentence does not make sense with *and* between *elegant* and *pearl*. Therefore, you should place the commas appropriately:

She looked longingly through the window at the <u>lovely, elegant pearl necklace</u>.

➤ **Rule 3** – Use a comma to separate various introductory elements from the rest of the sentence. Introductory elements include prepositional phrases, subordinating clauses, transitional words or phrases, and verbal phrases.

A *prepositional phrase* begins with a preposition and includes any modifiers or objects. Prepositional phrases usually signal a relationship, particularly a relationship of time or location.

Examples:
Spoiler Alert: <u>In the movie *Titanic*</u>, Leonardo di Caprio's character dies.
<u>Since the accident last year</u>, she has been afraid to drive on the highway.

Both introductory clauses in these examples begin with prepositions. The clauses indicate a relationship of location (*In the movie*...) and time (*Since the accident*...) between the introductory phrases and the independent clause that follows. Therefore, commas must separate them.

A *subordinating clause* begins with a *subordinator*, which is a word that indicates a relationship—usually a relationship of time or location—between the clause and the independent clause that follows. This relationship makes a subordinating clause similar to a prepositional phrase. However, unlike a prepositional phrase, a subordinating clause can also be referred to as a dependent clause because it has both a subject and a verb.

Example:
When I first entered the workforce, we didn't have all the modern technological conveniences that make today's business world move at such a rapid pace.

Here the phrase *When I first entered the workforce* begins with the subordinator *When*, which signals a time relationship between the subordinating clause and the independent clause that follows. Although this clause has a subject (*I*) and a verb (*entered*), it cannot stand alone as a sentence and requires the independent clause to complete the thought.

Transitional words and phrases add coherence to your writing. They help connect one sentence to the next, but beware; transitional words and phrases are often un-needed outside of formal writing, so they should be used with caution.

Here are some of the most commonly used transitional words: *finally*, *furthermore*, *moreover*, and *next* indicate sequence; *again*, *likewise*, and *similarly* indicate comparison; *although*, *but*, *however*, *by contrast*, and *on the other hand* indicate contrast; *for example*, *in fact*, and *specifically* indicate examples; *accordingly*, *as a result*, *consequently*, and *therefore* indicate cause and effect.

Example:
Dear Employees,

I am writing to tell you about a new incentive program we are beginning here at ABC Company. Specifically, this incentive program will focus on rewarding sales. Our customer base has dropped drastically this year. Consequently, we must look for new ways to increase sales. Although we have offered incentives in the past, this program will be different because it will reward you for improvement in sales rather than for your sales numbers. Furthermore, you will not only be able to earn monetary rewards, but you may also be awarded with extra vacation days.

Happy selling,
Mr. Smith

In the above text, transitional words and phrases are used to make the text flow more smoothly. A comma is required after each transitional word or phrase.

Verbal phrases contain verb elements but function as nouns, adjectives or adverbs rather than verbs. There are two kinds of verbal phrases that can act as introductory phrases and therefore must be set off by commas: participial phrases and infinitive phrases.

Participial phrases are made up of a present participle (the *–ing* form of a verb) or a past participle (the *–ed* form of a verb) as well as any modifiers or objects. Participial phrases act as adjectives because they describe, or modify, the subject in the independent clause.

Examples:
Standing alone by the door, Ricky watched the rest of the boys dance with their dates.
Angered by the kids' cutting remarks, Naomi stormed out of the room and then burst into tears.

The first example contains a participial phrase that contains the present participle *Standing*. The introductory phrase *Standing alone by the door* describes Ricky. In the second example, the past participle *Angered* makes up the participial phrase, and the full introductory phrase describes Naomi.

Infinitive phrases are made up of an infinitive (a verb taking its root form, e.g., *to drink, to live, to be*) as well as any modifiers or objects.

Examples:
To win a gold medal, you must work very hard.
To earn a high score on the ACT, you must study this guide thoroughly.

To win is the infinitive in the first sentence, and *To earn* is the infinitive in the second sentence. Both infinitives serve as part of the introductory phrase, which must be set off by commas.

✔ Check your work
To find introductory phrases that should be set off with a comma, first look for the subject and verb of the independent clause — the core sentence. Then note any words that precede the subject and verb. Other than articles (*a, an, the*) and adjectives, any words or phrases that precede the subject and verb make up the introductory phrase.

Example:
Knowing that the strongest qualities of a teacher are patience and understanding, Beth highlighted these qualities on her résumé.

Beth is the subject and *highlighted* is the verb. The phrase *Knowing that the strongest qualities of a teacher are patience and understanding* is a participial phrase and therefore should be set off with a comma.

Note that introductory preposition phrases of four words or less don't require a comma.

Example:
This morning I stopped at the bagel shop for coffee.

A comma is acceptable after *This morning*, but it's not required. When in doubt, however, use a comma.

➢ **Rule 4** – Use a comma to set off nonrestrictive clauses and phrases — clauses and phrases that are not essential modifiers. Adjectival clauses and appositives (words that rename a noun) are most often nonrestrictive.

Adjectival clauses are phrases that begin with *who, whom, whose, which, that, when, where,* or *why*. In many cases, an adjectival clause is nonrestrictive such as in the following example:

The heart, which pumps the body's blood, is necessary to sustain life.

In this sentence, the adjectival clause *which pumps the body's blood* is set off by commas because it is not essential to the sentence. It's separated because the sentence would have the same meaning without the clause. By contrast, the adjectival clause in the next sentence is restrictive because it is necessary to convey the meaning of the sentence:

> The police <u>who are investigating the murders in Maryland</u> are using geographic profiling to aid in their search for the perpetrator.

The adjectival clause *who are investigating the murders in Maryland* is necessary to provide the reader with full details about the police and the murderer for whom they are searching. Without this phrase, the reader would not know that the police are in Maryland and that they are investigating a murderer. *Appositives* act as nouns or noun substitutes by modifying the noun that precedes the appositive. Just as with adjectival clauses, nonrestrictive appositives are set off by commas, whereas restrictive appositives are not.

> **Nonrestrictive examples:**
> My high school English teacher, <u>Mr. Roper</u>, taught me how to use commas properly.
> She drove her new car, <u>a Honda Accord</u>, to the senior center to pick up her grandmother.
> The book club will be meeting this Wednesday to discuss the latest book, <u>Grisham's Rainmaker</u>.

In these examples, the underlined phrases are nonrestrictive appositives, which rename the noun preceding them. These phrases add interesting details to the sentences, but are not necessary to make the sentences complete and understandable. On the other hand, some appositives are essential to capture the full meaning of the sentence. Such restrictive appositives should not be set off with commas.

> My son <u>Michael</u> is two years old, and my other son <u>Jacob</u> is five months old.
> Meet me at 6:00 at the new restaurant <u>*Vinny's Vittles*</u> that just opened on Main Street.
> My friend <u>Tammy</u> met me at the beach yesterday.

The appositives in these examples are necessary in specifying the subjects. This information is necessary so the reader has a clear understanding of the subject involved in the text.

✓ <u>Check your work</u>
Review each sentence in your writing. Identify the adjectival phrases and appositives and the nouns they modify. For each adjectival phrase or appositive, ask yourself if the phrase provides important identifying information about the noun, or if it just provides "extra" information. If you are still unsure, read the sentence without the adjectival phrase or appositive. Does the sentence still have its full meaning? If so, set the phrase off with commas. If not, omit the commas.

> ➤ **Rule 5** – Use a comma to set off interjections and transitional phrases. Use a comma only if the transition or interjection could be removed without changing the basic meaning of the sentence.

An *interjection* is usually one or two words that interrupt the flow of a sentence and give extra information about the content of the sentence. Although an interjection provides added detail that enhances the reader's knowledge, generally the information provided by an interjection could be omitted with little or no effect on the meaning of the sentence.

> I could probably take, <u>say</u>, five people in my van for the carpool.
> She was, <u>oddly enough</u>, the only one who entered the contest.

A *transitional phrase* directs the flow of an essay. Often, transitional phrases are helpful in leading to a conclusion and therefore should not be set off with commas such as in these two examples:

> His strategy was to impress the boss and <u>thus</u> receive the promotion.
> I was tired and <u>therefore</u> did not want to go to the party.

There are instances, however, where a transitional word could be omitted without affecting the meaning of the sentence.

> **Examples:**
> I was not confident, <u>however</u>, that he knew the answer.
> The message went on to say, <u>furthermore</u>, that he would not be coming home for dinner.

The transitional words in these examples enhance the text by emphasizing the direction in which the meaning of the sentence is moving. However, the meaning of the sentences would be the same without the transitional words.

✓ Check your work

To double-check your use of commas with interjections, identify any word or words that interrupt your sentence and have little or no effect to the meaning of the sentence. Set these words off with commas. Next, check for transitional words, keeping in mind the list of common transitional phrases we discussed earlier. Once you have identified the transitional words, ask yourself if the words are necessary to convey the meaning of the sentence. If they are, don't set them off with commas; if they aren't, use commas.

> ➤ **Rule 6** – Use a comma before a coordination conjunction (*and, but, or, nor, for, so, yet*) that joins two independent clauses.

An *independent clause* is a group of words that contain both a subject and a verb and can stand alone as a sentence.

> **Example:**
> I drove my car to work. (*I* is the subject, and *drove* is the verb.)

A *coordinating conjunction* is a word that serves as a link between a word or group of words. These conjunctions are easy to remember by using the acronym BOYFANS:

> **B**ut
> **O**r
> **Y**et
> **F**or
> **A**nd
> **N**or
> **S**o

Short, choppy sentences can make your writing tedious to read. To provide some interest and variety, join some of the sentences in your essays. To do so, you will need to use a comma and a coordinating conjunction. Let's look at some examples:

Too choppy:

I took a long lunch. I went back to work. I got behind on my work. I had to stay late.

Better:

I took a long lunch, and I went back to work. I got behind on my work, so I had to stay late.

Too choppy:

My guests were arriving in an hour. I wanted to throw a memorable New Year's Eve party. I made the punch and hors d'oeuvres ahead of time. I found that I still had a lot to get done to get ready. I didn't have enough time. I decided to put the ice in the punch early. Then, I discovered that my icemaker was broken. I didn't have time to go to the store. I wasn't prepared to serve anything else. The punch would just have to be room temperature.

Better:

My guests were arriving in an hour, and I wanted to throw a memorable New Year's Eve party, so I made the punch and hors d'oeuvres ahead of time. I found, however, that I still had a lot to get ready and not enough to do it all, so I decided to put the ice in the punch early. Then, I discovered that my icemaker was broken, but I still didn't have time to go to the store, nor was I prepared to serve anything else, so the punch would just have to be room temperature.

In both examples, combining sentences with commas and conjunctions make them more interesting and conversational. We will learn more ways to create interest in your writing when we discuss writing style later on.

✓ Check your work

To properly combine two independent clauses with a comma and a conjunction, you must check to make sure that the clauses joined by the comma and conjunction are indeed independent clauses. To do this, first find all the conjunctions. Then look at the clauses on either side of each conjunction. Does each clause have a subject and a verb? Can each clause stand alone as sentences? If so, the conjunction is properly placed and a comma should precede the conjunction.

Incorrect:

We went to the mall last night, and bought some new dresses for work.

Correct:

We went to the mall last night and bought some new dresses for work.

Correct:

We went to the mall last night, and Terri bought some new dresses for work.

In the first example, *and* is the conjunction. *We went to the mall last night* is an independent clause (*we* is the subject, *went* is the verb). However, *bought some new dresses for work* is not an independent clause because there is no subject. Therefore, the sentence can be corrected by simply omitting the comma as seen in the second example. Or, if there is a possible subject for the sentence, it can be added and the comma can stay as seen in the third example. Here is another example where the same guidelines apply:

Incorrect:
He committed the crime, but didn't think the judge's ruling was fair.

Correct:
He committed the crime but didn't think the judge's ruling was fair.

Correct:
He committed the crime, but he didn't think the judge's ruling was fair.

Semicolons

What's stronger than a comma yet weaker than a period? A semicolon.

A *semicolon* indicates a major pause or break between thoughts, yet it also shows that the thoughts are logically related. If you want to master the mysterious semicolon, there are, again, only a few simple rules to remember.

> **Rule 1** – Use a semicolon to join two independent clauses if they aren't joined by a coordinating conjunction (*and, but, or, nor for, yet*) and are closely related to each other.

Sometimes a period seems like too strong of a pause when separating two closely related sentences. Equally, a comma doesn't always emphasize both sentences adequately. In cases like this, you should use a semicolon to join both independent clauses, giving you, as the writer, a subtle way of showing a close relationship between complete thoughts, especially if the second sentence restates the first or more clearly defines it by giving an example or presenting a contrast.

Example:
Loyalty is the foundation upon which relationships are built; without loyalty, friendships and marriages crumble.

The puppy scooted blindly across the floor; his eyes hadn't opened yet, leaving him totally dependent on his mother.

Using a semicolon with a transitional word is also a good way to join contrasting clauses.

These days there is a cure for every ailment; however, the side effects of many medications are worse than the condition for which the medication is prescribed.

A transitional word may also serve to emphasize a cause-effect relationship.

The drought has greatly affected many farmers; therefore, the price of produce is expected to rise.

The choice to join two clauses with a semicolon and a transitional word may be a stylistic choice rather than a grammatical one. Likewise, adding variety to your writing may be the purpose when it comes to replacing a comma and conjunction with a semicolon.

Correct:
The slippery rock presented the climbers with a challenge, <u>so</u> they watched their footing very closely.

Correct:
The slippery rock presented the climbers with a challenge; they watched their footing very closely.

Sometimes, however, it is necessary to replace the comma with a semicolon in order to provide clarity. In these cases, you may or may not omit the conjunction.

Confusing:
From such a great distance, the man could not make out the faces of the evil, crafty conspirators, but, if he moved any closer, he would be taking an unnecessary, careless risk.

Better:
From such a great distance, the man could not make out the faces of the evil, crafty conspirators; but, if he moved any closer, he would be taking an unnecessary, careless risk.

✔ <u>Check your work</u>

To use a semicolon to join two independent clauses, analyze the two clauses carefully to make sure there is a close relationship between the two before placing the semicolon. Be careful not to misuse semicolons, especially when you use them with a transitional word or in place of a comma and conjunction.

Incorrect:
I was forced; therefore, to take the detour around the construction site.

Correct:
I was forced, therefore, to take the detour around the construction site.

In this example, *therefore* is a transitional word and should be set off with commas. Furthermore, the clause *I was forced* is an independent clause and *to take the detour around the construction site* is not, so the clauses cannot be set apart by a semicolon.

Take the same caution when replacing a comma and conjunction with a semicolon. Remember that, to join two clauses with a comma and a conjunction, both clauses must be independent. Each clause must be able to stand alone as a separate sentence.

Incorrect:
He completed the yard work, and then enjoyed a lemonade break with his mom.

Incorrect:
He completed the yard work; and then enjoyed a lemonade break with his mom.

Correct:
He completed the yard work and then enjoyed a lemonade break with his mom.

The subject in this sentence is *He* and the compound verb is *completed* and *enjoyed*. There is no subject in the second part of the sentence, so it is incorrect to use a comma and conjunction in the sentence. Likewise, a semicolon cannot be used.

> **Rule 2** – Use semicolons to join more than two independent clauses.

In Rule 1, we discussed using a semicolon to join two independent clauses. Semicolons can also be used to join multiple independent clauses in more complex sentences:

Example:
Over the past few years, violence has adopted a new calling card; it is more random, gruesome and sinister than ever. In this country of freedom, violence has made its presence known in all areas of life. In schools, students take the lives of other students before taking their own; a close-knit community is gripped by fear because of random shootings; a father kills another father over their sons' hockey game.

This example could be written as a few separate sentences; however, since the independent clauses are all closely related, it is acceptable to link them with semicolons. Joining multiple independent clauses is often a stylistic choice and an effective one because it makes an impact by more closely connecting the sentences.

✓ Check your work
To join multiple independent clauses with a semicolon, make sure the clauses you are joining are closely related. When used conservatively, semicolons can add a great deal of impact while also adding clarity to comma riddled sentences. To avoid overusing semicolons, reread your text and make sure your use of semicolons is sporadic; semicolons should never appear as often as commas or periods.

Too many semicolons:
My next interviewee came in and sat across from me; she tried to put on a confident face; but I could tell she was nervous; she played anxiously with her ring; she shifted positions every few seconds.

Better:
My next interviewee came in and sat across from me. She tried to put on a confident face, but I could tell she was nervous; she played anxiously with her ring and shifted positions every few seconds.

> **Rule 3** – Use semicolons to separate a series of items that contain commas.

Use of the semicolon in this manner prevents confusion.

Confusing:
I boarded a flight in Los Angeles, California, had a two-hour layover in Detroit, Michigan, and finally landed in London, England.

Better:
I boarded a flight in Los Angeles, California; had a two-hour layover in Detroit, Michigan; and finally landed in London, England.

Too many commas cause confusion, so in order to simplify the sentence and make it clearer, semicolons must be used to separate the clauses.

> All employees must bring a pen, paper, and a notebook to the first day of training; a laptop, highlighter and paperclips to day two; and a sample report, pie chart and three markers to the last day.

✓ Check your work

Check each of the independent clauses you have joined with commas. Do any of the independent clauses contain commas? If so, joining the independent clauses with a semicolon instead of a comma might make the sentence clearer.

> **Confusing:**
> My pottery class is on Mondays, Wednesdays, and Fridays, and I babysit my nephew, niece, and neighbor's son on Tuesdays and Thursdays.

> **Better:**
> My pottery class is on Mondays, Wednesdays and Fridays; and I babysit my nephew, niece and neighbor's son on Tuesdays and Thursdays.

If, after reviewing your writing, you feel you have used semicolons too often, consider using other methods to join phrases. For example, you might use a period to divide clauses into separate sentences. Semicolons can make a big impact but only when used conservatively and correctly.

Colons

A colon means, in effect, "Note what follows," and is generally considered a very formal mark of punctuation.

> ➤ **Rule 1** – Use a colon to join two independent clauses when introducing an explanation or example.

When a comma does not place adequate emphasis on the relationship between two independent clauses, use a semicolon. When a semicolon does not provide adequate emphasis, use a colon.

> **Example:**
> When I picture my dream house, I can almost envision all the beautiful scenery: the beach or mountains, for example, would be perfect.

A colon can also introduce an explanation such as in the following:

> Dave and Stephanie's presentation lacked the usual enthusiasm: probably because they were up all night working on the ad campaign again.

✓ Check your work

Just as with semicolons, the choice to use colons can be a stylistic one. If you do choose to use a colon to introduce an explanation or example, make sure that both the preceding clause and the clause that follows are independent clauses.

Capitalize the clause that follows a colon if it is a formal statement or if the content that is introduced contains more than one sentence.

> **Example (formal statement):**
> Our club bylaws shall set forth the following: Rules for meetings, code of conduct, and membership procedures.

> **Example (more than one clause):**
> When thinking of a future career, there are many choices: Becoming a lawyer would be a good financial decision. On the other hand, teaching may provide more personal satisfaction.

> ➤ **Rule 2** – Use a colon to introduce a series, list, or formal quotation.

Use a colon to introduce a series or list.

> **Examples:**
> We need to get several things done before our trip: pay the bills, water the plants, and take the dog to the kennel.
>
> Before we can take off, you must do the following: fasten your seat belt, turn off your cell phone, and return your tray table to its upright position.
>
> The names of the people who made the volleyball team are as follows: Ruth, Mary Lynn, Amy, Sarah, Alicia, and Elizabeth.

Note that when the word *following* or *follows* is used to introduce a list or series you must use a colon. You should also use a colon to introduce a quotation.

> **Example:**
> As people seek to build relationships and, in so doing, break down the walls of racism, they should remember Martin Luther King, Jr.'s famous words: "I have a dream that [we] will one day live in a nation where [we] will not be judged by the color of [our] skin but by the content of [our] character."

✓ Check your work

When introducing a series or list, always use a colon if the clause that introduces the list or series contains the term *follows* or *following*.

> **Example:**
> The following improvements need to be made to your house before you try to sell it: new carpet should be installed, the outside trim should be painted, and the fixtures in the downstairs bathroom should be replaced.

Do not use a colon if the list or series is introduced by phrases such as *especially, such as, namely, for instance, for example,* or *that is* unless the series is made up of one or more independent clauses.

Incorrect (colon introducing a series of phrases):
Some of my life goals, for example: to ski in the Alps, bungee jump from Victoria Falls, and visit the Great Wall of China.

Correct (colon introducing a series of independent clauses):
I have set some goals that I wish to achieve before I get too old to do so. For example: I want to ski in the Alps, bungee jump from Victoria Falls, and visit the Great Wall of China.

Note that a comma would work in this sentence as well, but the colon following *For example* places more emphasis on the text that follows.

Do not use a colon after a form of the verb *to be*.

Incorrect:
My favorite marks of punctuation are: the dash, the semicolon, and the exclamation point.

Correct:
My favorite marks of punctuation are the dash, the semicolon, and the exclamation point.

You may use a colon to introduce a quotation and, in this instance, you must capitalize the first word of the quotation.

Example:
The principles of this country are founded on the *Declaration of Independence* and its famous words: "We hold these truths to be self-evident, that all men are created equal, that they are endowed by their Creator with certain unalienable Rights, that among these are Life, Liberty and the pursuit of Happiness."

Dashes

Many writers misunderstand dashes. They sprinkle their writing with dashes to indicate pauses where commas, periods, or semicolons should be, but the dash is not a super-powered mark of punctuation that saves the writer from the trouble of determining what other mark is appropriate. A dash merely indicates a break in thought or structure of the sentence.

> **Rule 1** – Use dashes for emphasis, to set off a repetition, or indicate an abrupt shift in the sentence structure or thought.

   Examples:
   If you are interested in martial arts — and who wouldn't be interested in such a disciplined art? — there are many centers for instruction.

   I was unable — unwilling, really — to head up the new committee at the office.

✓ Check your work

Although commas may be used to set off phrases that interrupt a sentence, dashes add emphasis to the set off clause. In addition, dashes set an informal tone in your writing. Because of their informality, dashes should be used sparingly, if ever, in graduate writing. When you do choose to use dashes, you may include question marks and exclamation points in the clauses that are set off by dashes (as in the first example above).

➢ **Rule 2** – Use dashes to set off parenthetical or explanatory information.

Example:
The editor of the *Banner Herald* often employs hyperbole — deliberate exaggeration or overstatement to show special emphasis or create humor — to express his political views.

Here dashes set apart the definition of *hyperbole*. Though not necessary to the meaning of the sentence, the definition adds useful information. Again, dashes are an informal way of setting off information; a comma could serve the same purpose here.

✓ Check your work

Review each sentence in your writing and identify any information that is parenthetical or that explains a topic in the sentence. You may set this information off with dashes. Remember, though, that dashes should seldom be used in formal writing. In formal writing, you should use commas to set off these elements from the rest of the sentence.

Apostrophes

While some would say that the use of an apostrophe is a mystery, it may, in fact, be the simplest mark of punctuation to truly master.

➢ **Rule 1** – Use an apostrophe to form a contraction, a word that is a shortened combination of two words.

Contractions are used in informal writing and serve to shorten two words by leaving out some letters and joining the two words.

Common Contractions:

Words that combine to form a contraction	Contractions
it is	it's
I am	I'm
he will	he'll
they are	they're
you are	you're
we will	we'll
could not	couldn't
would not	wouldn't
cannot	can't
does not	doesn't
do not	don't
will not	won't
let us	let's
I would	I'd
they would	they'd
was not	wasn't
I will	I'll
should not	shouldn't
we had	we'd
they will	they'll

✓ Check your work

The use of contractions is quite simple: if you wish to shorten two words into one, you must simply replace the words with the correct contraction. There are, however, some common mistakes people make when using contractions. A few contractions sound like possessive words, and these are often confused.

Example (they're):
I don't know where they think *they're* going, but *they're* going to end up at a dead end.

Example (their):
When I saw them heading toward the dead end, I assumed they did not know *their* way.

Example (they're and their):
They're going to run into a dead end because they don't know *their* way.

Remember that *they're* is short for *they are*. *Their* is the third person plural possessive. The next pair of words to watch out for is the contraction *you're* and the possessive *your*.

Example (you're):
You're not going to succeed in school if you don't study hard.

Example (your):
Your success in school is dependent upon hard work.

Example (you're and your):
You're not going to succeed in school if you don't try *your* best.

You're is short for *you are*, and *your* is the second person singular possessive. The final pair of words that can be confusing are *it's* and *its*.

Example (it's):
It's seemingly impossible for a cat to travel that far to get home.

Example (its):
A cat will travel a long way to find *its* home.

Example (it's and its):
It's amazing the distance a cat will travel to find *its* way back home.

Be careful when you use *it's* or *its*; remember that *it's* is the contraction for *it is* and *its* is the third person singular possessive.

✓ Check your work

To check for proper use of a contraction, especially those that can be tricky, substitute the words that have been replaced by the contraction. If the full-length word makes sense, the contraction is correct. If not, you need to check your spelling. Once again, though, keep in mind that contractions are more appropriate for use in informal writing.

➤ **Rule 2** – Use an apostrophe to show possession.

To show the possessive form of singular nouns, add an apostrophe and an –s.

Examples:
Teddy cleaned the *dog's* house before he and his family went on vacation.
The teacher used *Julia's* homework as an example because it was exceptional.
She didn't feel comfortable borrowing *Harris's* car.

To show the possessive form of plural nouns, add an –s and an apostrophe.

Examples:
Coach Hannigan distributed the *girls'* uniforms at soccer practice.

Some plural nouns, however, do not end in –s. In these instances, add an apostrophe and an –s.

Examples:
The *women's* meeting will be held in the gymnasium on Thursday night.
All of the *children's* bikes were parked in the driveway.
Competition between *men's* sports teams is fierce.

✓ Check your work
Check for the correct use of apostrophes with possessives by first identifying the nouns that show possession. Then identify whether the noun is singular or plural. If the noun is singular, add an apostrophe and an –s. If the noun is plural, add an –s and an apostrophe. Finally, take note of any irregular plural nouns that do not end in –s. Add an apostrophe and an –s to irregular nouns.

Quotation Marks

Use quotation marks to set off direct quotations and dialogue.

> **Example (quotation):**
> In his famous inaugural address, President John F. Kennedy implored, "My fellow Americans, ask not what your country can do for you: Ask what you can do for your country."

> **Example (dialog):**
> "Where are you going tonight?" asked Greg.
> "Beth and I are going to the library to get some research done," Susan replied. "Then we're heading to the mall to do some shopping."

➢ **Rule 1** – Commas and periods should be placed inside quotation marks.

> **Example:**
> "I don't understand what you're trying to say," Glen said. "You need to speak up."

Don't use a comma and quotation marks for indirect quotes.

> **Example (direct quote):**
> He said, "I don't have time to take the car for an oil change today."

> **Example (indirect quote):**
> He said that he didn't have time to take the car for an oil change today.

✓ Check your work
To determine if a quote is a direct or indirect quote, ask yourself if the quote comes directly from the speaker and if the quote contains the exact words of the speaker. If so, place quotation marks around the quote. If not, there should be no comma or quotation marks.

➢ **Rule 2** – Place semicolons and colons outside quotation marks.

> **Example (semicolon):**
> My mom always used to say, "A stitch in time saves nine"; I always remember that quote when I am tempted to procrastinate.

> **Example (colon):**
> Patrick Henry made a strong statement when he said, "Give me liberty or give me death": he felt that it would be better to die than to live in a country without freedom.

✓ Check your work

When you use quotation marks with a semicolon or colon, first determine whether you are using the semicolon or colon correctly. Then make sure you place the semicolon or colon outside the quotation marks.

> **Rule 3** – Place question marks and exclamation points outside quotation marks unless they are a part of the quotation.

> **Examples (question mark):**
> Did you hear Professor Johnston say, "You must read the first 500 pages for a quiz on Monday"?
>
> Stunned, she implored, "Why didn't you tell me you were leaving for good?"

In the first example, the quotation is a statement that does not require a question mark; however, the overall sentence that contains the quotation is a question. Therefore, the question mark goes outside the quotation marks. In the second example, though, the quotation is a question, so the question mark goes inside the quotation marks.

> **Examples (exclamation point):**
> I can't believe she finally said, "I love you"!
>
> The woman ran after the thief yelling, "Hey, come back with my purse!"

Overall, the first sentence is an exclamatory sentence, but the phrase *I love you* is not; therefore, the exclamation point goes outside the quotation marks. *Hey, come back with my purse* in the second sentence, however, is an exclamation, so the exclamation point goes inside the quotation marks.

✓ Check your work

Examine all quotations in your writing. If the quotation itself is a question or exclamation, place the appropriate punctuation mark inside the quotation marks. If, however, the overall sentence is a question or exclamation but the actual quote is not, the punctuation should be placed outside the quotation marks.

Sentence Fragments

A *sentence fragment* is an incomplete sentence. Sentence fragments are ungrammatical because they lack one or more of the three elements of a complete sentence: a subject, predicate (a fancy name for a verb or group of words that act as a verb), or a complete thought.

> **Example (independent clause):**
> I ran down the road.
>
> **Examples (sentence fragments):**
> Ran down the road.
>
> Running down the road.

Fragments generally occur when modifying phrases or dependent clauses aren't attached to an independent clause. To correct sentence fragments in your writing, you must first identify them and then add the right punctuation.

➢ **Step 1** – Identifying sentence fragments.

To find sentence fragments in your writing, first analyze each sentence. If a sentence doesn't have a subject or a verb, or if the sentence is actually a dependent clause that doesn't make sense on it's own, it's probably a fragment.

Fragment:
On our way to the store tomorrow. We need to stop at the bank

Complete sentence:
On our way to the store tomorrow, we need to stop at the bank.

Fragments:
Providing equal opportunity to all citizens. Is of utmost importance.

Complete sentence:
Providing equal opportunity to all citizens is of utmost importance.

In the first example, *On our way to the store tomorrow* is a prepositional phrase that can't stand on its own. In the second example, both sentences are fragments. *Providing equal opportunity to all citizens* is a gerund that acts as the noun of the sentence; therefore, it must be combined with the second sentence to be reunited with its long-lost verb *is*.

➢ **Step 2** – Revising sentence fragments: there are two ways to do this.

- Combine sentences to make them complete.

Example:
(Fragments) Because I was at the office working. I didn't make it to dinner.

(Revised) Because I was at the office working, I didn't make it to dinner.

- Add the necessary elements to the fragment to make it complete.

Example:
(Fragments) From the beginning. Wanted to practice law in a small town.

(Revised) From the beginning, he wanted to practice law in a small town.

Once you have made your revisions, make sure you reread your writing. Identify that there is a subject and verb in each sentence, but beware of subordinating clauses! They have both a subject and a verb, yet they do not complete a thought.

Example:
When we ran through the hallway.

Sentences that don't complete a thought but that have a subject and a verb are still sentence fragments.

Run-On Sentences

It's a common misconception that run-on sentences are just wordy sentences that "run-on" too long; however, that's not the case. In fact, it's not uncommon to see sentences that have the length of entire paragraphs without being run-on sentences.

A *run-on sentence* refers to two or more sentences written as one.

> **Example:**
> David went on a field trip to an aquarium with his classmates and they saw a large variety of fish.

In this example, two independent clauses are joined with a coordinating conjunction, but there is no comma. This type of run-on sentence is called a *fused* sentence. A fused sentence can also lack both a comma and a conjunction.

> The debate over alien existence will probably continue for years some are sure they have seen aliens.

This next sentence contains a comma but no coordinating conjunction.

> Many people believe in the powers of a psychic, sometimes even detectives depend on psychics to help solve crimes.

Because this sentence contains a comma but no coordinating conjunction, it is called a *comma splice*.

To correct run-on sentences in your writing, you must — you guessed it! — identify them and revise them.

> **Step 1** – Identify run-on sentences in your writing.

To find run-on sentences in your writing, first analyze each sentence. In your analysis, mark the subject and verb by underlining the subject once and the verb twice.

> **Examples:**
> Osteoporosis is very common among women but drinking milk and taking calcium supplements can help prevent it.
>
> History provides us with interesting stories, it also helps us in the future because we can learn from mistakes made in history.

These examples contain two independent clauses that are not combined correctly. Many writers also link multiple clauses incorrectly. If you are prone to this error, it is important that you take the time to go through each sentence and identify the subjects and verbs.

> **Step 2** – Revise your run-on sentences by using one of five methods:

- Separate the clauses into complete sentences.

    Example:
    (Run-on) Working together as a team is more productive than working individually, a team can get more accomplished than one person.

    (Revised) Working together as a team is more productive than working individually. A team can get more accomplished than one person.

- Link the clauses with a semicolon.

    Example:
    (Run-on) Writing is great therapy letting off steam through the written word is a good way to work through frustration.

    (Revised) Writing is great therapy; letting off steam through the written word is a good way to work through frustration.

- Link the clauses with a comma and a coordinating conjunction.

    Example:
    (Run-on) I went to Florida last week to go to Disney World with a friend but it rained the whole time.

    (Revised) I went to Florida last week to go to Disney World with a friend, but it rained the whole time.

- Rewrite the clauses to form just one independent clause.

    Example:
    (Run-on) This summer has been a very hot one, it has been humid also.

    (Revised) This summer has been a very hot and humid.

- Rewrite the clauses to form one independent clause with an introductory dependent clause.

    Example:
    (Run-on) We re-painted our house, the old paint was peeling and fading.

    (Revised) Because the old paint was peeling and fading, we re-painted our house.

✓ Check your work

Make sure you review your work after making revisions to ensure that all run-on sentences have indeed been corrected. In addition, try to use all five methods of revision in your writing; don't correct each run-on with the same method. Using different forms of revision will result in varying sentence patterns, which will enhance your writing style. We will talk more about writing style shortly; but first, let's make sure you can properly apply the rules of punctuation we just covered.

Punctuation Drills

> Directions: Grab a blank sheet of paper, read each sentence, and then make necessary punctuation and spelling corrections. Pay special attention to sentence fragments and run-on sentences and re-write them so that they are grammatically correct. Answers and solutions begin after the test.

1. Dana is a foster mother. Takes care of newborns. When babies are put up for adoption a social worker places the baby in Dana's house where the baby stays until the adoption is completed usually the baby stays no longer than six weeks unless there is no adoptee lined up yet.

2. Buying a new car is a big decision their are many factors to consider dependability for example is a key factor in choosing the car to suit your needs.

3. The energetic boisterous boy climbed the jungle gym hung from the monkey bars jumped down and then ran to the merry-go-round.

4. What do you think he meant when he said, "Your going to have to figure that one out on you're own"

5. A cool sparkling stream meandered through the peaceful forest and some deer stopped to take a drink and glanced up for a moment to look at me they disappeared into the trees.

6. Some people claim even boast that they've never read an entire book. This is there loss because reading leads to knowledge knowledge leads to power power enables people to influence those around them.

7. The mens' group did charity work this weekend they completed the following projects they helped rebuild a church that had been damaged in a tornado they completed some of the landscaping on the church grounds and they began repairs to the pastors home nearby the church.

8. Many people suffer from "diet fatigue" they try diet after diet only to meet failure with each one. What they should be focusing on instead is nutritional eating and fitness nutritional eating consists of eating well-balanced servings of meats vegetables fruits and grains drinking lots of water and indulging in junk food sparingly. Proper fitness can come in the form of aerobic exercise walking sports or weight training making just a few adjustments in daily eating and exercise habits can make all the difference in a persons physical and emotional well-being.

9. The beautiful grand stain-glassed windows added a majestic feeling to the old cathedral.

Punctuation

Solutions to Punctuation Drills

1. Dana is a foster <u>mother who takes</u> care of newborns. When babies are put up for <u>adoption,</u> a social worker places the baby in Dana's house where the baby stays until the adoption is <u>completed. Usually</u> the baby stays no longer than six weeks unless there is no adoptee lined up yet.

   Takes care of newborns is a fragment; it was corrected by joining it to the first clause *Dana is a foster mother*. *When babies are put up for adoption* is an introductory dependent clause and should be followed by a comma. The last clause is a run-on sentence, and it was corrected by placing a period after *completed*.

2. Buying a new car is a big <u>decision. There</u> are many factors to <u>consider: dependability, for example,</u> is a key factor in choosing the car to suit your needs.

   The first clause is a run-on sentence and should be divided into two sentences; thus, a period was placed between *decision* and *There*. Moreover, *their* was replaced with the correct word *there*. Once you have divided the sentence into two separate clauses, notice that *dependability* is an example. Therefore, a colon should follow *consider*. In addition, *for example* should be set off by commas because it is an interjection.

3. The <u>energetic, boisterous</u> boy climbed the jungle <u>gym, hung</u> from the monkey <u>bars, jumped</u> <u>down, and</u> then ran to the merry-go-round.

   Energetic and *boisterous* are adjectives that modify *boy*. Because there are two adjectives modifying the same noun, they should be separated by a comma. In addition, a set of four phrases follows— *climbed the jungle gym*, *hung from the monkey bars*, *jumped down*, and *then ran to the merry-go-round*—and should also be separated by commas.

4. What do you think he meant when he said, "<u>You're</u> going to have to figure that one out on <u>your</u> <u>own</u>"?

   Your and *you're* are misspelled. The contraction *you're* should be the first word in the quotation, and the possessive *your* should precede *own*. The question mark in the sentence should be placed outside the quotation marks because the quotation itself is not a question; however, the complete sentence is a question.

5. A <u>cool, sparkling</u> stream meandered through the peaceful <u>forest. Some</u> deer stopped to take a drink. <u>Before they disappeared into the trees, they glanced up for a moment to look at me.</u>

   First, a comma should separate the series of adjectives *cool* and *sparkling*. Second, this clause is a run-on sentence and was corrected by dividing it into two independent clauses by placing a period between *forest* and *Some*. Finally, a third clause was created by converting the sentence fragment into an introductory clause.

6. Some people claim, even boast, that they have never read an entire book. This is their loss because reading leads to knowledge; knowledge leads to power; power enables people to influence those around them.

   Even boast is an interjection and should be set apart by commas. You should use commas instead of dashes because the topic of the sentences is formal. The contraction *they've* should be changed to *they have* to maintain the formality. The next sentence should contain the possessive *their*. Finally, the last clause is a run-on sentence. Because the clauses are closely related, they should be separated by semicolons.

7. The men's group did charity work this weekend. They completed the following projects: they helped rebuild a church that had been damaged in a tornado, they completed some of the landscaping on the church grounds, and they began repairs to the pastor's home nearby the church.

   Because the word *men* is a plural noun that does not end in *–s*, its possessive should be spelled with an apostrophe and then an *–s*. Also, the first clause is a run-on, so there should be a period between *weekend* and *They*. Next, there should be a colon after *projects* in order to introduce the series of clauses that follow. The word *following* is your clue to use a colon in this instance. A comma should separate each clause in the series that follows. Finally, *pastor's* is possessive and should contain an apostrophe.

8. Many people suffer from "diet fatigue"; they try diet after diet only to meet failure with each one. What they should be focusing on instead is nutritional eating and fitness. Nutritional eating consists of eating well-balanced servings of meats, vegetables, fruits, and grains; drinking lots of water; and indulging in junk food sparingly. Proper fitness can come in the form of aerobic exercise, walking, sports, or weight training. Making just a few adjustments in daily eating and exercise habits can make all the difference in a person's physical and emotional well-being.

   The first clause is a run-on and should be divided into two separate sentences; since they're so closely related, you may use a semicolon. The semicolon should be placed outside the quotation marks around *diet fatigue*. A period should follow *fitness* in order to separate the next run-on sentence into separate sentences. In the third sentence, you are presented with a series of clauses; one of the clauses contains a list of words that require commas to separate them. Because so many commas can be confusing, semicolons should separate the series of clauses. Commas should separate the series of words in the sentence that follows as well. A final sentence should be set off starting at *Making*. Finally, the possessive of *person's* must contain an apostrophe.

9. The beautiful, grand stain-glassed windows added a majestic feeling to the old cathedral.

   A comma should separate *beautiful* and *grand*. Notice that there is no comma after *grand*. You can double-check this by placing *and* between each adjective: *The beautiful and grand and stain-glassed window*. The *and* between *grand* and *stain-glassed* does not make sense; therefore, there should be no comma preceding *stain-glass*.

Grammar

The field of grammar is a huge and complex world — entire books have been written about it, all with slightly differing opinions. This complexity should be no surprise since grammar deals with the process of English communication.

Grammar can be divided into two parts: Mechanics and Usage.

Mechanics concerns punctuation and capitalization, which we discussed earlier in this chapter, and it is not tested on the ACT to the same extent as usage. So don't spend too much time worrying whether a comma is in the right place or whether a particular word should be capitalized.

Usage deals with how we choose our words and how we express our thoughts. In other words, are the connections between the words in a sentence logically sound? Are they expressed in a way that conforms to standard diction? This is the part of grammar that is most important on the ACT. Six major categories of usage are tested:

- **Pronouns**
- **Subject-Verb Agreement**
- **Misplaced and Redundant Modifiers**
- **Parallelism**
- **Verb Tense**
- **Diction**

The more familiar you are with the parts of speech (*nouns, verbs, pronouns, adjectives, adverbs*, and so forth) and how they function in a sentence, the easier the test will be for you. Let's take a look at some of the rules that dictate proper usage in the English language.

Pronouns

A *pronoun* is a word that takes the place of a noun. In fancy grammatical terms, the noun is the antecedent of the pronoun. There are a few things to keep in mind when it comes to pronouns:

> **Rule 1** – A pronoun must have the same number (singular or plural) as the noun or noun phrase it is replacing.

>> **Examples:**
>> Steve has yet to receive *his* degree.
>> Everybody is on *his* (not *their*) best behavior during the ACT.

Because the word *everybody* is referring to a singular group of people and not multiple groups, it is almost always a singular noun. Even though the pronoun *their* sounds right, it's not. Whenever you see the word *everybody,* triple-check the pronoun to make sure that it is singular.

> **Rule 2** – A pronoun must have the same gender (feminine, masculine, or neuter) as the noun it is replacing.

>> **Example:**
>> Even though Pat knew *her* wedding was in less than an hour, *she* still didn't feel nervous.

Because *Pat* is a female, the pronouns *she* and *her* were used.

Following is a list of the most commonly used pronouns:

PRONOUNS

Singular	Plural	Both Singular and Plural
I, me	we, us	any
she, her	they	none
he, him	them	all
it	these	most
anyone	those	more
either	some	who
each	that	which
many	both	what
nothing	ourselves	you
one	any	
another	many	
everything	few	
mine	several	
his, hers	others	
this		
that		

> **Rule 3** – A pronoun should refer to one, and only one, noun or compound noun.

This is probably the most common error on the ACT. If a pronoun follows two nouns, it is often unclear which of the nouns the pronoun refers to.

Incorrect:
The breakup of the Soviet Union has left <u>nuclear weapons</u> in the hands of unstable, nascent <u>countries</u>. It is imperative to world security that *they* be destroyed.

<u>George</u> asked <u>Phil</u> to pick up *his* laundry.

An unclear pronoun often requires major sentence surgery to repair.

<u>George,</u> tired of seeing Phil's laundry on the floor, asked <u>Phil</u> to pick *it* up.

Sometimes, however, the pronoun should just be replaced with a clarifying noun.

The breakup of the Soviet Union has left <u>nuclear weapons</u> in the hands of unstable, nascent <u>countries</u>. It is imperative to world security that ***these weapons*** be destroyed.

> **Rule 4** – A pronoun must be in the proper case: subjective (*I, you, he, she, it, we, they*), objective (*me, you, him, her, it, us, them*), or possessive (*my, mine, your, yours, his, her, hers, its, our, ours, their, theirs*).

A pronoun following any form of the verb *to be,* is going to be in the subjective form. This form often sounds weird and pretentious, but it is correct. To do well on the ACT, you should store the following phrases in your mental bank:

Phrases:
It is I.
It was he.
It could be they.
It was she who...
This is he.
It was they.

Example:
After much interrogation, I finally confessed to my roommate that <u>it was I</u> who drank the last cup of coffee.

Subject-Verb Agreement

> **Rule 1** – A singular subject requires a singular verb.

> **Example:**
> Jack Johnson's <u>music</u> *is* (not are) relaxing.

Some words are singular, but they try to pose as plural words, with their plural-sounding, tricky ways. Don't be fooled, however. The following words are always singular and therefore always require a singular verb: *each, every, collection, group, public, club, government, organization,* and *union*.

> **Rule 2** – A plural subject requires a plural verb.

> **Example:**
> The <u>works</u> of Stephen King and Ted Dekker *are* (not is) terrifying and suspenseful.

The following words are always plural and require a plural verb: *few, both, several, many*.

> **Rule 3** – A compound subject, two or more subjects connected by the word *and*, requires a plural verb.

> **Example:**
> The *Iliad* and *The Odyssey* are two of the known epics written by Homer.

> **Rule 4** – Intervening clauses and phrases, the most common of these prepositional phrases, do not affect subject-verb agreement.

> **Example:**
> Only <u>one</u> ~~of the President's nominees~~ *was* confirmed.

Here, the singular verb *was* agrees with its singular subject *one*. The intervening prepositional phrase *of the President's nominees* has no effect on the number or person of the verb.

Collective nouns followed by intervening phrases are particularly easy to miss.

> **Example:**
> The <u>content</u> ~~of the boxes~~ *is* what she wants.
> The <u>meaning</u> ~~of her sentences~~ *is* not clear.

Be careful when a phrase beginning with *as well as, along with, together with, in addition to,* or a similar expression follows a simple subject. Be sure the verb agrees with the simple subject, not with a noun in the intervening phrase.

> **Example:**
> Our <u>Senator</u>, ~~along with most congressmen~~, *opposes* the bill.

Here, the singular verb *opposes* agrees with its singular subject *Senator*. The intervening phrase *along with most congressmen* has no effect on the number or person of the verb.

√ Check your work

In most writing, and on the ACT, sentences will not always follow the same pattern. That is to say, the subject will not always be closely followed by the verb and vise versa. In order to ease some of this confusion, mark a line through any prepositional phrases, like in the above examples, and simply read the noun (subject) next to the verb.

> **Rule 5** – When subject and verb are reversed, they still must agree in number and person.

   Example:
   Attached are <u>copies</u> ~~of the contract~~.

Here, the plural verb *are attached* agrees with its plural subject *copies*. The sentence could be rewritten as

   Copies of the contract are attached.

Although it may seem obvious that when reversing the normal order of the subject and the verb their agreement must be preserved, this obvious error is easy to miss.

   Incorrect:
   Attached ~~to the email~~ *is* <u>the graphic file and the agreement.</u>

This ungrammatical sentence sounds natural perhaps because its error is committed so often. The compound subject of the sentence is *the graphic file and the agreement*, which must take a plural verb:

   Correct
   Attached ~~to the email~~ *are* (not is) <u>the graphic file and the agreement.</u>

Be careful when an inverted subject-verb order is introduced by a construction such as *there is, there are, here is, here are*.

   There is much disagreement between the parties.

The word *there* introduces the singular verb *is*, which agrees with the singular subject of the sentence *disagreement*.

It's tempting to mistakenly use a singular verb before the plural subject.

   There is <u>a wallet and a key</u> on the dresser.

The compound (plural) subject of this sentence is *a wallet and a key*, so it requires a plural verb.

   <u>There are</u> a wallet and a key on the dresser.

Because the verb has to be chosen before we fully form the subject in our minds, this error occurs daily in speech, which makes the mistake all the more easy to commit in writing

Modifiers

A *modifier* is a phrase or a clause that describes something. A misplaced modifier, therefore, is one that describes the wrong item in a sentence, often creating an illogical statement.

> **Rule 1** – A modifier should be placed as close as possible to what it is modifying.

> **Example:**
> Following are some useful tips for protecting your person and property from the FBI.

This sentence implies that the FBI is a threat to your person and property. To correct the sentence put the modifier *from the FBI* next to the word it modifies, *tips*.

> Following are some useful tips from the FBI for protecting your person and property.

> **Example:**
> I saw the senators debating while watching television.

Here again, this sentence implies that senators were debating and watching TV at the same time. To improve the sentence, simply put the modifier *while watching television* next to the word it modifies, *I*.

> While watching television, I saw the senators debating.

The sentence can be made even clearer and more direct without the modifier:

> I saw the senators debating on television.

> **Rule 2** – When a phrase begins a sentence, make sure that it modifies the subject of the sentence.

> **Example:**
> Coming around the corner, a few moments passed before I could recognize my old home.

Is it possible for moments to come around the corner? Maybe, but that's probably not what the author is trying to say.

> Coming around the corner, I paused a few moments before I could recognize my old home.

Here's another example:

> While at summer camp, my family moved.

Does the family live at summer camp? If not, then the above sentence doesn't make much sense. It can, however, be corrected.

> While I was at summer camp, my family moved.

➢ **Rule 3** – When a prepositional phrase begins a sentence, make sure it modifies the *true* subject of phrase. Beware though: this error is easy to miss.

> **Example:**
> As the top programmer, I feel that only Steve can handle this project.

Who is the top programmer in this sentence, *Steve* or *I*? Since only *Steve* can handle the project, it's likely that he is the top programmer.

> As the top programmer, only Steve can handle this project.

> **Or**

> I feel that as the top programmer only Steve can handle this project.

➢ **Rule 4** – When a verbal phrase ends a sentence, make sure that it cannot modify more than one idea in the main clause.

> **Example:**
> Oddly, the senator known for his ability to close well performed poorly in the final two debates, causing a drop in his poll numbers.

There are two conflicting ideas expressed in the main clause of this sentence: the senator is a strong closer and he did poorly in the final debates. It's not clear which one caused the drop in his poll numbers (though logically the drop was caused by his poor performance). The sentence should be made clearer, often by removing the interfering verbal phrase.

> Though known to be a strong closer, the senator's poor performance in the final two debates caused his poll numbers to drop.

> **Or**

> The senator's poor performance in the final two debates caused his poll numbers to drop, even though he is known to be a strong closer.

➢ **Rule 5** – Do not modify a word with a word that means the same thing.

> **Example:**
> The old heirlooms are priceless.

By definition, heirlooms (valuables handed down from generation to generation) are old. The sentence can be corrected by dropping the word *old*.

Parallelism

Writers often try to summarize a thought or describe a situation by listing items in a series that are similar in content or function. When all of these parts share the same grammatical form, we say that they are parallel; hence, parallelism. Faulty parallelism occurs when units with similar functions in a sentence are not written with the same structure. Lucky for you, this error is easily fixed and fairly easy to spot. After all, faulty parallelism just doesn't sound right.

> **Rule 1** – When two adjectives modify the same noun, they must share a similar form.

> **Awkward:**
> The topology course was both rigorous and a challenge.

> **Parallel:**
> The topology course was both rigorous and *challenging*.

> **Rule 2** – When a series of adjective modify the same noun, they must share a similar form.

> **Awkward:**
> The interim Prime Minister is strong, compassionate, and wants to defeat the insurgency with a minimum of civilian casualties.

> **Parallel:**
> The interim Prime Minister is strong, compassionate, and *determined* to defeat the insurgency with a minimum of civilian casualties.

Often, this imbalance in complexity can make a sentence stilted, and the lesser adjectives will need to be subordinated.

> The interim Prime Minister, *who is strong and compassionate*, wants to defeat the insurgency with a minimum of civilian casualties.

However, the first rewrite is more natural, active and powerful.

> **Rule 3** – When a series of clauses is listed, the verbs in each clause must have the same form.

> **Awkward:**
> During his trip to Europe, the President will discuss ways to stimulate trade, offer economic aid, and trying to forge a new coalition with moderate forces in Russia.

> **Parallel:**
> During his trip to Europe, the President will discuss ways to stimulate trade, offer economic aid, and *try* to forge a new coalition with moderate forces in Russia.

> **Rule 4** – When the first half of a sentence has a certain structure, the second half should preserve that structure.

Awkward:
To acknowledge that one is an alcoholic is taking the first and hardest step to recovery.

Parallel:
To acknowledge that one is an alcoholic is *to take* the first and hardest step to recovery.

✓ Check your work

To correct an unparalleled structure, fist try giving the similar parts the same structure. For instance, change an adjective and a noun to two adjectives. However, this can sometimes also make the sentence more awkward. In these cases, you may need to subordinate one part to another.

Example:
He ranks as one of the top volleyball players in the country and is often solicited by clothing companies for his endorsement.

The first clause in this sentence uses the active verb *ranks*, and the second clause uses the passive verb *solicited*. Making the first clause passive can make the sentence parallel.

He *is ranked* as one of the top volleyball players in the country and is often solicited by clothing companies for his endorsement.

Be careful though; in writing, the active is preferred over the passive.

He *ranks* as one of the top volleyball players in the country, and clothing companies often *solicit* him for his endorsement.

But now the sentence sounds awkward. So instead of forcing a parallel structure here, let's just subordinate the first clause to the second clause:

As one of the top volleyball players in the country, he is often solicited for his endorsement.

➢ **Rule 5** – Correlative conjunctions should be preceded and followed by parallel constructions.

Following are some common correlative conjunctions:

both . . . and . . .
either . . . or . . .
neither . . . nor . . .
not only . . . but also . . .
whether . . . or . . .

Awkward:
It was a long vacation *and* very boring.

Parallel:
It was a long *and* very boring vacation.

Awkward:
The game was *not only* a financial success, *but* it *also* succeeded as art.

Parallel:
The game was *not only* a financial success *but also* an artistic success.

Verb Tense

A verb is usually defined as a word that expresses action or state of being. Oddly, this definition is simultaneously nebulous and too precise: "state of being" is vague, and words other than verbs can also carry the weight of action within a sentence. However, any attempt to better define the concept of a verb will lead us into far more detail than we have room to discuss. Let's just use the above definition to reinforce our understanding of the meaning and function of a verb in a sentence.

A verb has four principal forms:

1. **Present Tense**
    a. Used to express present tense: *He studies hard*

    b. Used to express general truths: *During a recession, people are cautious about their money.*

    c. Used with *will* or *shall* to express future time: *He will take the ACT next year.*

2. **Past Tense**
    a. Used to express past tense: *He took the ACT last year.*

3. **Past Participle**
    a. Used to form the *present perfect tense*, which indicates that an action was started in the past and its effects are continuing in the present. It is formed using *have* or *has* and the past participle of the verb: *He has prepared thoroughly for the ACT.*

    b. Used to form the *past perfect tense*, which indicates that an action was completed before another past action. It is formed using *had* and the past participle of the verb: *He had prepared thoroughly before taking the ACT.*

    c. Used to form the *future perfect tense*, which indicates that an action will be completed before another future action. It is formed using *will have* or *shall have* and the past participle of the verb: *He will have completed the ACT by now.*

4. **Present Participle**
    a. Used to form the *present progressive tense*, which indicates that an action is ongoing. It is formed using *is, am,* or *are* and the present participle of the verb: *He is preparing for the ACT.*

    b. Use to form the *past progressive tense*, which indicates that an action was in progress in the past. It is formed using *was* or *were* and the present participle of the verb: *He was preparing for the ACT.*

    c. Used to form the *future progressive tense*, which indicates that an action will be in progress in the future. It is formed using *will be* or *shall be* and the present participle of the verb: *He will be preparing for the ACT tonight.*

Much like a talented voice actor, verbs can also change their voice to suit a situation. But unlike a talented voice actor, verbs really only have two flavors to choose from.

The *passive voice* weakens a sentence by removing the subject of the sentence. Instead, the object of the sentence becomes the subject, and the subject becomes encased in a prepositional phrase.

The *active voice* is simply that. The verb shows the action that the subject is performing.

> **Passive Voice:**
> The bill *was resubmitted by* the Senator.
>
> **Active Voice:**
> *The Senator resubmitted* the bill.

Unless you want to de-emphasize the doer of an action, you should favor the active voice. Passive sentences are usually considered weak and timid. Notice in the above example that the sentence with the active verb is more powerful.

✓ Check your work

When passive construction is used in a sentence, the prepositional phrase often points to the wrong doer of action. Not only does this mistake make the writer seem unprofessional, but it will also lead to confusion for the reader.

> **Example:**
> The head of the insurgency of *was reported killed* in the first day of action by the press.

This sentence seems to imply that the press killed the head of the insurgency. The sentence is better expressed in the active voice:

> The press *reported* that the head of the insurgency *was killed* in the first day of action

Diction

By definition, *diction* is the choice and use of words and phrases in speech or writing. Often, these choices sound alike or even mean similar things. Because of this, diction errors occur daily in speech and writing. Fortunately for the writer, the most common diction errors can be pinpointed and fixed.

Accept/Except

Accept means to receive something that is offered or agree to something.

> The European powers would have *accepted* Iran's offer if it had included on-site and unrestricted inspections.

Except means to leave out or exclude something.

> All the world's industrial powers signed the treaty to reduce global warming *except* the United States.

Affect/Effect

Affect, usually a verb, means to influence or concern. *Effect*, usually a noun, means the cause or result.

> The anti-venom had the desired *effect*, and the boy fully recovered.

Here, *effect* is a noun meaning result.

> The negotiators were not *affected* by the large, violent street protests.

Here, *affected* is a verb meaning influence.

Among/Between

Between compares exactly two things. *Among* compares more than two things.

> The young lady must choose *between* two suitors.

Among compares more than two things.

> The fault is spread evenly *among* the three defendants.

As/Like

A frequent mistake is to use *like* when *as* is needed. If you are connecting a clause to its subject, use *as*. If you merely need a preposition to introduce a noun, use *like*.

> It appears *as* though the peace plan has failed.

As is introducing the clause *the peace plan has failed*.

It looks *like* rain.

Like is introducing the noun *rain*

As to

This phrase is usually imprecise. In almost all cases, it should replace with a more precise preposition or deleted.

Poor:
The prosecuting attorney left little doubt *as to* the defendant's motive for the murder.

Better:
The prosecuting attorney left little doubt *about* defendant's motive for the murder.

Poor:
The question *as to* whether it's better to let the bill die in committee or be voted down on the floor of the house is purely political.

Better:
The question *whether* it's better to let the bill die in committee or be voted down on the floor of the house is purely political.

Being that vs. Since

Being that is nonstandard and should be replaced by *since*.

Beside/Besides

Adding an *s* to *beside* completely changes its meaning: *Beside* means next to.

We sat *beside* (next to) the host.

Besides means in addition.

Besides (in addition), money was not even an issue in the contract negotiations.

Center on vs. Center around

Center around is colloquial. It should not be used in formal writing.

Incorrect:
The dispute *centers around* the effects of undocumented workers.

Correct:
The dispute *centers on* the effects of undocumented workers.

Conform to (not with)
>Stewart's writing does not *conform to* standard literary conventions.

Consensus of opinion
Consensus of opinion is redundant: consensus means general agreement, so *of opinion* is not necessary in the phase.

Correspond to/with
Correspond to means in agreement with.

>The penalty does not the severity of the crime.

Correspond with means to exchange letters.

>He *corresponded with* many of the top European leaders of his time.

Farther/Further
Farther refers to a measurable distance, and *further* refers to a figurative degree or quantity that can't be measured.

>**Examples:**
>They went no *further* (degree) than necking.
>He threw the discs *farther* (distance) than the top seated competitor.

Fewer/Less
Use *fewer* when referring to a number of items. Use *less* when referring to a continuous quantity.

>**Examples:**
>In the past, we had *fewer* options.
>The impact was *less* than what was expected.

Identical with (not to)
>This bid is *identical with* (not to) the one submitted by you.

In contrast to (not of)
>In *contrast to* (not of) the conservative attitudes of her time, Mae West was quite provocative.

Independent of (not from)
>The judiciary is *independent of* (not from) the other branches of government.

On account of vs. Because
Because is always better than *on account of*.

Poor:
On account of his poor behavior, he was expelled.

Better:
Because he behaved poorly, he was expelled.

One another/Each other
Use *each other* when referring to two things and *one another* when referring to more than two things.

Examples:
The members of the basketball team (more than two) congratulated *one another* on their victory.
The business partners (two) congratulated *each other* on their successful first year.

Plus vs. And
Do not use *plus* as a conjunction meaning *and*.

Incorrect:
His contributions to this community are considerable, *plus* his character is beyond reproach.

Correct:
His contributions to this community are considerable, *and* his character is beyond reproach.

Plus can be used to mean *and* as long as it is not being used as a conjunction.
His generous financial contribution *plus* his donated time has made this project a success.

Regard vs. Regards
Unless you are giving best wishes to someone, you should use *regard*.

Regardless vs. Irregardless
Regardless means "not withstanding." Hence, the "ir" in *irregardless* is redundant. *Irregardless* is not a real word and, therefore, should not be used under any circumstances.

Speak to/with
To *speak to* someone is to tell them something.

We *spoke to* Jennings about the alleged embezzlement.

To *speak with* someone is to discuss something with him or her.

Steve *spoke with* his friend Dave for hours yesterday.

Whether vs. As to whether
As to whether is wordy and should be replaced with *whether*.

Whether vs. If
Whether introduces a choice; *if* introduces a condition. A common mistake is to use *if* to present a choice.

> **Incorrect:**
> He inquired *if* we had decided to keep the gift.
>
> **Correct:**
> He inquired *whether* we had decided to keep the gift.

✓ <u>Check your work</u>
At times, grammar can seem impossible to conquer, especially when regularly accepted, spoken terms are often incorrect when written down on paper. But if you can remember a few key phrases and rules, you'll be mastering the written word in no time.

Points to Remember

1. A pronoun should be plural when it refers to two nouns joined by *and*.
2. A pronoun should be singular when it refers to two nouns joined by *or* or *nor*.
3. A pronoun should refer to one, and only one, noun or compound noun.
4. A pronoun must agree with its antecedent in both number and person.
5. The subject and verb must agree both in number and person.
6. Intervening phrases and clauses have no effect on subject-verb agreement.
7. When the subject and verb are reversed, they still must agree in both number and person.
8. As a general rule, a modifier should be placed as close as possible to what it modifies.
9. When a phrase begins a sentence, make sure that it modifies the subject of the sentence.
10. For a sentence to be parallel, similar elements must be expressed in similar form.
11. When two adjectives modify the same noun, they should have similar forms.
12. When a series of clauses is listed, the verbs must be in the same forms.
13. When the first half of a sentence has a certain structure, the second half should preserve that structure.
14. An adverb modifies a verb, an adjective, or another adverb.
15. A verb has four principal forms:
    I. Present Tense
        a. Used to express something that is occurring now.
        b. Used to express general truths.
        c. Used with *will* or *shall* to express future time.

    II. Past Tense
        a. Used to express something that occurred in the past.

    III. Past Participle
        a. Used to form the *present perfect tense*, which indicates that an action was started in the past and its effects are continuing in the present. It is formed using *have* or *has* and the past participle of the verb.
        b. Used to form the *past perfect tense*, which indicates that an action was completed before another past action. It is formed using *had* and the past participle of the verb.
        c. Used to form the *future perfect tense*, which indicates that an action is ongoing. It is formed using *is*, *am*, or *are* and the present participle of the verb.

    IV. Present Participle (*-ing* form of the verb)
        a. Used to form the *present progressive tense*, which indicates that an action is ongoing. It is formed using *is*, *am*, or *are* and the present participle of the verb.
        b. Used to form the *past progressive tense*, which indicates that an action was in progress in the past. It is formed using *was* or *were* and the present participle of the verb.
        c. Used to form the *future progressive tense*, which indicates that an action will be in progress in the future. It is formed using *will be* or *shall be* and the present participle of the verb.

16. Unless you intend to de-emphasize the doer of an action in a sentence, you should favor the active voice.

17. Attack strategy for identifying misplaced modifiers:
    I.   Find the subject and the verb.
    II. Isolate the subject and the verb by deleting intervening phrases.
    III. Follow the rule of proximity: Modifiers should describe what they are next to in a sentence.
    IV. Check the punctuation. Punctuation should create coherence and not confusion.

Grammar Practice Drills

> In each of the following sentences, part or all of the sentence is underlined. The answer-choices offer five ways of phrasing the underlined part. If you think the sentence as written is better than the alternatives, choose A, which merely repeats the underlined part; otherwise choose one of the alternatives.

1. Had the President's Administration not lost the vote on the budget reduction package, his first year in office would have been rated an A.
   (A) NO CHANGE
   (B) If the Administration had not lost the vote on the budget reduction package, his first year in office would have been rated an A.
   (C) Had the President's Administration not lost the vote on the budget reduction package, it would have been rated an A.
   (D) Had the President's Administration not lost the vote on its budget reduction package, his first year in office would have been rated an A.
   (E) If the President had not lost the vote on the budget reduction package, the Administration's first year in office would have been rated an A.

2. The new law requires a manufacturer to immediately notify their customers whenever the government is contemplating a forced recall of any of the manufacturer's products.
   (A) NO CHANGE
   (B) to immediately notify customers whenever the government is contemplating a forced recall of their products.
   (C) to immediately, and without delay, notify its customers whenever the government is contemplating a forced recall of any of the manufacture's products.
   (D) to immediately notify whenever the government is contemplating a forced recall of any of the manufacturer's products that the customers may have bought.
   (E) to immediately notify its customers whenever the government is contemplating a forced recall of any of the manufacturer's products.

3. World War II taught the United States the folly of punishing a vanquished aggressor; so after the war, they enacted the Marshall Plan to rebuild Germany.
   (A) NO CHANGE
   (B) after the war, the Marshall Plan was enacted to rebuild Germany.
   (C) after the war, the Marshall Plan was enacted by the United States to rebuild Germany.
   (D) after the war, the United States enacted the Marshall Plan to rebuild Germany.
   (E) after the war, the United States enacted the Marshall Plan in order to rebuild Germany.

4. In the 1950's, integration was an anathema to most Americans; now, however, most Americans accept it as desirable.
   (A) NO CHANGE
   (B) to most Americans, now, however, most Americans accept it.
   (C) to most Americans; now, however, most Americans are desirable of it.
   (D) to most Americans; now, however, most Americans accepted it as desirable.
   (E) to most Americans. Now, however, most Americans will accept it as desirable.

5. Geologists in California have discovered a fault near the famous San Andreas Fault, one that they believe to be a trigger for major quakes on the San Andreas.
   (A) NO CHANGE
   (B) one they believe to be a trigger for
   (C) one that they believe triggers
   (D) that they believe to be a trigger for
   (E) one they believe acts as a trigger for

6. The rising cost of government bureaucracy have made it all but impossible to reign in the budget deficit.
   (A) NO CHANGE
   (B) Since the rising costs
   (C) Because of the rising costs
   (D) The rising costs
   (E) Rising cost

7. In a co-publication agreement, ownership of both the material and its means of distribution are equally shared by the parties.
   (A) NO CHANGE
   (B) its means of distribution are shared equally by each of the parties.
   (C) its means of distribution is equally shared by the parties.
   (D) their means of distribution is equally shared by the parties.
   (E) the means of distribution are equally shared by the parties.

8. The rise in negative attitudes toward foreigners indicate that the country is becoming less tolerant, and therefore that the opportunities are ripe for extremist groups to exploit the illegal immigration problem.
   (A) NO CHANGE
   (B) indicates that the country is becoming less tolerant, and therefore
   (C) indicates that the country is becoming less tolerant, and therefore that
   (D) indicates that the country is being less tolerant, and therefore
   (E) indicates that the country is becoming less tolerant of and therefore that

9. The harvest of grapes in the local valleys decreased in 1990 for the third straight year but were still at a robust level.
   (A) NO CHANGE
   (B) The harvest of grapes in the local valleys began to decrease in 1990 for the third straight year but were
   (C) In 1990, the harvest of grapes in the local valleys decreased for the third straight year but were
   (D) The harvest of grapes in the local valleys decreased for the third straight year in 1990 but was
   (E) The harvest of grapes in the local valleys began decreasing in 1990 for the third straight year but was

10. More important than winning is developing the ability to work with others and developing leadership skills.
    (A) NO CHANGE
    (B) More important than winning are the ability to work with others and leadership skills.
    (C) Developing the ability to work with others and developing leadership skills is more important than winning.
    (D) More important than winning are developing the ability to work with others and developing leadership skills.
    (E) More important than winning has been the development of the ability to work with others and the development leadership skills.

11. There is a number of solutions to the problem of global warming that have not been considered by this committee.
    (A) NO CHANGE
    (B) There are a number of solutions
    (C) There was a number of solutions
    (D) There were a number of solutions
    (E) There have been a number of solutions

12. By focusing on poverty, the other causes of crime—such as the breakup of the nuclear family, changing morals, the loss of community, etc.—have been overlooked by sociologists.
    (A) NO CHANGE
    (B) the other causes of crime have been overlooked by sociologists—such as the breakup of the nuclear family, changing morals, the loss of community, etc.
    (C) there are other causes of crime that have been overlooked by sociologists—such as the breakup of the nuclear family, changing morals, the loss of community, etc.
    (D) crimes—such as the breakup of the nuclear family, changing morals, the loss of community, etc.—have been overlooked by sociologists.
    (E) sociologists have overlooked the other causes of crime—such as the breakup of the nuclear family, changing morals, the loss of community, etc.

13. Using the Hubble telescope, previously unknown galaxies are now being charted.
    (A) NO CHANGE
    (B) Previously unknown galaxies are now being charted, using the Hubble telescope.
    (C) Using the Hubble telescope, previously unknown galaxies are now being charted by astronomers.
    (D) Using the Hubble telescope, astronomers are now charting previously unknown galaxies.
    (E) With the aid of the Hubble telescope, previously unknown galaxies are now being charted.

14. The bitter cold the Midwest is experiencing is potentially life threatening to stranded motorists unless well-insulated with protective clothing.
    (A) NO CHANGE
    (B) stranded motorists unless being insulated
    (C) stranded motorists unless they are well-insulated
    (D) stranded motorists unless there is insulation
    (E) the stranded motorist unless insulated

15. Traveling across and shooting the vast expanse of the Southwest, in 1945 Ansel Adams began his photographic career.
    (A) NO CHANGE
    (B) In 1945, Ansel Adams began his photographic career, traveling across and shooting the vast expanse of the Southwest.
    (C) Having traveled across and shooting the vast expanse of the Southwest, in 1945 Ansel Adams began his photographic career.
    (D) Ansel Adams, in 1945 began his photographic career, traveling across and shooting the vast expanse of the Southwest.
    (E) Traveling across and shooting the vast expanse of the Southwest, Ansel Adams began his photographic career in 1945.

16. The Harmony virus will destroy a computer system unless inoculated by an anti-harmony program.
    (A) NO CHANGE
    (B) a computer system unless the system is inoculated
    (C) a computer system unless it is inoculated
    (D) a computer system unless inoculation occurred
    (E) a system unless it's being inoculated

17. As head of the division, we believe you should make the decision whether to retake the rebel stronghold.
    (A) NO CHANGE
    (B) Seeing as you are the head of the division, we believe
    (C) Being the head of the division, we believe
    (D) As head of the division, we are inclined to believe
    (E) We believe that as head of the division

18. It is well established that the death of a parent during childhood can cause insecurity in adults.
    (A) NO CHANGE
    (B) It is well established that the death of a parent when a child can cause insecurity in adults.
    (C) It is well established that the death of a parent occurring when a child can cause insecurity in adults.
    (D) It is well established that people who during childhood experience the death of a parent can be insecure as adults.
    (E) That people who during childhood experience the death of a parent can be insecure as adults is well established.

Grammar Practice Drills

19. <u>Based on the yarns of storytellers, linguistic archeologists are compiling a written history of Valhalla and are realizing</u> that much of what was considered myth is in fact true.
    (A) NO CHANGE
    (B) Basing on the yarns of storytellers, linguistic archeologists are compiling a written history of Valhalla and are realizing
    (C) Using the yarns of storytellers, linguistic archeologists are compiling a written history of Valhalla and are realizing
    (D) Based on the yarns of storytellers, linguistic archeologists are compiling a written history of Valhalla and are coming to the realization
    (E) Deriving it from the yarns of storytellers, linguistic archeologists are compiling a written history of Valhalla and are realizing

20. Common knowledge tells us that sensible exercise and <u>eating properly will result</u> in better health.
    (A) NO CHANGE
    (B) proper diet resulted
    (C) dieting will result
    (D) proper diet results
    (E) eating properly results

21. This century began with <u>war brewing in Europe, the industrial revolution well-established, and a nascent communication age.</u>
    (A) NO CHANGE
    (B) war brewing in Europe, the industrial revolution surging, and a nascent communication age.
    (C) war in Europe, the industrial revolution well-established, and a nascent communication age.
    (D) war brewing in Europe, the industrial revolution well-established, and the communication age beginning.
    (E) war brewing in Europe, the industrial revolution well-established, and saw the birth of the communication age.

22. It is often better <u>to try repairing an old car than to junk it.</u>
    (A) NO CHANGE
    (B) to repair an old car than to have it junked.
    (C) to try repairing an old car than to junking it.
    (D) to try and repair an old car than to junk it.
    (E) to try to repair an old car than to junk it.

23. <u>Jurassic Park, written by Michael Crichton, and which was first printed in 1988,</u> is a novel about a theme park of the future in which dinosaurs roam free.
    (A) NO CHANGE
    (B) Jurassic Park, written by Michael Crichton and first printed in 1988,
    (C) Jurassic Park, which was written by Michael Crichton, and which was first printed in 1988,
    (D) Written by Michael Crichton and first printed in 1988, Jurassic Park
    (E) Jurassic Park, which was written by Michael Crichton and first printed in 1988,

The following passage is a first draft of an essay. Some parts of the passage need to be rewritten.

(1) Nestled in the foothills of the Smoky Mountains, *Getaway Lodge* offers its guests hospitality, comfort, and living in luxury. (2) Guests are greeted at the door and ushered to their rooms where they are welcomed with a large gift basket filled with scrumptious snacks and bath oils. (3) Every room has magnificent, breathtaking views of the surrounding mountains. (4) The mountains offer a myriad of activities for travelers including hiking and rock climbing. (5) If outdoor recreation is not appealing, guests can lounge by the free-form pool or soak in the hot tub.

(6) After a full day's activities, dinner is served in a romantic dining room adjacent to a waterfall. (7) By the glow of candlelight, diners will enjoy savory entrees and decadent desserts. (8) After dinner, guests may enjoy a stroll through the garden or sitting by the fireplace. (9) With so many pleasurable activities, guests can easily pass a memorable week at the *Getaway Lodge*.

24. What is the best way to deal with sentence 1 (reproduced below)?

    Nestled in the foothills of the Smoky Mountains, Getaway Lodge offers its guests hospitality, comfort, and living in luxury.

    (A) NO CHANGE
    (B) Change *its* to *their*.
    (C) Change *hospitably* to *hospitable living*.
    (D) Change *comfort* to *comfortable living*.
    (E) Change *living in luxury* to *luxurious living*.

25. Which of the following is the best revision of sentence 4 to better link it to sentence 3?
    (A) Every room also has magnificent, breathtaking views of the surrounding mountains.
    (B) Moreover, every room has magnificent, breathtaking views of the surrounding mountains.
    (C) Guests are also treated to magnificent, breathtaking views of the surrounding mountains.
    (D) In addition, guests are also shown magnificent, breathtaking views of the surrounding mountains.
    (E) Also, guests may view magnificent, breathtaking views of the surrounding mountains.

26. What is the best way to deal with sentence 8 (reproduced below)?

    After dinner, guests may enjoy a stroll through the garden or sitting by the fireplace.

    (A) NO CHANGE
    (B) Change *enjoy* to *take*.
    (C) Change *a stroll* to *strolling*.
    (D) Change *sitting* to *taking a seat*.
    (E) Place *after dinner* at the end of the sentence.

27. In the past few years and to this day, many teachers of math and science <u>had chosen to return to the private sector.</u>
    (A) NO CHANGE
    (B) having chosen to return to the private sector.
    (C) chose to return to the private sector.
    (D) have chosen to return to the private sector.
    (E) have chosen returning to the private sector.

28. Most of the homes that were destroyed in last summer's brush fires were built with wood-shake roofs.
    (A) NO CHANGE
    (B) Last summer, brush fires destroyed most of the homes that were
    (C) Most of the homes that were destroyed in last summer's brush fires had been
    (D) Most of the homes that the brush fires destroyed last summer's have been
    (E) Most of the homes destroyed in last summer's brush fires were being

29. Although World War II ended nearly a half century ago, Russia and Japan still have not signed a formal peace treaty; and both countries have been reticent to develop closer relations.
    (A) NO CHANGE
    (B) did not signed a formal peace treaty; and both countries have been
    (C) have not signed a formal peace treaty; and both countries being
    (D) have not signed a formal peace treaty; and both countries are
    (E) are not signing a formal peace treaty; and both countries have been

30. The Democrats have accused the Republicans of resorting to dirty tricks by planting a mole on the Democrat's planning committee and then used the information obtained to sabotage the Democrat's campaign.
    (A) NO CHANGE
    (B) used the information they had obtained to sabotage
    (C) of using the information they had obtained to sabotage
    (D) using the information obtained to sabotage
    (E) to have used the information obtained to sabotage

31. Unless you maintain at least a 2.0 GPA, you will not graduate medical school.
    (A) NO CHANGE
    (B) you will not be graduated from medical school.
    (C) you will not be graduating medical school.
    (D) you will not graduate from medical school.
    (E) you will graduate medical school.

32. The studio's retrospective art exhibit refers back to a simpler time in American history.
    (A) NO CHANGE
    (B) The studio's retrospective art exhibit harkens back to
    (C) The studio's retrospective art exhibit refers to
    (D) The studio's retrospective art exhibit refers from
    (E) The studio's retrospective art exhibit looks back to

33. Due to the chemical spill, the commute into the city will be delayed by as much as 2 hours.
    (A) NO CHANGE
    (B) The reason that the commute into the city will be delayed by as much as 2 hours is because of the chemical spill.
    (C) Due to the chemical spill, the commute into the city had been delayed by as much as 2 hours.
    (D) Because of the chemical spill, the commute into the city will be delayed by as much as 2 hours.
    (E) The chemical spill will be delaying the commute into the city by as much as 2 hours.

The following passage is a first draft of an essay. Some parts of the passage need to be rewritten.

(1) A best-selling book offers "Seven Ways to Become a Better Person." **(2)** A radio ad promises you will feel great in 30 days or less just by taking some pills. **(3)** "If you buy our exercise equipment," a TV ad guarantees, "you'll have the body you've always wanted." **(4)** In today's society, we are continually bombarded with the latest techniques of how to better ourselves, a focus which some feel is unhealthy. **(5)** Additionally, a focus on self-improvement is very important in helping people grow in character.

(6) Self-improvement helps build character. **(7)** Building character involves taking a person's strengths and building on them. **(8)** Such strengths as unselfishness can be developed into a lifelong habit of generosity, a positive spirit into an unfailing compassion for others. **(9)** Everyone has strength in character and the ability to build on these strengths through self-improvement.

(10) Weaknesses are not flaws, but rather negative traits that, through self-improvement, can be developed into more positive traits. **(11)** For example, impatience can be turned into determination to accomplish goals. **(12)** Strong will turns into perseverance. **(13)** If a person can just find a way to capitalize on a weakness, it can be turned into a strength. **(14)** Self-improvement is the best way to do this.

34. What is the best word or phrase to use in place of the word *additionally* in sentence 5 (reproduced below)?

    Additionally, a focus on self-improvement is very important in helping people grow in character.

    (A) Moreover
    (B) On the contrary
    (C) Along those lines
    (D) Consequently
    (E) Accordingly

35. What is the best way to deal with sentence 12 (reproduced below)?

    Strong will turns into perseverance.

    (A) NO CHANGE
    (B) Add *is* before *turns* and change *turns* to *turned*.
    (C) Add *shall* before *turns* and change *turns* to *turn*.
    (D) Change *turns into* to *becomes*.
    (E) Add *can be* before *turns* and change *turns* to *turned*.

Solutions to Grammar Practice Drills

1. Had the President's Administration not lost the vote on the budget reduction package, his first year in office would have been rated an A.
   (A) NO CHANGE
   (B) If the Administration had not lost the vote on the budget reduction package, his first year in office would have been rated an A.
   (C) Had the President's Administration not lost the vote on the budget reduction package, it would have been rated an A.
   (D) Had the President's Administration not lost the vote on its budget reduction package, his first year in office would have been rated an A.
   (E) If the President had not lost the vote on the budget reduction package, the Administration's first year in office would have been rated an A.

The answer is (E).

Choice (A) is incorrect because *his* appears to refer to *the President*, but the subject of the subordinate clause is *the President's Administration*, not *the President*.

Choice (B) changes the structure of the sentence, but retains the same flawed reference.

In choice (C), *it* can refer to either *the President's Administration* or *the budget reduction package*. Thus, the reference is ambiguous.

Choice (D) adds another pronoun, *its*, but still retains the same flawed reference.

Choice (E) corrects the flawed reference by removing all pronouns.

2. The new law requires a manufacturer to immediately notify their customers whenever the government is contemplating a forced recall of any of the manufacturer's products.
   (A) NO CHANGE
   (B) to immediately notify customers whenever the government is contemplating a forced recall of their products.
   (C) to immediately, and without delay, notify its customers whenever the government is contemplating a forced recall of any of the manufacture's products.
   (D) to immediately notify whenever the government is contemplating a forced recall of any of the manufacturer's products that the customers may have bought.
   (E) to immediately notify its customers whenever the government is contemplating a forced recall of any of the manufacturer's products.

The answer is (E).

Choice (A) is incorrect because the plural pronoun *their* cannot have the singular noun *a manufacturer* as its antecedent.

Although choice (B) corrects the given false reference, it introduces another one. *Their* can now refer to either *customers* or *government*, neither of which would make sense in this context.

Choice (C) also corrects the false reference, but it introduces a redundancy: *immediately* means "without delay."

Choice (D) corrects the false reference, but its structure is very awkward. The direct object of a verb should be as close to the verb as possible. In this case, the verb *notify* is separated from its direct object *customers* by the clause *that the government is contemplating a forced recall of any of the manufacturer's products that*.

Choice (E) is correct because the singular pronoun *its* has the singular noun *a manufacturer* as its antecedent.

3. World War II taught the United States the folly of punishing a vanquished aggressor; so <u>after the war, they enacted the Marshall Plan to rebuild Germany.</u>
   (A) NO CHANGE
   (B) after the war, the Marshall Plan was enacted to rebuild Germany.
   (C) after the war, the Marshall Plan was enacted by the United States to rebuild Germany.
   (D) after the war, the United States enacted the Marshall Plan to rebuild Germany.
   (E) after the war, the United States enacted the Marshall Plan in order to rebuild Germany.

The answer is (D).

Choice (A) is incorrect. Since *United States* is denoting the collective country, it is singular and therefore cannot be correctly referred to by the plural pronoun *they*.

Choice (B) is not technically incorrect, but it lacks precision since it does not state who enacted the Marshall Plan. Further, it uses a passive construction: *was enacted*.

Choice (C) states who enacted the Marshall Plan, but it retains the passive construction *was enacted*.

Choice (E) does not violate the rules of grammar (though some strict grammarians do object to its use in this context). It is the second-best answer-choice. The phrase "*in order*" is unnecessary. In this context, the phase "*in order to*" has the same meaning as just the word "*to*." Choice (D) is the same as Choice (E), except for the redundant words "in order," so it is a better answer.

Choice (D) corrects the false reference by replacing *they* with *the United States*. Further, it uses the active verb *enacted* instead of the passive verb *was enacted*.

4. In the 1950's, integration was an anathema <u>to most Americans; now, however, most Americans accept it as desirable.</u>
   (A) NO CHANGE
   (B) to most Americans, now, however, most Americans accept it.
   (C) to most Americans; now, however, most Americans are desirable of it.
   (D) to most Americans; now, however, most Americans accepted it as desirable.
   (E) to most Americans. Now, however, most Americans will accept it as desirable.

The sentence is correct as written. The answer is (A).

Choice (B) creates a run-on sentence by replacing the semicolon with a comma. Without a connecting word (*and, or, but*, etc.) two independent clauses must be joined by a semicolon or written as two separate sentences. Also, deleting *as desirable* changes the meaning of the sentence.

Choice (C) uses a very awkward construction: *are desirable of it*.

Choice (D) contains an error in tense. The sentence progresses from the past to the present, so the verb in the second clause should be *accept*, not *accepted*.

Choice (E) writes the two clauses as separate sentences, which is allowable, but it also changes the tense of the second clause to the future: *will accept*.

5. Geologists in California have discovered a fault near the famous San Andreas Fault, <u>one that they believe to be a trigger for</u> major quakes on the San Andreas.
   (A) NO CHANGE
   (B) one they believe to be a trigger for
   (C) one that they believe triggers
   (D) that they believe to be a trigger for
   (E) one they believe acts as a trigger for

The answer is (B).

Choice (A) is incorrect since the relative pronoun *that* is redundant: the pronoun *one*, which refers to the newly discovered fault, is sufficient.

Although choice (C) reads more smoothly, it still contains the double pronouns.

Choice (D) is incorrect. Generally, relative pronouns such as *that* refer to whole ideas in previous clauses or sentences. Since the second sentence is about the fault and not its discovery, the pronoun *that* is appropriate.

Choice (E) is very tempting. It actually reads better than choice (A), but it contains a subtle flaw. *One* is the direct object of the verb *believes* and therefore cannot be the subject of the verb *acts*. Since *they* clearly is not the subject, the verb *acts* is without a subject.

Choice (B) has both the correct pronoun and the correct verb form.

6. <u>The rising cost</u> of government bureaucracy have made it all but impossible to reign in the budget deficit.
   (A) NO CHANGE
   (B) Since the rising costs
   (C) Because of the rising costs
   (D) The rising costs
   (E) Rising cost

The answer is (D).

Choice (A) is incorrect because the plural verb *have* does not agree with its singular subject *the rising cost*.

Both (B) and (C) are incorrect because they turn the sentence into a fragment.

Choice (E) is incorrect because *rising cost* is still singular.

Choice (D) is the correct answer since now the plural verb *have* agrees with its plural subject *the rising costs*.

7. In a co-publication agreement, ownership of both the material and <u>its means of distribution are equally shared by the parties.</u>
   (A) NO CHANGE
   (B) its means of distribution are shared equally by each of the parties.
   (C) its means of distribution is equally shared by the parties.
   (D) their means of distribution is equally shared by the parties.
   (E) the means of distribution are equally shared by the parties.

The answer is (C).

Choice (A) is incorrect. Recall that intervening phrases have no effect on subject-verb agreement. In this sentence, the subject *ownership* is singular, but the verb *are* is plural.

Choice (B) is incorrect. Neither adding *each of* nor interchanging *shared* and *equally* addresses the issue of subject-verb agreement.

Choice (D) contains a faulty pronoun reference. The antecedent of the plural pronoun *their* would be the singular noun *material*.

Choice (E) is incorrect since it still contains the plural verb *are*.

8. The rise in negative attitudes toward foreigners <u>indicate that the country is becoming less tolerant, and therefore that</u> the opportunities are ripe for extremist groups to exploit the illegal immigration problem.
   (A) NO CHANGE
   (B) indicates that the country is becoming less tolerant, and therefore
   (C) indicates that the country is becoming less tolerant, and therefore that
   (D) indicates that the country is being less tolerant, and therefore
   (E) indicates that the country is becoming less tolerant of and therefore that

The answer is (B).

Choice (A) has two flaws. First, the subject of the sentence *the rise* is singular, and therefore the verb *indicate* should not be plural. Second, the comma indicates that the sentence is made up of two independent clauses, but the relative pronoun *that* immediately following *therefore* forms a subordinate clause.

Choice (C) corrects the number of the verb, but retains the subordinating relative pronoun *that*.

Choice (D) corrects the number of the verb and eliminates the subordinating relative pronoun *that*. However, the verb *being* is less descriptive than the verb *becoming*: As negative attitudes toward foreigners increase, the country becomes correspondingly less tolerant. *Being* does not capture this notion of change.

Choice (E) corrects the verb's number, and by dropping the comma, makes the subordination allowable. However, it introduces the preposition *of* which does not have an object: less tolerant of what?

Choice (B) both corrects the verb's number and removes the subordinating relative pronoun *that*.

9. The harvest of grapes in the local valleys decreased in 1990 for the third straight year but were still at a robust level.
   (A) NO CHANGE
   (B) The harvest of grapes in the local valleys began to decrease in 1990 for the third straight year but were
   (C) In 1990, the harvest of grapes in the local valleys decreased for the third straight year but were
   (D) The harvest of grapes in the local valleys decreased for the third straight year in 1990 but was
   (E) The harvest of grapes in the local valleys began decreasing in 1990 for the third straight year but was

The answer is (D).

Choice (A) is incorrect since the singular subject *the harvest* requires a singular verb, not the plural verb *were*.

Choice (B) is illogical since it states that the harvest began to decrease in 1990 and then it states that it was the third straight year of decrease.

In choice (C) the plural verb *were* still does not agree with its singular subject *the harvest*.

Choice (E) contains the same flaw as choice (B).

Choice (D) has the singular verb *was* agreeing with its singular subject *the harvest*. Further, it places the phrase *in 1990* more naturally.

10. More important than winning is developing the ability to work with others and developing leadership skills.
    (A) NO CHANGE
    (B) More important than winning are the ability to work with others and leadership skills.
    (C) Developing the ability to work with others and developing leadership skills is more important than winning.
    (D) More important than winning are developing the ability to work with others and developing leadership skills.
    (E) More important than winning has been the development of the ability to work with others and the development leadership skills.

The answer is (D).

Choice (A) is incorrect since the compound subject *developing the ability to work with others and developing leadership skills* requires a plural verb, not the singular verb *is*.

Choice (B) uses the correct plural verb *are* but deletes the word *developing*, making the meaning of the sentence less clear.

Choice (C) uses a the natural order of subject then verb, but it is incorrect since the compound subject *developing the ability to work with others and developing leadership skills* requires a plural verb, not the singular verb *is*.

Choice (D) has the plural verb *are* agreeing with its compound subject *developing the ability to work with others and developing leadership skills*.

Choice (E) is incorrect since the compound subject *the development of the ability to work with others and the development leadership skills* requires a plural verb, not the singular verb *has*.

11. There is a number of solutions to the problem of global warming that have not been considered by this committee.
    (A) NO CHANGE
    (B) There are a number of solutions
    (C) There was a number of solutions
    (D) There were a number of solutions
    (E) There have been a number of solutions

The answer is (B).

Choice (A) is incorrect since the plural subject *a number* requires a plural verb, not the singular verb *is*.

Choice (B) is the answer because it correctly uses the plural verb *are* with the plural subject *a number*.

Choice (C) is incorrect since the plural subject *a number* requires a plural verb, not the singular verb *was*. Further, the shift in verb tense from *was* to *have not been* is awkward.

Choice (D) is incorrect because the shift in verb tense from *were* to *have not been* is awkward.

Choice (E) is incorrect because it is awkward and changes the meaning of the sentence.

12. By focusing on poverty, the other causes of crime—such as the breakup of the nuclear family, changing morals, the loss of community, etc.—have been overlooked by sociologists.
    (A) NO CHANGE
    (B) the other causes of crime have been overlooked by sociologists—such as the breakup of the nuclear family, changing morals, the loss of community, etc.
    (C) there are other causes of crime that have been overlooked by sociologists—such as the breakup of the nuclear family, changing morals, the loss of community, etc.
    (D) crimes—such as the breakup of the nuclear family, changing morals, the loss of community, etc.—have been overlooked by sociologists.
    (E) sociologists have overlooked the other causes of crime—such as the breakup of the nuclear family, changing morals, the loss of community, etc.

The answer is (E).

Choice (A) is incorrect since it implies that *the other causes of crime* are doing the focusing.

Choice (B) has the same flaw as Choice (A).

Choice (C) is incorrect. The phrase *by focusing on poverty* must modify the subject of the sentence, but *there* cannot be the subject since the construction *there are* is used to introduce a subject.

Choice (D) implies that *crimes* are focusing on poverty.

Choice (E) correctly puts the subject of the sentence *sociologists* immediately next to its modifying phrase *by focusing on poverty*.

13. Using the Hubble telescope, previously unknown galaxies are now being charted.
    (A) NO CHANGE
    (B) Previously unknown galaxies are now being charted, using the Hubble telescope.
    (C) Using the Hubble telescope, previously unknown galaxies are now being charted by astronomers.
    (D) Using the Hubble telescope, astronomers are now charting previously unknown galaxies.
    (E) With the aid of the Hubble telescope, previously unknown galaxies are now being charted.

The answer is (D).

Choice (A) is incorrect because the phrase *using the Hubble telescope* does not have a noun to modify.

Choice (B) is incorrect because the phrase *using the Hubble telescope* still does not have a noun to modify.

Choice (C) offers a noun, *astronomers*, but it is too far from the phrase *using the Hubble telescope*.

Choice (D) offers a noun, *astronomers*, and correctly places it immediately after the modifying phrase *using the Hubble telescope*.

In choice (E), the phrase *with the aid of the Hubble telescope* does not have a noun to modify.

14. The bitter cold the Midwest is experiencing is potentially life threatening to <u>stranded motorists unless well-insulated</u> with protective clothing.
    (A) NO CHANGE
    (B) stranded motorists unless being insulated
    (C) stranded motorists unless they are well-insulated
    (D) stranded motorists unless there is insulation
    (E) the stranded motorist unless insulated

The answer is (C).

Choice (A) is incorrect. As worded, the sentence implies that the cold should be well-insulated.

Choice (B) is awkward; besides, it still implies that the cold should be well-insulated.

Choice (C) is the answer since it correctly implies that the stranded motorists should be well-insulated with protective clothing.

Choice (D) does not indicate what should be insulated.

Choice (E), like choices (A) and (B), implies that the cold should be well-insulated.

15. <u>Traveling across and shooting the vast expanse of the Southwest, in 1945 Ansel Adams began his photographic career.</u>
    (A) NO CHANGE
    (B) In 1945, Ansel Adams began his photographic career, traveling across and shooting the vast expanse of the Southwest.
    (C) Having traveled across and shooting the vast expanse of the Southwest, in 1945 Ansel Adams began his photographic career.
    (D) Ansel Adams, in 1945 began his photographic career, traveling across and shooting the vast expanse of the Southwest.
    (E) Traveling across and shooting the vast expanse of the Southwest, Ansel Adams began his photographic career in 1945.

The answer is (E).

Choice (A) has two flaws. First, the introductory phrase is too long. Second, the subject Ansel Adams should immediately follow the introductory phrase since it was Ansel Adams—not the year 1945—who was traveling and shooting the Southwest.

Choice (B) is incorrect because the phrase *traveling across . . . Southwest* is too far from its subject Ansel Adams. As written, the sentence seems to imply that the photographic career was traveling across and shooting the Southwest.

Choice (C) is inconsistent in verb tense. Further, it implies that Adams began his photographic career after he traveled across the Southwest.

Choice (D) is awkward.

Choice (E) is the best answer.

16. The Harmony virus will destroy <u>a computer system unless inoculated</u> by an anti-harmony program.
    (A) NO CHANGE
    (B) a computer system unless the system is inoculated
    (C) a computer system unless it is inoculated
    (D) a computer system unless inoculation occurred
    (E) a system unless it's being inoculated

The answer is (B).

Choice (A) is incorrect because it implies that the Harmony virus should be inoculated when it's the computer system that needs to be protected.

Choice (B) is the answer since it correctly implies that the computer system should be inoculated, not the virus.

Choice (C) sounds better, but it is not clear what the pronoun *it* is referring to, the virus or the computer. Hence, it is not clear whether it's the virus or the computer that needs to be inoculated.

Choice (D) is awkward, and it implies that the Harmony virus should be inoculated when it's the computer system that needs to be protected.

Choice (E) is awkward, and it implies that the Harmony virus should be inoculated when it's the computer system that needs to be protected.

17. <u>As head of the division, we believe</u> you should make the decision whether to retake the rebel stronghold.
    (A) NO CHANGE
    (B) Seeing as you are the head of the division, we believe
    (C) Being the head of the division, we believe
    (D) As head of the division, we are inclined to believe
    (E) We believe that as head of the division

The answer is (E).

Choice (A) is incorrect because it implies that *we* are the head of the division instead of the actual head of the division *you*.

Although Choice (B) makes clear who is the head of the division (*you* not *we*), the structure *Seeing as you...* is too lose and informal.

Choice (C) makes the same mistake as the original sentence: It implies that *we* are the head of the division instead of the actual head of the division *you*.

Choice (D) is incorrect because it merely adds unnecessary words *are inclined to* which does not correct the flaw in the original sentence: It still implies that *we* are the head of the division instead of the actual head of the division *you*.

Choice (E) is the answer because the clause *that as head of the division* correctly modifies the head of the division *you*.

18. It is well established that the death of a parent during childhood can cause insecurity in adults.
    (A) NO CHANGE
    (B) It is well established that the death of a parent when a child can cause insecurity in adults.
    (C) It is well established that the death of a parent occurring when a child can cause insecurity in adults.
    (D) It is well established that people who during childhood experience the death of a parent can be insecure as adults.
    (E) That people who during childhood experience the death of a parent can be insecure as adults is well established.

The answer is (D).

Choice (A) is incorrect because the phrase *during childhood* modifies *parent* illogically implying that the parent died during childhood.

Choice (B) is incorrect because the phrase *when a child* modifies *parent* illogically implying that the parent died during childhood.

Choice (C) is incorrect because the phrase *occurring when a child* modifies *parent* illogically implying that the parent died during childhood.

Choice (D) is the answer. Now, the phrase *during childhood* correctly modifies *people*.

Choice (E) is very awkward. The long clause *That people who . . . as adults* is the subject of the sentence. Although perhaps not ungrammatical, Choice (E) is very hard to read.

19. Based on the yarns of storytellers, linguistic archeologists are compiling a written history of Valhalla and are realizing that much of what was considered myth is in fact true.
    (A) NO CHANGE
    (B) Basing on the yarns of storytellers, linguistic archeologists are compiling a written history of Valhalla and are realizing
    (C) Using the yarns of storytellers, linguistic archeologists are compiling a written history of Valhalla and are realizing
    (D) Based on the yarns of storytellers, linguistic archeologists are compiling a written history of Valhalla and are coming to the realization
    (E) Deriving it from the yarns of storytellers, linguistic archeologists are compiling a written history of Valhalla and are realizing

The answer is (C).

Choice (A) is incorrect because the phrase *Based on yarns of storytellers* modifies *linguistic archeologists* illogically implying that the archeologists are based on the yarns of storytellers.

Choice (B) is incorrect because the phrase *Basing on the yarns of storytellers* modifies *linguistic archeologists* illogically implying that the archeologists are based on the yarns of storytellers. Further, the phrase *Basing on the yarns of storytellers* is very awkward.

Choice (C) is the answer. The clause *Using the yarns of storytellers* correctly modifies *linguistic archeologists,* showing how they are using the yarns. The clause can also be placed after the subject it modifies: Linguistic archeologists using the yarns of storytellers . . ..

Choice (D) is incorrect because the phrase *coming to the realization* is wordy. Further, the phrase *Based on the yarns of storytellers* modifies *linguistic archeologists* illogically implying that the archeologists are based on the yarns of storytellers.

Choice (E) is incorrect because it is awkward and vague: What is *it* referring to?

20. Common knowledge tells us that sensible exercise and <u>eating properly will result</u> in better health.
    (A) NO CHANGE
    (B) proper diet resulted
    (C) dieting will result
    (D) proper diet results
    (E) eating properly results

The answer is (D).

Choice (A) is incorrect since *eating properly* (verb-adverb) is not parallel to *sensible exercise* (adjective-noun).

Choice (B) offers two parallel nouns, *exercise* and *diet*. However, a general truth should be expressed in the present tense, not in the past tense.

Choice (C) is not parallel since it pairs the noun *exercise* with the gerund (a verb acting as a noun) *dieting*.

Choice (E) makes the same mistake as choice (A).

Choice (D) offers two parallel nouns—*exercise* and *diet*—and two parallel verbs—*tells* and *results*.

21. This century began with <u>war brewing in Europe, the industrial revolution well-established, and a nascent communication age.</u>
   (A) NO CHANGE
   (B) war brewing in Europe, the industrial revolution surging, and a nascent communication age.
   (C) war in Europe, the industrial revolution well-established, and a nascent communication age.
   (D) war brewing in Europe, the industrial revolution well-established, and the communication age beginning.
   (E) war brewing in Europe, the industrial revolution well-established, and saw the birth of the communication age.

The answer is (D).

Choice (A) is incorrect. Although the first two phrases, *war brewing in Europe* and *the industrial revolution well-established*, have different structures, the thoughts are parallel. However, the third phrase, *and a nascent communication age*, is not parallel to the first two.

Choice (B) does not make the third phrase parallel to the first two.

Choice (C) changes the meaning of the sentence: the new formulation states that war already existed in Europe while the original sentence states that war was only developing.

Choice (E) is not parallel. The first two phrases in the series are noun phrases, but the final phrase *saw the birth of the communication age* is a verb phrase.

Choice (D) offers three phrases in parallel form.

22. It is often better <u>to try repairing an old car than to junk it.</u>
   (A) NO CHANGE
   (B) to repair an old car than to have it junked.
   (C) to try repairing an old car than to junking it.
   (D) to try and repair an old car than to junk it.
   (E) to try to repair an old car than to junk it.

The answer is (E).

Choice (A) is incorrect since the verb *repairing* is not parallel to the verb *junk*.

In choice (B), the construction *have it junked* is awkward. Further, it changes the original construction from active to passive.

Choice (C) offers a parallel construction (*repairing/junking*), but it is awkward.

Choice (D) also offers a parallel construction (*repair/junk*), but the construction *try and* is not proper diction.

Choice (E) offers a parallel construction (*repair/junk*), and the formal structure—*try to*.

23. Jurassic Park, written by Michael Crichton, and which was first printed in 1988, is a novel about a theme park of the future in which dinosaurs roam free.
    (A) NO CHANGE
    (B) Jurassic Park, written by Michael Crichton and first printed in 1988,
    (C) Jurassic Park, which was written by Michael Crichton, and which was first printed in 1988,
    (D) Written by Michael Crichton and first printed in 1988, Jurassic Park
    (E) Jurassic Park, which was written by Michael Crichton and first printed in 1988,

The answer is (B).

Choice (A) is incorrect since the verb *written* is not parallel to the construction *which was ... printed*.

Choice (B) is the correct answer since the sentence is concise and the verb *written* is parallel to the verb *printed*.

Choice (C) does offer a parallel structure (*which was written/which was printed*); however, choice (B) is more concise.

Choice (D) rambles. The introduction *Written by ... 1988* is too long.

Choice (E) also offers a parallel structure (*which was written/which was printed*); however, choice (B) is more concise.

24. What is the best way to deal with sentence 1 (reproduced below)?

    Nestled in the foothills of the Smoky Mountains, Getaway Lodge offers its guests hospitality, comfort, and living in luxury.

    (A) NO CHANGE
    (B) Change *its* to *their*.
    (C) Change *hospitality* to *hospitable living*.
    (D) Change *comfort* to *comfortable living*.
    (E) Change *living in luxury* to *luxurious living*.

The answer is (E).

Choice (A) is incorrect. We cannot leave the sentence as it is because the elements of the sentence need to be parallel in structure.

Choice (B) is incorrect. The subject of the sentence is *Getaway Lodge*. The correct pronoun is *its* not *their*.

Choice (C) is incorrect because it makes an unnecessary change. *Hospitality* functions better than *hospitable living*, so why change it?

Choice (D) is incorrect for the same reason as Choice (C). *Comfort* is much more effective here than *comfortable living*.

Choice (E) is the correct answer. As it is, *living in luxury* is not parallel to *hospitality* and *comfort*. We need to change it to *luxurious living*.

25. Which of the following is the best revision of sentence 4 to better link it to sentence 3?
    (A) Every room also has magnificent, breathtaking views of the surrounding mountains.
    (B) Moreover, every room has magnificent, breathtaking views of the surrounding mountains.
    (C) Guests are also treated to magnificent, breathtaking views of the surrounding mountains.
    (D) In addition, guests are also shown magnificent, breathtaking views of the surrounding mountains.
    (E) Also, guests may view magnificent, breathtaking views of the surrounding mountains.

The answer is (C).

Choice (A) is incorrect. The passage thus far has focused on the guests rather than the subject of the room.

Choice (B) is incorrect for the same reason as Choice (A).

Choice (D) is incorrect because it implies that guests were simply *shown* their gift baskets. The passage clearly implies that the gift baskets are given to the guests.

Choice (E) is not correct. It is a poorly constructed sentence, and it does not provide an effective transition from the subject of gift baskets to mountain views.

Choice (C) is correct. Just as guests were *treated* to gift baskets, the mountain views serve as a treat as well. It works well to tie the sentences together. Additionally, the guests are the focus in this sentence just as in sentence three.

26. What is the best way to deal with sentence 8 (reproduced below)?

    After dinner, guests may enjoy a stroll through the garden or sitting by the fireplace.

    (A) NO CHANGE
    (B) Change *enjoy* to *take*.
    (C) Change *a stroll* to *strolling*.
    (D) Change *sitting* to *taking a seat*.
    (E) Place *after dinner* at the end of the sentence.

The answer is (C).

Choice (A) is incorrect. All element of the sentence need to be parallel; they are not parallel, so we cannot leave it as it is.

Choice (B) is incorrect. Not only does the solution not address the problem of parallel structure in the sentence, but it takes away some of the interest of the sentence by replacing the word *enjoy* with *take*.

Choice (D) is incorrect. It changes the wording of a part of the sentence that is not parallel, but the rewrite does not change the structure of the sentence.

Choice (E) is incorrect because the solution does not correct the problem of balancing the parallelism of the sentence. Moreover, changing the order of the sentence takes away much of the interest of the sentence.

Choice (C) is the correct answer. In this sentence, we needed to make *stroll through the garden* and *sitting by the fireplace* parallel. We could have corrected this by addressing *stroll* or *sitting*. This answer-choice offers a solution by changing *stroll* to *strolling*.

27. In the past few years and to this day, many teachers of math and science had chosen to return to the private sector.
    (A) NO CHANGE
    (B) having chosen to return to the private sector.
    (C) chose to return to the private sector.
    (D) **have chosen to return to the private sector.**
    (E) have chosen returning to the private sector.

The answer is (C).

Choice (A) is incorrect because it uses the past perfect *had chosen*, which describes an event that has been completed before another event. But the sentence implies that teachers have and are continuing to return to the private sector. Hence, the present perfect tense should be used.

Choice (B) is incorrect because it uses the present progressive tense *having chosen*, which describes an ongoing event. Although this is the case, it does not capture the fact that the event began in the past.

Choice (C) is incorrect because it uses the simple past *chose*, which describes a past event. But again, the sentence implies that the teachers are continuing to opt for the private sector.

Choice (D) is the correct answer because it uses the present perfect *have chosen* to describe an event that occurred in the past and is continuing into the present.

Choice (E) is incorrect because it leaves the thought in the sentence uncompleted.

28. Most of the homes that were destroyed in last summer's brush fires were built with wood-shake roofs.
    (A) NO CHANGE
    (B) Last summer, brush fires destroyed most of the homes that were
    (C) **Most of the homes that were destroyed in last summer's brush fires had been**
    (D) Most of the homes that the brush fires destroyed last summer's have been
    (E) Most of the homes destroyed in last summer's brush fires were being

The answer is (C).

Choice (A) is incorrect because the simple past *were* does not express the fact that the homes had been built before the fire destroyed them.

Choice (B) merely rearranges the wording while retaining the simple past *were*.

Choice (C) is the correct answer because it uses the past perfect *had been* to indicate that the homes were completely built before they were destroyed by the fire.

Choice (D) is incorrect because it uses the present perfect *have been*, which implies that the homes were destroyed before being built.

Choice (E) is incorrect. Although removing *that were* makes the sentence more concise, the past progressive *were being* implies that the homes were destroyed while being built.

ACT Verbal Prep Course

29. Although World War II ended nearly a half century ago, Russia and Japan still have not signed a formal peace treaty; and both countries have been reticent to develop closer relations.
    (A) NO CHANGE
    (B) did not signed a formal peace treaty; and both countries have been
    (C) have not signed a formal peace treaty; and both countries being
    (D) have not signed a formal peace treaty; and both countries are
    (E) are not signing a formal peace treaty; and both countries have been

The sentence is grammatical as written, so the answer is (A). The present perfect verb *have ... signed* correctly indicates that they have not signed a peace treaty and are not on the verge of signing one. Further, the present perfect verb *have been* correctly indicates that in the past both countries have been reluctant to develop closer relations and are still reluctant.

In choice (B), the simple past *did* does not capture the fact that they did not sign a peace treaty immediately after the war and still have not signed one.

Choice (C) is very awkward, and the present progressive *being* does not capture the fact that the countries have been reluctant to thaw relations since after the war up through the present.

In choice (D), the present tense *are* leaves open the possibility that in the past the countries may have desired closer relations but now no longer do.

In choice (E), the present progressive tense *are ... signing*, as in choice (D), leaves open the possibility that in the past the countries may have desired closer relations but now no longer do.

30. The Democrats have accused the Republicans of resorting to dirty tricks by planting a mole on the Democrat's planning committee and then used the information obtained to sabotage the Democrat's campaign.
    (A) NO CHANGE
    (B) used the information they had obtained to sabotage
    (C) of using the information they had obtained to sabotage
    (D) using the information obtained to sabotage
    (E) to have used the information obtained to sabotage

The answer is (C).

Choice (A) is incorrect because the simple past *obtained* does not express the fact that the information was obtained before another past action—the sabotage.

Choice (B) is incorrect because *used* is not parallel to *of resorting*.

Choice (C) is correct because the phrase *of using* is parallel to the phrase *of resorting*. Further, the past perfect *had obtained* correctly expresses that a past action—the spying—was completed before another past action—the sabotage.

Choice (D) is incorrect because *using* is not parallel to *of resorting* and the past perfect is not used.

Choice (E) is incorrect because *to have used* is not parallel to *of resorting* and the past perfect is not used.

31. Unless you maintain at least a 2.0 GPA, you will not graduate medical school.
   (A) NO CHANGE
   (B) you will not be graduated from medical school.
   (C) you will not be graduating medical school.
   (D) you will not graduate from medical school.
   (E) you will graduate medical school.

The answer is (D).

Choice (A) is incorrect. In this context, *graduate* requires the word *from*: "you will not *graduate from* medical school."

The use of the passive voice in choices (B) and (C) weakens the sentence.

Choice (D) is the answer since it uses the correct diction *graduate from*.

Choice (E) changes the meaning of the sentence and does not correct the faulty diction.

32. The studio's retrospective art exhibit refers back to a simpler time in American history.
   (A) NO CHANGE
   (B) The studio's retrospective art exhibit harkens back to
   (C) The studio's retrospective art exhibit refers to
   (D) The studio's retrospective art exhibit refers from
   (E) The studio's retrospective art exhibit looks back to

The answer is (C).

Choice (A) is incorrect. *Retrospective* means looking back on the past. Hence, in the phrase *refers back*, the word *back* is redundant.

Choice (B) is incorrect because *harkens back* is also redundant.

Choice (C) is correct. Dropping the word *back* eliminates the redundancy.

Choice (D) is incorrect because the preposition *from* is non-idiomatic.

Choice (E) is incorrect because *looks back* is also redundant.

33. Due to the chemical spill, the commute into the city will be delayed by as much as 2 hours.
    (A) NO CHANGE
    (B) The reason that the commute into the city will be delayed by as much as 2 hours is because of the chemical spill.
    (C) Due to the chemical spill, the commute into the city had been delayed by as much as 2 hours.
    (D) **Because of the chemical spill, the commute into the city will be delayed by as much as 2 hours.**
    (E) The chemical spill will be delaying the commute into the city by as much as 2 hours.

The answer is (D).

Choice (A) is incorrect. Although many educated writers and speakers begin sentences with *due to*, it is almost always incorrect.

Choice (B) is incorrect: it is both redundant and awkward.

Choice (C) is incorrect. The past perfect *had been delayed* implies the delay no longer exists. Hence, the meaning of the sentence has been changed.

Choice (D) is correct. In general, *due to* should not be used as a substitute for *because of, by reason of*, etc.

Choice (E) is incorrect. The future progressive *will be delaying* is unnecessary and ponderous. Had choice (E) used the simple future *will delay*, it would have been better that choice (D) because then it would be more direct and active.

34. What is the best word or phrase to use in place of the word *additionally* in sentence 5 (reproduced below)?

    Additionally, a focus on self-improvement is very important in helping people grow in character.

    (A) Moreover
    (B) **On the contrary**
    (C) Along those lines
    (D) Consequently
    (E) Accordingly

The answer is (B).

Choice (A) is incorrect. Sentence four ends with *a focus that some feel is unhealthy*. Sentence five says that *a focus on self-improvement is very important in helping people grow in character*. The content of sentence five is in contrast to the content of sentence four, so we need a transition that shows contrast. *Moreover* is a transitional word used to show agreement.

Choice (C) is incorrect for the same reason as Choice (A).

Choice D is incorrect because *consequently* is a transitional word that precedes a result in a cause-effect relationship.

Choice (E) is incorrect for the same reason as Choice (A) and (C).

Choice (B) is correct because *on the contrary* shows the contrast between what is said in sentence four and what is said in sentence five.

35. What is the best way to deal with sentence 12 (reproduced below)?

    Strong will turns into perseverance.

    (A) NO CHANGE
    (B) Add *is* before *turns* and change *turns* to *turned*.
    (C) Add *shall* before *turns* and change *turns* to *turn*.
    (D) Change *turns into* to *becomes*.
    (E) Add *can be* before *turns* and change *turns* to *turned*

The answer is (E).

Choice (A) is incorrect. We need to make sure that sentence 12 is parallel in structure to sentence 11 which says *impatience can be turned...* As it is now, sentence 12 is not parallel to sentence 11, so we cannot leave it as it is.

Choice (B) is incorrect because the resulting new sentence would be *Strong will is turned into perseverance*. Again, this is not parallel to sentence 11, so this is not our solution.

Choice (C) is not correct either. Let's look at the proposed new construction of the sentence: *Strong will shall turn into perseverance*. This again is not parallel.

Choice (D) is incorrect. *Strong will becomes perseverance* is not parallel in structure.

Choice (E) is the correct answer. Let's check the new sentence: *Strong will can be turned into perseverance*. This is parallel to *...impatience can be turned into determination...*

Rhetoric

Now that you know when to use a semicolon instead of a comma, and now that you know how to repair faulty grammar within a sentence, the final section the English test will test you on is rhetoric.

Rhetoric is literally the art of effective or persuasive writing, and it can be broken down into a few primary areas: style, structure, and strategy.

Style

The way a writer uses words and phrases to add personality to his writing is called *style*. A writer is to style as a figure skater is to skating. A writer can learn all the rules to make his writing correct, just as a figure skater can learn how to accomplish her jumps and footwork. But just learning the rules of grammar is not enough to create a well-written piece; learning just the rules of skating is not enough to earn a gold medal. The writer must bring his own methods and personality to his writing, just as a skater must invest her own personality and flair to her performance.

Many elements combine to form the writer's style; and, although style can be identified and examined, true style will only develop through practice. Let's look at some specific elements of style.

➢ **Transitions**—Transitional phrases are an important element of formal writing because they create coherence. They guide the reader from point A to point B. Look at the lists below for some examples of transitional words and phrases that help achieve cohesiveness.

> **Agreement:** *also, plus, in addition, further, furthermore, moreover, additionally, to add to that, next, in accordance with, accordingly, in agreement, finally, for instance, for example, in exemplification, exemplifying that, in fact, factually speaking, in terms of, and so forth, in coordination with, along those lines, collectively speaking, generally speaking, indeed, undoubtedly, obviously, to be sure, equally*
>
> **Contrast:** *however, in contrast, on the contrary, on the other hand, from a different angle, nonetheless, nevertheless, but, yet, a catch to this is, sadly enough, as a hindrance, oddly enough, instead, in direct opposition, still, rather*
>
> **Result:** *as a result, as a consequence, consequently, thus, therefore, hence, thereby, resulting in, ultimately, in the end, finally, in the overall analysis, in hindsight, in retrospect, retrospectively, vicariously, the long term effect, as a short term result, significantly, as a major effect, effectively, heretofore, hereafter, thereafter, in short, generally, over all, concluding*

✓ Check your work
Transitional words and phrases are helpful not only in linking ideas between sentences, but also in providing cohesiveness from paragraph to paragraph. Without this clarity, an essay will likely be choppy and difficult to read and understand. A word of caution, though: Be careful not to overuse transitional words and phrases. Overuse can make you sound like a pedantic writer rather than an intelligent one.

> **Varying Sentences**—No matter how well an essay flows, the reader will easily get bored if it consists only of sentences that contain the same words and follow the same structure.

> **Example:**
> Dogs help blind people. Dogs also help epileptic people. Dogs can sense when an epileptic person is about to have a seizure. Dogs are also used in rescue work. They help rescue skiers. They also help in catastrophic events. They rescue people after earthquakes.

There are several things wrong with this paragraph:
- Almost every sentence is the same length.
- The structure in each sentence is almost identical: Subject + Verb + Direct Object.
- The same words are used over and over: *dogs, they, rescue, help, people*.
- No description is used to further illustrate the writer's points.

✓ Check your work
To add more interest, try varying sentence length and structure. Try different sentence styles, employ a variety of words and use these words to paint a vivid picture of the subject. For example, you could begin your sentence with a subject and a predicate and then build on them using various words and phrases.

> **Cumulative sentence:**
> The energetic children played hard, chasing each other in all directions, occasionally falling and then scrambling to their feet, giggling at each other's antics and never stopping for even a moment to catch their breath.

> **Periodic sentence:**
> With flour in her hair, dough in between her fingers and sauce all over her face, she attempted to make a gourmet pizza.

Both of the above sentences not only add variety, but also bring rhythm and cadence to writing. This rhythm creates interest and is pleasant to read. Additionally, descriptive words paint a clear picture for the reader.

> **Figurative Language**—Another excellent way to paint a vivid picture is to use figures of speech. Figures of speech—like similes, metaphors, analogies, personification, hyperbole, irony, and allusion—when used correctly, add extra flair to writing. They add an extra element that takes writing from ordinary to extraordinary.

> - *Similes* show a marked comparison between two things by using the phrases *like, as,* or, *as if:*
>
>   The cat stood poised and *still as a statue*, waiting for the opportune moment to pounce.

- *Metaphors* show absolute comparison by omitting *like, as,* or, *as if:*

  She is Mother Theresa when it comes to her generosity and compassion.

Here the comparison is absolute because the writer states that this person *is* Mother Theresa, even though she is not actually Mother Theresa.

- *Analogies* compare the similar features of two dissimilar things, and they often bring clarity to writing by showing the reader another way of seeing something. Analogies are not limited to a sentence; sometimes an analogy streams its way through an entire piece of writing.

  Example:
  Office cooperation is like a soccer game. Each employee has a position on the playing field, and each position dictates an employee's function. Working together, the office completes passes by communicating well within each department. Shots on goal are taken when employees meet with prospective clients to pitch ideas, and the whole office triumphs when a goal is scored and a prospect becomes a client.

Although an office and a soccer team are two very unrelated things, the writer sees similarities between the two and uses these similarities to clearly show how an office works.

- *Personification* gives human characteristics to animals, inanimate objects and ideas in order to make them more real and understandable:

  The rusty car groaned, coughed, then gave one last sputter and died.

The car in this sentence comes to life even as it "dies" because of the human characteristics it is given.

- *Hyperbole* uses deliberate exaggeration or overstatement to show special emphasis or create humor.

  Example:
  Fat-free foods have become so popular that soon all vendors will want to sell them. Before you know it, Kentucky Fried Chicken will have fat-free fried chicken. Big Macs will contain 0 grams of fat. And the amount of fat in a Pizza Hut cheese pizza? You guessed it—none!

In order to show how excessive people's obsession with fat-free foods has become, this description purposefully exaggerates a world where the most unlikely things are fat-free.

- *Irony* uses language to make a suggestion that directly contrasts with the literal word or idea. It can offer humor to writing, or a bitter tone when it is used in sarcasm.

  Example:
  Scientists have worked hard to develop ways to decrease infant mortality rates and increase longevity. As a result, more people are living longer and scientists will soon have to develop some methods with which to control overpopulation.

This sentence uses irony by predicting that, because scientists have now discovered ways to increase a person's life span, they will soon have to deal with another problem—overpopulation.

- *Allusion* makes indirect reference to known cultural works, people or events. The familiarity allusions bring to writing helps the writer make connections with the reader:

I have so much to do today, I feel like David must have felt as he approached Goliath.

David must have felt a bit intimidated when facing the giant, Goliath—a feeling this writer alludes to when thinking about everything that needs to be done.

✔ Check your work

Your goal as a writer is to create interest and coherence through your unique writing style. Using figures of speech and maintaining consistent use of tone, diction, and person are effective ways to create interest; and using transitional words help to create coherence. Remember, though, that part of creating coherence is being concise. Use only the details that are necessary to support your topic and avoid tedious descriptions. This isn't to say that you should avoid vivid imagery, but only that you should take care to ensure that the above methods add to your writing rather than detract from it.

The most important aspect to remember is that style can only develop through practice. Practice your writing and proofread, proofread, proofread. If you do all of these things, you'll be well on your way to becoming an effective, skillful writer.

Structure

Although style usually takes the front seat when it comes to rhetoric, structure is just as important.

In his book, *The Elements of Style,* William Strunk wrote that, "The more clearly the writer perceives the shape (of an essay), the better are the chances of success." No truer words have ever been spoken in regard to composition. Sure, it can be a pain to create a full outline. Sure, some writer's write better by the seat of their pants. But, for the most part, planning must be a deliberate prelude to writing. And since nearly half of the questions in the English section test rhetoric—writing style, structure, and strategy—it's important to understand the structure of an essay.

The two most important elements of structure are the introduction and the conclusion.

> **Introduction**—The introduction serves two structural purposes: It restates the topic so that the reader need not review the given question, and it offers a clear thesis—the main idea—so that the reader can discover the purpose of the essay.

> **Example:**
> Does the adoption of covenants in housing communities result in rising property values? In a letter to the residents of Rivermill Subdivision, a small group of homeowners stated that property values in nearby Providence were double the property values in Rivermill because of such a covenant.

Not only did the above example restate the topic, but it also sparked interest in the issue.

It may seem like a tall order to have to examine a passage and determine if it restates the topic, creates a thesis, AND makes the content captivating; but, if the writer uses one of the following techniques to start their essay, then it's a good bet that the rest of the essay will follow in good form.

- Begin the introduction with a question. Naturally, when a question is posed to the reader, he or she will want to keep reading to find out the answer.
- Begin the introduction with a quote.
- Begin with an anecdote. An anecdote is entertaining and will thus draw in the reader.
- Begin with an illustration or a hypothetical example based on the topic.
- Begin with a true-to-life example.
- Begin with vivid description of something pertaining to the topic.

> **Conclusion**—The conclusion of an essay is just as important as the introduction. It should wrap up the writer's thoughts and leave the reader satisfied that a convincing discussion has just taken place. The conclusion should include a restatement of the thesis and end with a general statement, perhaps a warning or a call to action.

✓ Check your work

It's important to understand the function of the introduction and conclusion of an essay. The ACT will often ask you to move a sentence to an area where it makes more sense, or it might ask you what the overall goal of an essay was and if the writer accomplished that goal.

Example:

(1) Stonehenge, one of the many magnificent wonders of the ancient world, has long been shrouded in mystery. (2) Its creation and purpose have generated numerous theories down the years. (3) One thing is for certain: it took many hours of manpower to develop this amazing site.

(4) Hundreds of men would have had to have helped with the construction because there were three phases of it. (5) In Phase 1, a circular ditch and bank were dug out of the ground, probably with the use of crude tools made from animal bones. (6) Phase 2 involved transporting approximately 80 stones, each weighing about 4 tons, from 240 miles away. (7) These stones were to be arranged in a circle, and, although such construction began, it was never finished. (8) Many speculate that a majority of the 4 ton stones that were hauled in were eventually removed and replaced by the larger stones used in Phase 3. (9) Approximately 30 stones were used in Phase 3, each weighing at least 25 tons and each originating 20 miles away from the Stonehenge site. (10) These stones were arranged in an outer circle and then capped with additional stones.

(11) How workers hoisted such heavy stones to their upright positions without modern-day cranes is one of the mysteries surrounding Stonehenge. (12) Without its enigma, however, it would not be the tourist attraction it is today.

1. What is the best version of sentence 4 (reproduced below)?

Hundreds of men would have had to have helped with the construction because there were three phases of it.

(A) Hundreds of men would have had to have helped with the construction because there were three phases of it.
(B) Hundreds of men must have helped with the construction because there were three phases of it.
(C) Hundreds of men must have helped with the construction because there were three phases of construction.
(D) Because there were three phases of construction, hundreds of men must have helped.
(E) Hundreds of men must have helped with the three phases of construction.

2. Which sentence would function best as a concluding sentence after sentence 12 (reproduced below)?

Without its enigma, however, it would not be the tourist attraction it is today.

(A) The purpose of Stonehenge is still an enigma too, although most believe that it was used as a sacred burial ground for prominent people.
(B) Thousands visit the site in Southern England each year, and work is in progress to better preserve Stonehenge so generations can enjoy the wonder.
(C) Tourists can stay in one of the many hotels that have been built within kilometers of Stonehenge.
(D) Many other tourist attractions are nearby as well.
(E) The sheer magnitude of the attraction is amazing.

3. Which transitional word or phrase would best work to improve the flow between sentences 7 and 8 (reproduced below)?

These stones were to be arranged in a circle, and, although such construction began, it was never finished. Many speculate that a majority of the 4 ton stones that were hauled in were eventually removed and replaced by the larger stones used in Phase 3.

(A) However, many speculate...
(B) Nevertheless, many speculate...
(C) Consequently, many speculate...
(D) Therefore, many speculate...
(E) In fact, many speculate...

Even though most questions on the English test will deal with punctuation and grammar, it will not be uncommon for you to come across strategy — or content — questions like the ones above. But we'll go more into detail on these during the Reading Test, which is next.

Part Two
Reading Test

- **INTRODUCTION**

- **READING METHODS**
  Why Speed Reading Doesn't Work
  Why Previewing Questions Doesn't Work
  Why Pre-reading Topic Sentences Works

- **THE SIX QUESTIONS**
  Main Idea Questions
  Description Questions
  Writing Technique Questions
  Extension Questions
  Application Questions
  Tone Questions

- **PIVOTAL WORDS**

- **THE THREE-STEP METHOD**
  Preview Topic Sentences
  Circle the Pivotal Words and Annotate
  Understand the Six Questions

- **PRACTICE READING TEST**

Introduction

As mentioned earlier, it's too late to fake amnesia. Everyone knows that you know how to read. So the only thing to do now is prepare for the ACT's 35 minutes of reading fun.

Format of the Reading Test

The Reading Test is 35-minutes long and consists of 40 multiple-choice questions. The questions are separated into four sections, and each section tests a different subject. The test contains one passage in each of the following areas:

- **Humanities:** This passage can be about music, dance, theater, art, architecture, language, ethics, literary criticism, and even philosophy.
- **Social Studies**: The social studies passage can include sociology, anthropology, history, geography, psychology, political science, and economics.
- **Natural Sciences:** The natural science passage can cover chemistry, biology, physics, and other physical sciences.
- **Prose Fiction:** The fiction passage can be taken from a novel or a short story; however, don't expect to have seen the passage before.

So, if my math's correct, you'll have 35-minutes to read four passages and answer 10 multiple-choice questions on each passage, which brings us to a grand total of 40 questions.

Watch Out For:

➤ **Vocabulary -** The reading section could partly be considered a vocabulary test. If you know the word, you will probably be able to answer the question correctly. Thus, it is crucial that you improve your vocabulary. Even if you already have a strong vocabulary, you will still encounter unfamiliar words on the ACT.

Toward the end of this book, you will find a list of 4000 essential words and study techniques that will help you discern the meaning of words you barely recognize. Granted, memorizing a list of words is rather dry, but it is probably one of the most effective ways to improve your performance on the reading test.

➤ **Pivotal Words -** *Pivotal words* mark natural places for questions to be drawn. At a pivotal word, the author changes direction. The ACT writers form questions at these junctures to test whether you turned with the author or if you continued to go straight. Rarely do the ACT writers let a pivotal word pass without drawing a question from its sentence.

> **Common Pivotal Words:**
> - But
> - However
> - Despite
> - Nonetheless
> - In contrast
> - Although
> - Yet
> - Nevertheless
> - Except
> - Even though

As mentioned earlier, you will have 35 minutes to read four passages and answer ten questions concerning each passage. That leaves you with about 8 1/2 minutes to spend on each passage and their following questions. It's essential, therefore, to identify the places from which questions will most likely be drawn and concentrate your attention there.

Read the pages that follow carefully. The better you understand how the reading test is written, the better are your chances of success.

Reading Methods

Reading styles are subjective: there is no best method for approaching the written word. A reading technique that works for one person can be awkward and unnatural for another. However, it's really hard to believe that so many books advocate methods that don't work and often cause more confusion than necessary.

Speed Reading

Some books recommend speed-reading the passages on timed tests. This is a mistake. Speed-reading is designed for ordinary, nontechnical material, not for the fluff-less material you'll encounter on the ACT.

The passages on the ACT are often quoted articles that have been condensed to about one-third of their original length. Which means that all the fluff in the original article gets cut, making more room for essential material. This is why speed-reading will not work: the passages on the ACT just contain too much information.

Previewing Questions

Many books also recommend that the questions be read before the passage. Not only does this method seem like a cruel joke, but it also seems like it's advocated merely to give the reader the feeling that he or she is getting the inside stuff on how to ace the test. But there are two big problems with this method. First, some of the questions are almost a paragraph long; reading a paragraph-long question twice will use up precious time. Second, there are up to ten questions per passage, and psychologists have shown that we can hold in our minds a maximum of about three thoughts at any one time (some of us have trouble simply remembering a single phone number). After reading all ten questions, the student will turn to a passage with his mind clouded by half-remembered thoughts. This is, at best, a waste of time. Rather than helping the student better comprehend the passage, it will more likely turn the passage into a disjointed mass of information.

Pre-Reading Topic Sentences

However, one technique that you may find helpful is to preview the passage by reading the first sentence of each paragraph. Generally, the topic of a paragraph is contained in the first sentence. The topic sentence acts, in essence, as a summary of the following text. Furthermore, since each passage is only four to eight paragraphs long, previewing the topic sentences will not use up an inordinate amount of time.

The Six Questions

The key to performing well on the reading test is not the particular reading technique you use (so long as it's neither speed reading nor pre-reading). Rather, the key is to become familiar with the question types on the test, so that you can anticipate the questions that *might* be asked and answer those that *are* asked more quickly and efficiently.

Although you may encounter many different types of questions on the ACT, the following passage will illustrate six of the most common offenders. Read the passage slowly to get a good understanding of the issues.

There are two major systems of criminal procedure in the modern world—the adversarial and the inquisitorial. The former is associated with common law tradition and the latter with civil law tradition. Both systems were historically preceded by the system of private vengeance in which the victim of a crime fashioned his own remedy and administered it privately, either personally or through an agent. The vengeance system was a system of self-help, the essence of which was captured in the slogan "an eye for an eye, a tooth for a tooth." The modern adversarial system is only one historical step removed from the private vengeance system and still retains some of its characteristic features. Thus, for example, even though the right to institute criminal action has now been extended to all members of society and even though the police department has taken over the pretrial investigative functions on behalf of the prosecution, the adversarial system still leaves the defendant to conduct his own pretrial investigation. The trial is still viewed as a duel between two adversaries, refereed by a judge who, at the beginning of the trial, has no knowledge of the investigative background of the case. In the final analysis the adversarial system of criminal procedure symbolizes and regularizes the punitive combat.

By contrast, the inquisitorial system begins historically where the adversarial system stopped its development. It is two historical steps removed from the system of private vengeance. Therefore, from the standpoint of legal anthropology, it is historically superior to the adversarial system. Under the inquisitorial system the public investigator has the duty to investigate not just on behalf of the prosecutor but also on behalf of the defendant. Additionally, the public prosecutor has the duty to present to the court not only evidence that may lead to the conviction of the defendant but also evidence that may lead to his exoneration. This system mandates that both parties permit full pretrial discovery of the evidence in their possession. Finally, in an effort to make the trial less like a duel between two adversaries, the inquisitorial system mandates that the judge take an active part in the conduct of the trial, with a role that is both directive and protective.

Fact-finding is at the heart of the inquisitorial system. This system operates on the philosophical premise that in a criminal case the crucial factor is not the legal rule but the facts of the case and that the goal of the entire procedure is to experimentally recreate for the court the commission of the alleged crime.

➢ **Main Idea Questions** - The process of writing is the process of communicating; all authors have a point that they want to make in their writing. *Main idea questions* test your ability to identify and understand an author's intent. Main idea questions are usually the first questions asked after you read the passage.

>   **Common Main Idea Questions:**
>   Which one of the following best expresses the main idea of the passage?
>   The primary purpose of the passage is to . . .
>   In the passage, the author's primary concern is to discuss . . .

Main idea questions are rarely difficult, especially if the author is a clear communicator. If, however, after reading the passage, you don't have a feel for the main idea, review the first and last sentence of each paragraph; these should provide you with a main idea quick fix.

✓ Check your work

Because main idea questions are relatively easy, the ACT writers try to obscure the correct answer by surrounding it with semi-correct choices (detractors) that either overstate or understate the author's main point. Choices that stress specifics tend to understate the main idea; choices that go beyond the scope of the passage tend to overstate the main idea. To answer main idea questions correctly, remember that the answer will summarize the author's argument, yet it won't be too specific or broad.

>   **Example:** (Refer to the original passage.)
>   The primary purpose of the passage is to
>   **(A)** explain why the inquisitorial system is the best system of criminal justice
>   **(B)** explain how the adversarial and the inquisitorial systems of criminal justice both evolved from the system of private vengeance
>   **(C)** show how the adversarial and inquisitorial systems of criminal justice are being combined into a new and better system
>   **(D)** analyze two systems of criminal justice and deduce which one is better

Choice (A) is incorrect because it overstates the scope of the passage with its use of the extreme word *best*. Choice (B) is incorrect because it understates the scope of the passage by neglecting to mention that the author is trying to prove which system is better. And Choice (C) can be quickly dismissed since it's not mentioned in the passage.

The passage does two things: it presents two systems of criminal justice and shows why one is better than the other. So choice (D) is the correct answer.

➢ **Description Questions** - Description questions, as with main idea questions, refer to a point made by the author. However, description questions refer to a minor point or to incidental information, not to the author's main point.

Common Description Questions:
   ➢ According to the passage . . .
   ➢ In line 37, the author mentions . . . for the purpose of . . .
   ➢ The passage suggests that which one of the following would . . .

The answer to a description question must refer <u>directly</u> to a statement in the passage, not to something implied by it. However, the correct answer will paraphrase a statement in the passage, not give an exact quote. In fact, exact quotes ("Same language" traps) are often used to bait wrong answers.

Caution: When answering a description question, you must find the point in the passage from which the question is drawn. Don't rely on memory—too many obfuscating tactics are used with these questions.

Not only must the correct answer refer directly to a statement in the passage, it must refer to the relevant statement. The correct answer will be surrounded by wrong choices which refer directly to the passage but don't address the question. These choices can be tempting because they tend to be quite close to the actual answer.

Once you spot the sentence to which the question refers, you still must read a few sentences before and after it, to put the question in context. If a question refers to line 20, the information needed to answer it can occur anywhere from line 15 to 25. Even if you have spotted the answer in line 20, you should still read a couple more lines to make certain you have the proper perspective.

Example: (Refer to the original passage.)
According to the passage, the inquisitorial system differs from the adversarial system in that
(F) it does not make the defendant solely responsible for gathering evidence for his case
(G) it does not require the police department to work on behalf of the prosecution
(H) it does not allow the victim the satisfaction of private vengeance
(J) it requires the prosecution to drop a weak case

This is a description question, so the information needed to answer it must be stated in the passage—though not in the same language as in the answer. The needed information is contained at the end of second paragraph, which states that the public prosecutor has to investigate on behalf of both society and the defendant. Thus, the defendant is not solely responsible for investigating his case. Furthermore, the paragraph's opening implies that this feature is not found in the adversarial system. This illustrates why you must determine the context of the situation before you can safely answer the question. The answer is (F).

The other choices can be easily dismissed. (G) is the second best answer. The passage states that in the adversarial system the police assume the work of the prosecution, and the passage states that the inquisitorial system begins where the adversarial system stopped; this implies that in both systems the police work for the prosecution. (H) uses a false claim ploy. The passage states that both systems are removed from the system of private vengeance. (J) is probably true, but it is neither stated nor directly implied by the passage.

Often you will be asked to define a word or phrase based on its context. For this type of question, again you must look at a few lines before and after the word. Don't assume that because the word is familiar you know the definition requested. Words often have more than one meaning, and the ACT often asks for a peculiar or technical meaning of a common word. For example, as a noun *champion* means "the winner," but as a verb *champion* means "to be an advocate for someone." You must consider the word's context to get its correct meaning.

On the ACT, the definition of a word will not use as simple a structure as was used above to define *champion*. One common way the ACT introduces a defining word or phrase is to place it in apposition to the word being defined.

Don't confuse "apposition" with "opposition": they have antithetical [exactly opposite] meanings. Words or phrases in apposition are placed next to each other, and the second word or phrase defines, clarifies, or gives evidence for the first word or phrase. The second word or phrase will be set off from the first by a comma, semicolon, hyphen, or parentheses. (Note: If a comma is not followed by a linking word—such as *and, for, yet*—then the following phrase is probably appositional.)

Example:
The discussions were acrimonious, frequently degenerating into name-calling contests.

After the comma in this sentence, there is no linking word (such as *and, but, because, although*, etc.). Hence, the phrase following the comma is in apposition to *acrimonious*—it defines or further clarifies the word. Now *acrimonious* suggests bitter, mean-spirited talk, which would aptly describe a name-calling contest.

> **Writing Technique Questions** - All coherent writing has a superstructure or blueprint. When writing, we don't just randomly jot down our thoughts; we organize our ideas and present them in a logical manner. For example, we may present evidence that builds up to a conclusion but intentionally leaves the conclusion unstated; or we may present a position and then contrast it with an opposing position; or we may even draw an extended analogy.

There are an endless number of writing techniques that authors use to present their ideas, so we cannot classify them all. However, some techniques are common enough on the ACT to acknowledge.

Compare & Contrast Technique - This technique has a number of variations, but the most common occurrence is when two ideas are developed and then contrasted.

Example: (Refer to the original passage.)

Which one of the following best describes the organization of the passage?

(A) Two systems of criminal justice are compared and contrasted, and one is deemed to be better than the other.
(B) One system of criminal justice is presented as better than another. Then evidence is offered to support that claim.
(C) Two systems of criminal justice are analyzed, and one specific example is examined in detail.
(D) A set of examples is furnished. Then a conclusion is drawn from them.

Clearly the author is comparing and contrasting two criminal justice systems; the opening makes this clear. The author opens the passage by developing (comparing) both systems and then shifts to developing just the adversarial system. He then opens the second paragraph by contrasting the two criminal justice systems and then further develops just the inquisitorial system. Finally, he closes by again contrasting the two systems and implying that the inquisitorial system is superior.

Only choices (A) and (B), have any real merit. They essentially say the same thing—though in different order.

In the passage, the author does not indicate which system is better until the end of paragraph one, and he does not make that certain until paragraph two. This contradicts the order given by choice (B). The answer is (A). (Note: In (A) the order is not specified and therefore is harder to attack, whereas in (B) the order is definite and therefore is easier to attack. Remember that a measured response is harder to attack and therefore is more likely to be the answer.)

Cause & Effect - In this technique, the author typically shows how a particular cause leads to a certain result or set of results. It's not uncommon for this method to introduce a sequence of causes and effects. A causes B, which causes C, which causes D, and so on. Hence B is both the effect of A and the cause of C. The variations on this rhetorical technique can be illustrated by the following schematics:

Example *(Short Passage)*:
Thirdly, I worry about the private automobile. It is a dirty, noisy, wasteful, and lonely means of travel. It pollutes the air, ruins the safety and sociability of the street, and exercises upon the individual a discipline which takes away far more freedom than it gives him. It causes an enormous amount of land to be unnecessarily abstracted from nature and from plant life and to become devoid of any natural function. It explodes cities, grievously impairs the whole institution of neighborliness, and fragmentizes and destroys communities. It has already spelled the end of our cities as real cultural and social communities, and has made impossible the construction of any others in their place. Together with the airplane, it has crowded out other, more civilized and more convenient means of transport, leaving older people, infirm people, poor people and children in a worse situation than they were a hundred years ago. It continues to lend a terrible element of fragility to our civilization, placing us in a situation where our life would break down completely if anything ever interfered with the oil supply.
George F. Kennan

Which of the following best describes the organization of the passage?
- **(F)** A problem is presented and then a possible solution is discussed.
- **(G)** The benefits and demerits of the automobile are compared and contrasted.
- **(H)** A topic is presented and a number of its effects are discussed.
- **(J)** A set of examples is furnished to support a conclusion.

This passage is laden with effects. Kennan introduces the cause, the automobile, in the opening sentence and from there on presents a series of effects—the automobile pollutes, enslaves, and so on. Hence the answer is (H). Choice (J) is the second-best choice, but it is disqualified by two flaws: First, in this context, the word *examples* is not as precise as *effects*. Second, the order is wrong: the conclusion, "I worry about the private automobile" is presented first and then the examples: it pollutes, it enslaves, etc.

Position & Evidence - This technique is common with opinionated passages. Equally common is the reverse order. That is, the supporting evidence is presented and then the position or conclusion is stated. Sometimes an author will even present evidence that builds up an unstated position. If this is done skillfully the reader's conclusion will more than likely be the author's conclusion, even though it is unstated.

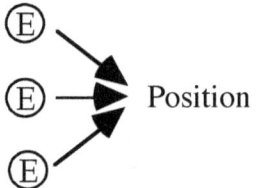
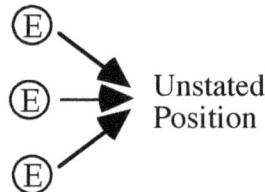

➤ **Extension Questions** - *Extension questions* are the most common question type on the reading test. They require you to go beyond what is stated in the passage, asking you to draw an inference from the passage, to make a conclusion based on the passage, or to identify one of the author's tacit assumptions.

>**Common Extension Questions:**
>It can be inferred from the passage that . . .
>The passage suggests that . . .

✔ Check your work

Since extension questions require you to go beyond the passage, the correct answer must say *more* than what is said in the passage. Beware of language traps when answering these questions. The correct answer will often both paraphrase and extend a statement in the passage, but it will not directly quote it. The answer should not require a quantum leap in thought, but it will add significantly to the ideas presented in the passage.

>**Example:** (Refer to the original passage.)
>The author views the prosecution's role in the inquisitorial system as being
>**(A)** an advocate for both society and the defendant
>**(B)** solely responsible for starting a trial
>**(C)** an investigator only
>**(D)** an aggressive but fair investigator

The author states that the prosecutor is bound to present any evidence that may prove the defendant innocent and that he must disclose all pretrial evidence (i.e., have no tricks up his sleeve). This is the essence of fair play. So the answer is probably (D).

Choice (A) overstates the case. Although the prosecutor must disclose any evidence that might show the defendant innocent, the prosecutor is still advocating society's case against the defendant, not for the defendant. As for choice (B): although it is implied that in both systems the right to initiate a case is extended to all people through the prosecutor, it is not stated or implied that this is the only way to start a case. Finally, choice (C) is not mentioned or implied in the passage. The answer, therefore, is (D).

Application: *(Short passage)*
Often, the central problem in any business is that money is needed to make money. The following discusses the sale of equity, which is one response to this problem.

Sale of Capital Stock: a way to obtain capital through the sale of stock to individual investors beyond the scope of one's immediate acquaintances. Periods of high interest rates turn entrepreneurs to this equity market. This involves, of necessity, a dilution of ownership, and many owners are reluctant to take this step for that reason. Whether the owner is wise in declining to use outside equity financing depends upon the firm's long-range prospects. If there is an opportunity for substantial expansion on a continuing basis and if other sources are inadequate, the owner may decide logically to bring in other owners. Owning part of a larger business may be more profitable than owning all of a smaller business.

Small-Business Management, 6th Ed., © 1983 by South-Western Publishing Co.
The passage implies that an owner who chooses not to sell capital stock despite the prospect of continued expansion is
(A) subject to increased regulation
(B) more conservative than is wise under the circumstances
(C) likely to have her ownership of the business diluted
(D) sacrificing security for rapid growth

(A): No. This is not mentioned in the passage. **(B): Yes.** The passage states that *"the owner may decide logically to bring in other owners"*; in other words, the owner would be wise to sell stock in this situation. (C): No. By NOT selling stock, the owner retains full ownership. (D) No. Just the opposite: the owner would be sacrificing a measure of security for growth if she did sell stock.

➤ **Application Questions** - *Application questions* differ from extension questions only in degree. Extension questions ask you to apply what you have learned from the passage to derive new information about the same subject, whereas application questions go one step further, asking you to apply what you have learned from the passage to a different or hypothetical situation.

> **Common Application Questions:**
> - Which one of the following is the most likely source of the passage?
> - Which one of the following actions would be most likely to have the same effect as the author's actions?
>
> **Or**
>
> - The author would most likely agree with which one of the following statements?
> - Which one of the following sentences would the author be most likely to use to complete the last paragraph of the passage?

✓ Check your work

To answer an application question, take the author's perspective and ask yourself, "What am I arguing for?" Or, "What might make my argument stronger? What might make it weaker?"

Because these questions go well beyond the passage, they tend to be the most difficult. And because application and extension questions require a deeper understanding of the passage, skimming (or worse yet, speed-reading) the passage is ineffective. Skimming may give you the main idea and structure of the passage, but it is unlikely to give you the subtleties of the author's attitude.

> **Example:** (Refer to the original passage.)
> Based on the information in the passage, it can be inferred that which one of the following would most logically begin a paragraph immediately following the passage?
> - **(F)** Because of the inquisitorial system's thoroughness in conducting its pretrial investigation, it can be concluded that a defendant who is innocent would prefer to be tried under the inquisitorial system, whereas a defendant who is guilty would prefer to be tried under the adversarial system.
> - **(G)** As the preceding analysis shows, the legal system is in a constant state of flux. For now the inquisitorial system is ascendant, but it will probably be soon replaced by another system.
> - **(H)** The accusatorial system begins where the inquisitorial system ends. So it is three steps removed from the system of private vengeance, and therefore historically superior to it.
> - **(J)** Because in the inquisitorial system the judge must take an active role in the conduct of the trial, his competency and expertise have become critical.

The example passage compares and contrasts two systems of criminal justice, implying that the inquisitorial system is superior. We expect the concluding paragraph to sum up this position. The system of justice under which an innocent person would choose to be judged is a logical place for the author to conclude. The answer is (A).

➤ **Tone Questions** - *Tone questions* ask you to identify the writer's attitude or perspective. Is the writer's feeling toward the subject positive, negative, or neutral? Does the writer give his own opinion, or does he objectively present the opinions of others? However, if you're having a hard time feeling out the writer's tone for the subject, check the adjectives that he wrote.

Adjectives and, to a lesser extent, adverbs express our feelings toward a subject. For instance, if we agree with a person who holds strong feelings about a subject, we may describe his opinions as impassioned. On the other hand, if we disagree with him, we may describe his opinions as excitable, which has the same meaning as impassioned but carries a negative connotation.

> **Example:** (Refer to the original passage.)
> The author's attitude toward the adversarial system can best be described as
> (A) encouraged that it is far removed from the system of private vengeance
> (B) concerned that it does not allow all members of society to instigate legal action
> (C) hopeful that it will be replaced by the inquisitorial system
> (D) doubtful that it is the best vehicle for justice

The author does not reveal his feelings toward the adversarial system until the end of paragraph one. The clause *the adversarial system of criminal procedure symbolizes and regularizes the punitive combat* indicates that he has a negative attitude toward the system. This is confirmed in the second paragraph when he states that the inquisitorial system is historically superior to the adversarial system. So he feels that the adversarial system is deficient.

Only choices (C) and (D) have any real merit. Both are good answers, but which one is better? To decide between two choices attack each: the one that survives is the answer.

A tone question should be answered from what is directly stated in the passage, not from what it implies. Although the author has reservations toward the adversarial system, at no point does he say that he hopes the inquisitorial system will replace it, he may prefer a third system over both. This eliminates (C), so the answer is (D).

The remaining choices are not supported by the passage. Choice (A), using the same language as in the passage, overstates the author's feeling. Remember: **Be wary of extreme words**. Choice (A) would be a better choice if *far* were dropped. And choice (B) and (C) make false claims.

✓ Check your work

Beware of answers that contain extreme emotions. Remember that the passages are taken from academic journals; strong emotions are considered inappropriate. The writers want to display opinions that are considered and reasonable, not spontaneous and off-the-wall. So if an author's tone is negative, it may be disapproving, not snide. Or if his tone is positive, it may be approving, not ecstatic.

Answers must also be indisputable. If answers were subjective, then the writers of the ACT would be deluged with letters from angry test takers, complaining that their test-scores are unfair. To avoid such a difficult position, the writers of the ACT never allow the correct answer to be either controversial or grammatically questionable.

Let's use these theories to answer the following questions.

Example:
Which one of the following most accurately characterizes the author's attitude with respect to Phillis Wheatley's literary accomplishments?
- (A) enthusiastic advocacy
- (B) qualified admiration
- (C) dispassionate impartiality
- (D) detached ambivalence

Even without reference to the passage, this is not a difficult question to answer.

Scholars may advocate each other's work, but they are unlikely to be enthusiastic advocates. Furthermore, the context stretches the meaning of advocacy—to defend someone else's cause or plight. So (A) is unlikely to be the answer.

(B) is the measured response and therefore is probably the answer.

"Dispassionate impartiality" is a rather odd construction; additionally, it is redundant. It could never be the answer to an ACT question. This eliminates (C).

"Detached ambivalence" is not as odd as "dispassionate impartiality," but it is unusual. So (D) is unlikely to be the answer.

Hence, even without the passage we can still find the answer, (B).

Example:
Which one of the following best describes the author's attitude toward scientific techniques?
- (A) critical
- (B) hostile
- (C) idealistic
- (D) neutral

(A) is one of two measured responses offered. Now a scholar may be critical of a particular scientific technique, but only a crackpot would be critical of *all* scientific techniques—eliminate (A).

"Hostile" is far too negative. Scholars consider such emotions juvenile—eliminate (B).

"Idealistic," on the other hand, is too positive; it sounds pollyannaish—eliminate (C).

(D) is the other measured response, and by elimination it is the answer.

Points to Remember

1. The order of questions roughly corresponds to the order of the passage.

2. The six question types are:
   Main Idea
   Description
   Writing Technique
   Extension
   Application
   Tone

3. The main idea of a passage is usually stated in the last, sometimes the first, sentence of the first paragraph. If it's not there, it will probably be the last sentence of the entire passage.

4. If after the first reading you don't have a feel for the main idea, review the first and last sentence of each paragraph.

5. The answer to a description question must refer directly to a statement in the passage, not to something implied by it. However, the correct answer will paraphrase a passage statement, not quote it exactly. In fact, exact quotes are used with these questions to bait wrong answers.

6. When answering a description question, you must find the point in the passage from which the question is drawn.

7. If a description question refers to line 20, the information needed to answer it can occur anywhere from line 15 to 25.

8. Some writing techniques commonly used in the ACT passages are
   A. Compare & Contrast
   B. Cause & Effect
   C. Position & Evidence

9. For extension questions, any answer that refers explicitly to or repeats a statement in the passage is probably be wrong.

10. Application questions differ from extension questions only in degree. Extension questions ask you to apply what you have learned from the passage to derive new information about the same subject, whereas application questions go one step further, asking you to apply what you have learned from the passage to a different or hypothetical situation.

11. To answer an application question, take the perspective of the author and ask yourself, "What am I arguing for? What might make my argument stronger?" And, "What might make it weaker?"

12. Because application questions go well beyond the passage, they tend to be the most difficult.

13. For tone questions, decide whether the writer's tone is positive, negative, or neutral before you look at the answers.

14. If you do not have a feel for the writer's attitude after the first reading, check the adjectives that he chooses.

15. Beware of answers that contain extreme emotion. If an author's tone is negative, it may be disapproving, not snide. If his tone is positive, it may be approving, not ecstatic.

16. Answers must be indisputable. A correct answer will never be controversial or grammatically questionable.

Mentored Exercise

> **Directions:** This passage is followed by a group of questions to be answered based on what is *stated* or *implied* in the passage. Choose the best answer - the one that most accurately and completely answers the question. Hints, insights, and answers immediately follow the questions.

From Romania to Germany, from Tallinn to Belgrade, a major historical process—the death of communism—is taking place. The German Democratic Republic no longer exists as a separate state. And the former German Democratic Republic will serve as the first measure of the price a post-Communist society has to pay for entering the normal European orbit. In Yugoslavia we will see whether the federation can survive without communism.

One thing seems common to all these countries: dictatorship has been defeated and freedom has won, yet the victory of freedom has not yet meant the triumph of democracy. Democracy is something more than freedom. Democracy is freedom institutionalized, freedom submitted to the limits of the law, freedom functioning as an object of compromise between the major political forces on the scene.

We have freedom, but we still have not achieved the democratic order. That is why this freedom is so fragile. In the years of democratic opposition to communism, we supposed that the easiest thing would be to introduce changes in the economy. In fact, we thought that the march from a planned economy to a market economy would take place within the framework of the bureaucratic system and that the market within the Communist state would explode the totalitarian structures. Only then would the time come to build the institutions of a civil society; and only at the end, with the completion of the market economy and the civil society, would the time of great political transformations finally arrive.

The opposite happened. First came the big political change, the great shock, which either broke the monopoly and the principle of Communist Party rule or simply pushed the Communists out of power. Then came the creation of civil society, whose institutions were created in great pain, and which had trouble negotiating the empty space of freedom. Only then, as the third moment of change, the final task was undertaken: that of transforming the totalitarian economy into a normal economy where different forms of ownership and different economic actors will live one next to the other.

Today we are in a typical moment of transition. No one can say where we are headed. The people of the democratic opposition have the feeling that we won. We taste the sweetness of our victory the same way the Communists, only yesterday our prison guards, taste the bitterness of their defeat. Yet, even as we are conscious of our victory, we feel that we are, in a strange way, losing. In Bulgaria the Communists have won the parliamentary elections and will govern the country, without losing their social legitimacy. In Romania the National Salvation Front, largely dominated by people from the old Communist bureaucracy, has won. In other countries democratic institutions seem shaky, and the political horizon is cloudy.

The masquerade goes on: dozens of groups and parties are created, each announces similar slogans, each accuses its adversaries of all possible sins, and each declares itself representative of the national interest. Personal disputes are more important than disputes over values. Arguments over values are fiercer than arguments over ideas.

1. The author originally thought that the order of events in the transformation of communist society would be represented by which one of the following?
   (A) A great political shock would break the totalitarian monopoly, leaving in its wake a civil society whose task would be to change the state-controlled market into a free economy.
   (B) The transformation of the economy would destroy totalitarianism, after which a new and different social and political structure would be born.
   (C) First the people would freely elect political representatives who would transform the economy, which would then undermine the totalitarian structure.
   (D) The change to a democratic state would necessarily undermine totalitarianism, after which a new economic order would be created.

The answer is (B).

This is a description question, so you should locate the point in the passage from which it was drawn. In the third paragraph, the author recalls his expectation that, by introducing the market system, the communist system would topple from within.

Watch out for choice (A). It chronicles how the events actually occurred, not how they were anticipated to occur. It's also baited with the words like *great shock, monopoly,* and *civil society*. Remember: In a description question, the correct answer will paraphrase a passage statement, not quote it exactly. Quoted answer-choices are used as bait for wrong answers.

2. Beginning in the second paragraph, the author describes the complicated relationship between freedom and democracy. In the author's view, which one of the following statements best reflects that relationship?
   (F) A country can have freedom without having democracy.
   (G) If a country has freedom, it necessarily has democracy.
   (H) A country can have democracy without having freedom.
   (J) A country can never have democracy if it has freedom.

The answer is (F).

This is an extension question, so the answer must say more than what is said in the passage, without requiring a quantum leap in thought. The needed reference is *Democracy is something more than freedom* (middle of second paragraph). Since freedom can exist without democracy, freedom alone does not insure democracy.

3. From the passage, a reader could conclude that which one of the following best describes the author's attitude toward the events that have taken place in communist society?
   (A) Relieved that at last the democratic order has surfaced.
   (B) Clearly wants to return to the old order.
   (C) Disappointed with the nature of the democracy that has emerged.
   (D) Surprised that communism was toppled through political rather than economic means.

The answer is (C).

This is a tone question. The key to answering this question is found in the closing comments. There the author states that *The masquerade goes on,* referring to nascent democracies. So he has reservations about the newly emerging democracies.

Watch out for answer-choices like choice (D). Although it is supported by the passage and is a right-enough-sounding answer, its placement in the passage is key. (D) is pulled from a supporting paragraph. The ideas in a concluding paragraph take precedence over those in a supporting paragraph.

Remember: Multiple answer-choices can be slightly correct. You must, however, choose the BEST answer.

4. A cynic who has observed political systems in various countries would likely interpret the author's description of the situation at the end of the passage as
   (F) a distorted description of the new political system.
   (G) a necessary political reality that is a prelude to democracy.
   (H) a fair description of many democratic political systems.
   (J) evidence of the baseness of people.

The answer is (H).

This is an application question. These are like extension questions, but they go well beyond what is stated in the passage. In this case we are asked to interpret the author's comments from a cynic's perspective. Because application questions go well beyond the passage, they are often difficult, as is this one.

A cynic looks at reality from a negative perspective, usually with a sense of dark irony and hopelessness.

Don't make the mistake of choosing (J). Although a cynic is likely to make such a statement, it does not address the subject of the passage—political and economic systems. The passage is not about human nature, at least not directly.

5. Which one of the following does the author imply may have contributed to the difficulties involved in creating a new democratic order in eastern Europe?
   I. *The people who existed under the totalitarian structure have not had the experience of negotiating the empty space of freedom.*
   II. *Mistaking the order in which political, economic, and social restructuring would occur.*
   III. *Excessive self-interest among the new political activists.*
   (A) I only
   (B) II only
   (C) II and III only
   (D) I, II, and III

The answer is (D).

This is an extension question. Statement I is true. In the fourth paragraph, the author implies that the institutions of the new-born, free society were created with great pain because the people lacked experience. Statement II is true. Expectations that the market mechanisms would explode totalitarianism and usher in a new society were dashed, and having to read just one's expectations certainly makes a situation more difficult. Finally, statement III is true. It summarizes the thrust of the passage's closing lines.

6. By stating *even as we are conscious of our victory, we feel that we are, in a strange way, losing* (fifth paragraph) the author means that
   (A) some of the old governments are still unwilling to grant freedom at the individual level.
   (B) some of the new governments are not strong enough to exist as a single federation.
   (C) some of the new democratic governments are electing to retain the old political parties.
   (D) no new parties have been created to fill the vacuum created by the victory of freedom.

The answer is (C).

This is a hybrid extension and description question. Because it refers to a specific point in the passage, you must read a few sentences before and after it. The answer can be found in the fifth paragraph.

Solo Exercise

> Directions: This passage is followed by a group of questions to be answered based on what is *stated* or *implied* in the passage. Choose the *best* answer - the one that most accurately and completely answers the question.

In the United States the per capita costs of schooling have risen almost as fast as the cost of medical treatment. But increased treatment by both doctors and teachers has shown steadily declining results. Medical expenses concentrated on those above forty-five have doubled several times over a period of forty years with a resulting 3 percent increase in the life expectancy of men. The increase in educational expenditures has produced even stranger results; otherwise President Nixon could not have been moved this spring to promise that every child shall soon have the "Right to Read" before leaving school.

In the United States it would take eighty billion dollars per year to provide what educators regard as equal treatment for all in grammar and high school. This is well over twice the $36 billion now being spent. Independent cost projections prepared at HEW and at the University of Florida indicate that by 1974 the comparable figures will be $107 billion as against the $45 billion now projected, and these figures wholly omit the enormous costs of what is called "higher education," for which demand is growing even faster. The United States, which spent nearly eighty billion dollars in 1969 for "defense," including its deployment in Vietnam, is obviously too poor to provide equal schooling. The President's committee for the study of school finance should ask not how to support or how to trim such increasing costs, but how they can be avoided.

Equal obligatory schooling must be recognized as at least economically unfeasible. In Latin America the amount of public money spent on each graduate student is between 350 and 1,500 times the amount spent on the median citizen (that is, the citizen who holds the middle ground between the poorest and the richest). In the United States the discrepancy is smaller, but the discrimination is keener. The richest parents, some 10 percent, can afford private education for their children and help them to benefit from foundation grants. But in addition they obtain ten times the per capita amount of public funds if this is compared with the per capita expenditure made on the children of the 10 percent who are poorest. The principal reasons for this are that rich children stay longer in school, that a year in a university is disproportionately more expensive than a year in high school, and that most private universities depend—at least indirectly—on tax-derived finances.

Obligatory schooling inevitably polarizes a society; it also grades the nations of the world according to an international caste system. Countries are rated like castes whose educational dignity is determined by the average years of schooling of its citizens, a rating which is closely related to per capita gross national product, and much more painful.

1. Which one of the following best expresses the main idea of the passage?
    (A) The educational shortcomings of the United States, in contrast to those of Latin America, are merely the result of poor allocation of available resources.
    (B) Defense spending is sapping funds which would be better spent in education.
    (C) Obligatory schooling must be scrapped if the goal of educational equality is to be realized.
    (D) Obligatory education does not and cannot provide equal education.

2. The author most likely would agree with which one of the following solutions to the problems presented by obligatory education?
    (F) Education should not be obligatory at all.
    (G) Education should not be obligatory for those who cannot afford it.
    (H) More money should be diverted to education for the poorest.
    (J) Future spending should be capped.

3. According to the passage, education is like health care in all of the following ways EXCEPT:
    (A) It has reached a point of diminishing returns, increased spending no longer results in significant improvement.
    (B) It is unfairly distributed between rich and poor.
    (C) The amount of money being spent on older students is increasing.
    (D) Its cost has increased nearly as fast.

4. Why does the author consider the results from increased educational expenditures to be "even stranger" than those from increased medical expenditures?
    (F) The aging of the population should have had an impact only on medical care, not on education.
    (G) The "Right to Read" should be a bare minimum, not a Presidential ideal.
    (H) Educational spending has shown even poorer results than spending on health care, despite greater increases.
    (J) It inevitably polarizes society.

5. Which one of the following most accurately characterizes the author's attitude with respect to obligatory schooling?
    (A) critical
    (B) neutral
    (C) ambivalent
    (D) resentful

ACT Verbal Prep Course

Answers and Solutions to Solo Exercise

1. The answer to a main idea question will summarize the passage, without going beyond it, so the answer is (D).
   (A) makes a false claim. The beginning of the third paragraph implies that the discrepancy in allocation of funds is greater in Latin America than the United States.
   (B) is implied in the passage but never fully developed.
   (C) is the second-best answer-choice. The answer to a main idea question, however, should sum up the passage, not make a conjecture about it. Clearly the author has serious reservations about obligatory schooling, but at no point does he state or imply that it should be scrapped.
   (D) aptly summarizes the passage, without going beyond it. The key to seeing this is the opening to paragraph three: *Equal obligatory schooling must be recognized as at least economically unfeasible.* In other words, regardless of any other failings, it cannot succeed economically and therefore cannot provide equal education.

2. This is an application question. These questions tend to be rather difficult, though this one is not. To answer an application question, put yourself in the author's place. If you were arguing his case, which of the solutions would you advocate? The answer is (F).
   (F) The author does not merely imply that obligatory education has some shortcomings; he suggests that it is fundamentally flawed. Again this is made clear by the opening to paragraph three, *Equal obligatory schooling must be recognized as at least economically unfeasible*.
   (G) is incorrect because nothing in the passage suggests that the author would advocate a solution that would polarize society even more.
   (H) is incorrect because it contradicts the author. Paragraph two is dedicated to showing that the United States is too poor to provide equal schooling. You can't divert money you don't have.
   (J) is the second-best answer-choice. Although the author probably believes that future spending should be restrained or capped, this understates the thrust of his argument.

3. This is a description question, so we must find the place from which it is drawn. Through the process of elimination, the answer is (B).
   (A) is eliminated by the first paragraph.
   (B) is correct. In paragraph three, the author does state that there is a keen discrepancy in the funding of education between rich and poor, but a survey of the passage shows that at no point does he mention that this is also the case with health care.
   (C) is eliminated by the first paragraph.
   (D) is eliminated by the opening.

4. This is an extension question. We are asked to interpret a statement by the author. The needed reference is the closing sentence to paragraph one. Remember: extension questions require you to go beyond the passage, so the answer won't be explicitly stated in the reference—we will have to interpret it.

The implication of President Nixon's promise is that despite increased educational funding many children cannot even read when they graduate from school. The answer is (G).

120

Don't make the mistake of choosing (H). The opening line to the passage states that educational costs have risen "almost as fast" as medical costs, not faster.

(F) is incorrect because the passage never mentions the aging of the population.

Many students who cannot solve this question choose (J)—don't. It uses bait language from the passage, *"inevitably polarizes a society."* The correct answer to an extension question will often both paraphrase and extend a passage statement but will not quote it directly, as in (J).

5. Like most tone questions this one is rather easy.

The author clearly does not admire the obligatory school system. This eliminates (B) and (C).

Although the author strongly opposes obligatory schooling, the word *resentful* in (D) is too strong and too personal. A scholar would never directly express resentment or envy, even if that is his true feeling. Hence, the answer is (A).

Pivotal Words

As mentioned earlier, you will have 35 minutes to read four passages and answer ten questions concerning each passage. That leaves you with about 8 1/2 minutes to spend on each passage and their following questions. It's essential, therefore, to identify the places from which questions will most likely be drawn and concentrate your attention there.

Pivotal words can help in this regard. Following are the most common pivotal words.

PIVOTAL WORDS

But	**Although**
However	**Yet**
Despite	**Nevertheless**
Nonetheless	**Except**
In contrast	**Even though**

As you may have noticed, these words indicate contrast. Pivotal words warn that the author is about to either make a U-turn or introduce a counter-premise (concession to a minor point that weakens the argument).

Example: (Counter-premise)

I submit that the strikers should accept the management's offer. Admittedly, it is less than what was demanded. But it does resolve the main grievance—inadequate health care. Furthermore, an independent study shows that a wage increase greater than 5% would leave the company unable to compete against Japan and Germany, forcing it into bankruptcy.

The conclusion, "the strikers should accept the management's offer," is stated in the first sentence. Then "Admittedly" introduces a concession (counter-premise); namely, that the offer was less than what was demanded. This weakens the speaker's case, but it addresses a potential criticism of his position before it can be made. The last two sentences of the argument present more compelling reasons to accept the offer and form the gist of the argument.

Pivotal words mark natural places for questions to be drawn. At a pivotal word, the author changes direction. The ACT writers form questions at these junctures to test whether you turned with the author or you continued to go straight. Rarely do the ACT writers let a pivotal word pass without drawing a question from its sentence.

Strategy: As you read a passage, circle the pivotal words and refer to them when answering the questions.

Let's apply this theory to the passage on criminal justice. For easy reference, the passage is reprinted here with explanations. The pivotal words are marked in bold.

****

There are two major systems of criminal procedure in the modern world—the adversarial and the inquisitorial. The former is associated with common law tradition and the latter with civil law tradition. Both systems were historically preceded by the system of private vengeance in which the victim of a crime fashioned his own remedy and administered it privately, either personally or through an agent. The vengeance system was a system of self-help, the essence of which was captured in the slogan "an eye for an eye, a tooth for a tooth." The modern adversarial system is only one historical step removed from the private vengeance system and still retains some of its characteristic features. Thus, for example, **even though** the right to institute criminal action has now been extended to all members of society and **even though** the police department has taken over the pretrial investigative functions on behalf of the prosecution, the adversarial system still leaves the defendant to conduct his own pretrial investigation. The trial is still viewed as a duel between two adversaries, refereed by a judge who, at the beginning of the trial has no knowledge of the investigative background of the case. In the final analysis the adversarial system of criminal procedure symbolizes and regularizes the punitive combat.

By contrast, the inquisitorial system begins historically where the adversarial system stopped its development. It is two historical steps removed from the system of private vengeance. Therefore, from the standpoint of legal anthropology, it is historically superior to the adversarial system. Under the inquisitorial system the public investigator has the duty to investigate not just on behalf of the prosecutor **but also** on behalf of the defendant. Additionally, the public prosecutor has the duty to present to the court not only evidence that may lead to the conviction of the defendant **but also** evidence that may lead to his exoneration. This system mandates that both parties permit full pretrial discovery of the evidence in their possession. Finally, in an effort to make the trial less like a duel between two adversaries, the inquisitorial system mandates that the judge take an active part in the conduct of the trial, with a role that is both directive and protective.

Fact-finding is at the heart of the inquisitorial system. This system operates on the philosophical premise that in a criminal case the crucial factor is not the legal rule but the facts of the case and that the goal of the entire procedure is to experimentally recreate for the court the commission of the alleged crime.

****

Even though—Here "even though" is introducing a concession. In the previous sentence, the author stated that the adversarial system is only one step removed from the private vengeance system. The author uses the two concessions as a hedge against potential criticism that he did not consider that the adversarial system has extended the right to institute criminal action to all members of society and that police departments now perform the pretrial investigation. But the author then states that the adversarial system still leaves the defendant to conduct his own pretrial investigation. This marks a good place from which to draw a question. Many people will misinterpret the two concessions as evidence that the adversarial system is two steps removed from the private vengeance system.

By contrast—In this case the pivotal word is not introducing a concession. Instead it indicates a change in thought: now the author is going to discuss the other criminal justice system. This is a natural place to test whether the student has made the transition and whether he will attribute the properties soon to be introduced to the inquisitorial system, not the adversarial system.

But also—In both places, "but also" indicates neither concession nor change in thought. Instead it is part of the coordinating conjunction "not only . . . but also . . . ." Rather than indicating contrast, it emphasizes the second element of the pair.

Let's see how these pivotal words can help answer the questions in the last section. The first is from the Description Section:

Example:
According to the passage, the inquisitorial system differs from the adversarial system in that
(A) it does not make the defendant solely responsible for gathering evidence for his case
(B) it does not require the police department to work on behalf of the prosecution
(C) it does not allow the victim the satisfaction of private vengeance
(D) it requires the prosecution to drop a weak case

The pivotal phrase "by contrast" flags the second paragraph as the place to begin looking. The pivotal phrase "but also" introduces the answer—namely that the prosecutor must also investigate "on behalf of the defendant." The answer is (A).

The next question is from the Writing Techniques Section:

Example:
Which one of the following best describes the organization of the passage?
(A) Two systems of criminal justice are compared and contrasted, and one is deemed to be better than the other.
(B) One system of criminal justice is presented as better than another. Then evidence is presented to support that claim.
(C) Two systems of criminal justice are analyzed, and one specific example is examined in detail.
(D) A set of examples is presented. Then a conclusion is drawn from them.

The pivotal phrase "by contrast" gives this question away. The author is comparing and contrasting two criminal justice systems, which the opening pivotal word introduces. Hence the answer is (A).

For our final example, consider the question from the Extension Section:

Example:
The author views the prosecution's role in the inquisitorial system as being
(A) an advocate for both society and the defendant
(B) solely responsible for starting a trial
(C) an investigator only
(D) an aggressive but fair investigator

The information needed to answer this question is introduced by the pivotal phrase, "but also." There it is stated that the prosecutor must present evidence that may exonerate the defendant; that is, he must act fairly. The answer is (D).

Points to Remember

1. Pivotal words indicate that the author is about to make a U-turn in thought or introduce a counter-premise (concession to a minor point that weakens the argument).

2. The following are the most common pivotal words:

    | **But** | **Although** | **Except** |
    | **However** | **Yet** | **Even though** |
    | **Despite** | **Nevertheless** | **In contrast** |
    | **Nonetheless** | | |

3. Pivotal words mark natural places for questions to be drawn. At a pivotal word, the author changes direction. The ACT writers form questions at these junctures to test whether you made the turn with the author or whether you continued to go straight. Rarely do the ACT writers pass a pivotal word without drawing a question from its sentence.

4. As you read each passage, circle the pivotal words.

ACT Verbal Prep Course

Mentored Exercise

> Directions: This passage is followed by a group of questions to be answered based on what is stated or implied in the passage. Choose the best answer; the one that most accurately and completely answers the question. Hints, insights, and answers are given.

The premise with which the multiculturalists begin is unexceptional: that it is important to recognize and to celebrate the wide range of cultures that exist in the United States. In what sounds like a reflection of traditional American pluralism, the multiculturalists argue that we must recognize difference, that difference is legitimate; in its kindlier versions, multiculturalism represents the discovery on the part of minority groups that they can play a part in molding the larger culture even as they are molded by it. And on the campus multiculturalism, defined more locally as the need to recognize cultural variations among students, has tried with some success to talk about how a racially and ethnically diverse student body can enrich everyone's education.

Phillip Green, a political scientist at Smith and a thoughtful proponent of multiculturalism, notes that for a significant portion of the students the politics of identity is all-consuming. Students he says "are unhappy with the thin gruel of rationalism. They require a therapeutic curriculum to overcome not straightforward racism but ignorant stereotyping."

(1) But multiculturalism's hard-liners, who seem to make up the majority of the movement, damn as racism any attempt to draw the myriad of American groups into a common American culture. For these multiculturalists, differences are absolute, irreducible, intractable—occasions not for understanding but for separation. The multiculturalist, it turns out, is not especially interested in the great American hyphen, in the syncretistic (and therefore naturally tolerant) identities that allow Americans to belong to more than a single culture, to be both particularists and universalists.

The time-honored American mixture of assimilation and traditional allegiance is denounced as a danger to racial and gender authenticity. This is an extraordinary reversal of the traditional liberal commitment to a "truth" that transcends parochialisms. In the new race/class/gender formation, universality is replaced by, among other things, feminist science Nubian numerals (as part of an Afro-centric science), and what Marilyn Frankenstein of the University of Massachusetts-Boston describes as "ethno-mathematics," in which the cultural basis of counting comes to the fore.

The multiculturalists insist on seeing all perspectives as tainted by the perceiver's particular point of view. Impartial knowledge, they argue, is not possible, because ideas are simply the expression of individual identity, or of the unspoken but inescapable assumptions that are inscribed in a culture or a language. The problem, **(2) however,** with this warmed-over Nietzscheanism is that it threatens to leave no ground for anybody to stand on. So the multi-culturalists make a leap, necessary for their own intellectual survival, and proceed to argue that there are some categories, such as race and gender, that do in fact embody an unmistakable knowledge of oppression. Victims are at least epistemologically lucky. Objectivity is a mask for oppression. And so an appalled former 1960s radical complained to me that self-proclaimed witches were teaching classes on witchcraft. "They're not teaching students how to think," she said, "they're telling them what to believe."

****

There are two critical pivotal words in this passage—(1) **But**, and (2) **however**.

(1) **But**. Until this point, the author did not reveal his feeling toward multiculturalism. He presented an objective, if not positive, view of the movement. However, "**But**" introduced an abrupt change in direction (a U-turn). Before he talked about the "kindlier" multiculturalism—to which he appears to be sympathetic. Now he talks about "hard-line" multiculturalism, which he implies is intolerant and divisive.

The pivotal word "**but**" doesn't just change the direction of the passage, it introduces the main idea: that multiculturalism has become an extreme and self-contradictory movement.

(2) **however**. This is the second critical pivotal word. The author opened this paragraph by presenting the multiculturalist's view; now he will criticize their positions.

1. Which one of the following ideas would a multiculturalist NOT believe?
   (A) That we should recognize and celebrate the differences among the many cultures in the United States.
   (B) That we can never know the "truth" because "truth" is always shaped by one's culture.
   (C) That "difference" is more important than "sameness."
   (D) That different cultures should work to assimilate themselves into the mainstream culture so that eventually there will be no excuse for racism.

   The sentence introduced by the pivotal word "**But**" gives away the answer to this question.

   The answer is (D).

2. According to a hard-line multiculturalist, which one of the following groups is most likely to know the "truth" about political reality?
   (A) Educated people who have learned how to see reality from many different perspectives.
   (B) A minority group that has suffered oppression at the hands of the majority.
   (C) High government officials who have privileged access to secret information.
   (D) Minorities who through their education have risen above the socioeconomic position occupied by most members of their ethnic group.

   This is a rather hard extension question.

   Hint: A subjugated minority group has at least the "unmistakable knowledge of oppression" (last paragraph)

   Don't make the mistake of choosing (D). Upper class minorities have simply exchanged one tainted point of view for another—and probably a more tainted one since the adopted position does not allow for knowledge of "oppression."

   The answer is (B).

3. The author states that in a "kindlier version" of multiculturalism, minorities discover "that they can play a part in molding the larger culture even as they are molded by it." If no new ethnic groups were incorporated into the American culture for many centuries to come, which one of the following would be the most probable outcome of this "kindlier version"?
   (A) At some point in the future, there would be only one culture with no observable ethnic differences.
   (B) Eventually the dominant culture would overwhelm the minority cultures, who would then lose their ethnic identities.
   (C) The multiplicity of ethnic groups would remain but the characteristics of the different ethnic groups would change.
   (D) The smaller ethnic groups would remain, and they would retain their ethnic heritage.

   This application question clearly goes well beyond the passage.

   If no new ethnic groups were incorporated into the American culture, then the interplay between the larger and smaller groups would continue, with both groups changing, until there would be only one common (and different from any original) group.

   The answer is (A).

ACT Verbal Prep Course

4. The author speaks about the "politics of identity" that Phillip Green, a political scientist at Smith, notes is all-consuming for many of the students. Considering the subject of the passage, which one of the following best describes what the author means by "the politics of identity"?

   (A) The attempt to discover individual identities through political action
   (B) The political agenda that aspires to create a new pride of identity for Americans
   (C) The current obsession for therapy groups that help individuals discover their inner selves
   (D) The trend among minority students to discover their identities in their ethnic groups rather than in their individuality

   This is an extension question. You may find the classification of the these problems as "application" or "extension" to be somewhat arbitrary or even disagree with a particular classification. As mentioned before, application and extension questions differ only in degree. Question 3 is clearly an application question; by asking you to make a conjecture about the future, it goes well beyond the passage. How to classify Question 4, however, is not so clear. We classified it as an extension question because it seems to be asking merely for the author's true meaning of the phrase "the politics of identity." That is, it stays within the context of the passage.

   Trap: Don't be led astray by (B); it uses the word "political" to tempt you. Although it is perhaps a good description, it is not within the context of the passage, which focuses on ethnic politics, not national identities through "roots."

   The answer is (D).

5. Which one of the following best describes the attitude of the writer toward the multicultural movement?

   (A) Tolerant. It may have some faults, but it is well-meaning overall.
   (B) Critical. A formerly admirable movement has been taken over by radical intellectuals.
   (C) Disinterested. He seems to be presenting an objective report.
   (D) Enthusiastic. The author embraces the multiculturalist movement and is trying to present it in a favorable light.

   Like most tone questions this one is rather easy.

   To get a feel for the author's attitude, check the adjectives he chooses. The author starts by introducing the "kindlier" version of multiculturalism and describes a proponent of multiculturalism, Phillip Green, as "thoughtful." Then he introduces the "hard liners" who "damn" any attempt at cultural assimilation. He feels that the movement has changed; that it has gone bad.

   The answer is (B).

6. "Multiculturalist relativism" is the notion that there is no such thing as impartial or objective knowledge. The author seems to be grounding his criticism of this notion on

    (A) the clear evidence that science has indeed discovered "truths" that have been independent of both language and culture.
    (B) the conclusion that relativism leaves one with no clear notions of any one thing that is true.
    (C) the absurdity of claiming that knowledge of oppression is more valid than knowledge of scientific facts.
    (D) the agreement among peoples of all cultures as to certain undeniable truths—e.g., when the sky is clear, day is warmer than night.

    This is an another extension question.

    Hint: The answer can be derived from the pivotal sentence containing "however" (2).

    The answer is (B).

ACT Verbal Prep Course

Solo Exercise

> Directions: This passage is followed by a group of questions to be answered based on what is *stated* or *implied* in the passage. Choose the *best* answer - the one that most accurately and completely answers the question.

According to usage and conventions which are at last being questioned but have by no means been overcome, the social presence of a woman is different in kind from that of a man. A man's presence is dependent upon the promise of power which he embodies. If the promise is large and credible his presence is striking. If it is small or incredible, he is found to have little presence. The promised power may be moral, physical, temperamental, economic, social, sexual—but its object is always exterior to the man. A man's presence suggests what he is capable of doing to you or for you. His presence may be fabricated, in the sense that he pretends to be capable of what he is not. But the pretense is always toward a power which he exercises on others.

By contrast, a woman's presence expresses her own attitude to herself, and defines what can and cannot be done to her. Her presence is manifest in her gestures, voices, opinions, expressions, clothes, chosen surroundings, taste—indeed there is nothing she can do which does not contribute to her presence. Presence for a woman is so intrinsic to her person that men tend to think of it as an almost physical emanation, a kind of heat or smell or aura.

To be born a woman has been to be born, within an allotted and confined space, into the keeping of men. The social presence of women has developed as a result of their ingenuity in living under such tutelage within such a limited space. But this has been at the cost of a woman's self being split into two. A woman must continually watch herself. Whilst she is walking across a room or whilst she is weeping at the death of her father, she can scarcely avoid envisaging herself walking or weeping. From earliest childhood she has been taught and persuaded to survey herself continually.

And so she comes to consider the *surveyor* and the *surveyed* within her as the two constituent yet always distinct elements of her identity as a woman.

She has to survey everything she is and everything she does because how she appears to others, and ultimately how she appears to men, is of crucial importance for what is normally thought of as the success of her life. Her own sense of being in herself is supplanted by a sense of being appreciated as herself by another. Men survey women before treating them. Consequently how a woman appears to a man can determine how she will be treated. To acquire some control over this process, women must contain it and internalize it. That part of a woman's self which is the surveyor treats the part which is the surveyed so as to demonstrate to others how her whole self would like to be treated. And this exemplary treatment of herself by herself constitutes her presence. Every woman's presence regulates what is and is not "permissible" within her presence. Every one of her actions—whatever its direct purpose or motivation—is also read as an indication of how she would like to be treated. If a woman throws a glass on the floor, this is an example of how she treats her own emotion of anger and so of how she would wish to be treated by others. If a man does the same, his action is only read as an expression of his anger. If a woman makes a good joke this is an example of how she treats the joker in herself and accordingly of how she as joker-woman would like to be treated by others. Only a man can make a good joke for its own sake.

1. According to "usage and conventions," appearance is NECESSARILY a part of reality for

    (A) men
    (B) women
    (C) both men and women
    (D) neither men nor women

2. In analyzing a woman's customary "social presence," the author hopes to

    (A) justify and reinforce it.
    (B) understand and explain it.
    (C) expose and discredit it.
    (D) demonstrate and criticize it.

3. It can be inferred from the passage that a woman with a Ph.D. in psychology who gives a lecture to a group of students is probably MOST concerned with

    (A) whether her students learn the material.
    (B) what the males in the audience think of her.
    (C) how she comes off as a speaker in psychology.
    (D) finding a husband.

4. The passage portrays women as

    (A) victims
    (B) liars
    (C) actresses
    (D) politicians

5. Which one of the following is NOT implied by the passage?

    (A) Women have split personalities.
    (B) Men are not image-conscious.
    (C) Good looks are more important to women than to men.
    (D) A man is defined by what he does, whereas a woman is defined by how she appears.

6. The primary purpose of the passage is to

    (A) compare and contrast woman's presence and place in society with that of man's.
    (B) discuss a woman's presence and place in society and to contrast it with a man's presence and place.
    (C) illustrate how a woman is oppressed by society.
    (D) explain why men are better than women at telling jokes.

Answers and Solutions to Exercise

This passage is filled with pivotal words, some of which are crucial to following the author's train of thought. We will discuss only the critical pivotal words. The first pivotal word, "but" (middle of the first paragraph), introduces a distinction between a man's presence and a woman's: a man's is external, a woman's internal. The second pivotal word, "by contrast," introduces the main idea of the passage. The author opened the passage by defining a man's presence; now she will define a woman's presence. The last pivotal word, "but" (middle of the third paragraph), also introduces a change in thought. Now the author discusses how a woman's presence has split her identity into two parts—the *surveyor* and the *surveyed*. By closing with, *"Only a man can make a good joke for its own sake,"* the author is saying a man can concentrate on the punch line, whereas a woman must concentrate on its delivery.

1. This is a description question. The needed reference is contained in the second paragraph: *"there is nothing [a woman] can do which does not contribute to her presence. Presence for a woman is intrinsic to her person . . ."* If something is intrinsic to you, then it necessarily is part of your reality. Hence the answer is (B).

Note the question refers to "usage and conventions" discussed in the passage, not to any other way of viewing the world—such as your own!

2. Although the author opens the passage with a hint that she doesn't like the customary sex roles (*"conventions which are at last being questioned"*), the rest of the passage is explanatory and analytical. So (C) and (D) are too strong. The answer is (B).

3. This is an application question; we are asked to apply what we have learned from the passage to a hypothetical situation.

The best way to analyze this question is to compare the speaker to a joke-teller. The passage paints a portrait of a woman as most concerned with the image she presents to the world. She is not concerned with the speech or joke, *per se*, rather with how she delivers it. *"Only a man can make a good joke for its own sake."* The answer is (C).

Don't make the mistake of choosing (B). Although men have, in the main, molded her self-image, she has gone beyond that; she now measures herself in the abstract: "how will I come off to the ultimately critical audience?" and not "how will actual audience members see me?"

4. This description question is a bit tricky because the second-best choice is rather good. Women are concerned with the image they present, so they cannot be themselves—they must act their part. Hence, the answer is (C).

You may have been tempted by (A). According to the passage, women are thrown into the role of an actress, "into the keeping of men." So, like victims, they are not responsible for their social position. However, nothing in the passage directly suggests that it is wrong for women to be in this position or that women attempt to refuse this role. According to the passage, therefore, women are not, strictly speaking, victims. (*Victim* means "someone not in control of something injurious happening to him or her.")

5. This is an extension question. The passage discusses the fact that a man may fabricate his image (first paragraph). This suggests that men *are* conscious of their images, but the passage also states that image is not intrinsic to their personalities, as it is for women. The answer is (B).

6. This is a rather hard main idea question because the second-best choice, (A), is quite good.

The passage does open with a discussion of a man's presence. But in paragraph two the pivotal phrase "by contrast" introduces a woman's presence; from there the discussion of a man's presence is only in regard to how it affects a woman's. So a woman's presence is the main idea; contrasting it with a man's presence is secondary. (B) gives the proper emphasis to these two purposes.

The Three-Step Method

If speed-reading doesn't work — ever — and guessing just isn't your style, then what does work? If we combine three of the pivotal points we discussed earlier — previewing topic sentences, circling pivotal words, and understanding the six most common question types — then we can create a reading method that works. Otherwise known as the Three-Step Method.

The Three-Step Method:
1. (Optional) Preview the first sentence of each paragraph.
2. Read the passage at a slightly faster pace, and annotate the passage or circle any pivotal words. Use your marks as reference points when answering the following questions. Following are some guidance marks for your annotation pleasure.
   A = Author's Attitude
   C = Complex point
   ? = Question? I don't understand this part (you can bet that this area will be important to at least one question)
   SP = Significant point
   ! = Exclamation! Strong opinion
   W = Weak, questionable or unsupported argument or premise
3. Stay alert to places from which any of the six questions might be drawn:
   d. Main Idea
   e. Description
   f. Writing Technique
   g. Extension
   h. Application
   i. Tone

The *three-step method* should be viewed as a dynamic — not a static — process. Steps will often overlap each other and will not always be performed in the same order. Analyzing a passage to understand how it is constructed can be compared to dismantling an engine to understand how it was built. Some may dismantle the entire engine and then label the parts, while others may label the parts as they take them off the engine. Likewise, with writing, each person's process will be different.

Let's apply the three-step method to the following passage. Begin by previewing the first sentence of each paragraph:

Passage:

That placebos can cure everything from dandruff to leprosy is well known. They have a long history of use by witch doctors, faith healers, and even modern physicians, all of whom refuse to admit their efficacy. Modern distribution techniques can bring this most potent of medicines to the aid of everyone, not just those lucky enough to receive placebos in a medical testing program.

Every drug tested would prove effective if special steps were not taken to neutralize the placebo effect. This is why drug tests give half the patients the new medication and half a harmless substitute. These tests prove the value of placebos because approximately five percent of the patients taking them are cured even though the placebos are made from substances that have been carefully selected to be useless.

Most people feel that the lucky patients in a drug test get the experimental drug because the real drug provides them a chance to be cured. **(1) Yet** analysis shows that patients getting the placebo may be the lucky ones because they may be cured without risking any adverse effects the new drug may have. Furthermore, the drug may well be found worthless and to have severe side effects. No harmful side effects result from placebos.

Placebos regularly cure more than five percent of the patients and would cure considerably more if the doubts associated with the tests were eliminated. Cures are principally due to the patient's faith, **(2) yet** the patient must have doubts knowing that he may or may not be given the new drug, which itself may or may not prove to be an effective drug. Since he knows the probability of being given the true drug is about fifty percent, the placebo cure rate would be more than doubled by removing these doubts if cures are directly related to faith.

The actual curing power of placebos probably stems from the faith of the patient in the treatment. This suggests that cure rates in the ten percent range could be expected if patients are given placebos under the guise of a proven cure, even when patients know their problems are incurable.

It may take a while to reach the ten percent level of cure because any newly established program will not have cultivated the word-of-mouth advertising needed to insure its success. One person saying "I was told that my problem was beyond medical help, but they cured me," can direct countless people to the treatment with the required degree of faith. Furthermore, when only terminal illnesses are treated, those not cured tell no one of the failure.

Unfortunately, placebo treatment centers cannot operate as nonprofit businesses. The nonprofit idea was ruled out upon learning that the first rule of public medicine is never to give free medicine. Public health services know that medicine not paid for by patients is often not taken or not effective because the recipient feels the medicine is worth just what it cost him. **(3) Even though** the patients would not know they were taking sugar pills, the placebos cost so little that the patients would have no faith in the treatment. Therefore, though it is against higher principles, treatment centers must charge high fees for placebo treatments. This sacrifice of principles, however, is a small price to pay for the greater good of the patients.

Topic Sentence Previews:

j. The sentence *"That placebos can cure everything from dandruff to leprosy is well known "* implies that the passage is about placebos and that they are perhaps cure-alls.

k. The sentence *"Every drug tested would prove effective if special steps were not taken to neutralize the placebo effect"* gives the first bit of evidence supporting the topic sentence.

l. The sentence *"Most people feel that the lucky patients in a drug test get the experimental drug because the real drug provides them a chance to be cured"* might be introducing a counter-premise or pivotal point. We won't know until we read the passage.

m. The sentence *"Placebos regularly cure more than five percent of the patients and would cure considerably more if the doubts associated with the tests were eliminated"* provides more support for the topic sentence.

n. The sentence *"The actual curing power of placebos probably stems from the faith of the patient in the treatment"* explains why the topic sentence is true.

o. The sentence *"It may take a while to reach the ten percent level of cure because any newly established program will not have cultivated the word-of-mouth advertising needed to insure its success"* is hard to interpret, and doesn't really help with getting a glimpse of the passage.

p. The sentence *"Unfortunately, placebo treatment centers cannot operate as nonprofit businesses"* seems to be off the subject. Again, this does not help us.

In summary, although the last two sentences were not useful, we now have a good idea of what the passage is about: *how* and *why* placebos are effective.

The next step in the Three-Step Method is to fully read the passage, all the while keeping an eye out for places where the writer's of the ACT might have drawn questions.

Go back to the passage. As you read it, circle pivotal words and annotate any key points that you think are relevant. I've already marked some pivotal word for you, so all you need to do is watch out for key points.

Done? Good. Remember: Don't be afraid to mark up the passages on the ACT. Not only will doing so help you understand the material you've just read, but it will also make the text easier to navigate the second time around, when answering questions.

ACT Verbal Prep Course

Let's apply your knowledge of the passage on to some questions. Answers will immediately follow the questions.

1. Which one of the following best expresses the main idea of the passage?
   (A) Placebo treatment is a proven tool of modern medicine and its expanded use would benefit society's health.
   (B) Because modern technology allows for distribution of drugs on a massive scale, the proven efficacy of the placebo is no longer limited to a privileged few.
   (C) The curative power of the placebo is so strong that it should replace proven drugs because the patients receiving the placebo will then be cured without risking any adverse side effects.
   (D) The price of placebo treatment must be kept artificially high because patients have little faith in inexpensive treatments.

This is a main idea question.

As we found by previewing the topic sentences, the passage is about the efficiency of placebo treatment. Careful reading shows that the passage also promotes expanded use of placebos. Hence, the answer is (A). The other choices can be quickly dismissed.

The other choices can be quickly dismissed. (B) is the second-best choice: the author *does* mention that modern distribution techniques can bring the curative power of placebos to everyone, but he does not fully develop that idea. This answer-choice is tempting because it is contained in the topic paragraph. As to (C), it overstates the author's claim. Although in the third paragraph, the author states that those who receive the placebos may be the lucky ones, this is referring to new, unproven drugs, not to established drugs. As to (D), it, like (B), is mentioned in the passage but is not fully developed. It's tempting because it appears in the last paragraph—a natural place for the conclusion. Finally, (E) is neither mentioned nor implied by the passage

2. Which one of the following is most analogous to the idea presented in the last paragraph?
   (F) Buying a television at a discount house
   (G) Making an additional pledge to charity
   (H) Choosing the most expensive dishwasher in a manufacturer's line
   (J) Waiting until a book comes out in paperback

This is an application question.

The information needed to answer this question is heralded by the pivotal phrase *Even though* (middle of last paragraph). The implication of that sentence is you get what you pay for. This would motivate one to buy the most expensive item in a manufacturer's line. The answer is (H).

3. According to the passage, when testing a new drug medical researchers give half of the subjects the test drug and half a placebo because
   (A) proper statistical controls should be observed.
   (B) this method reduces the risk of maiming too many subjects if the drug should prove to be harmful.
   (C) all drugs which are tested would prove to be effective otherwise.
   (D) most drugs would test positively otherwise.

This is a description question.

Since this is a description question, you must refer to the passage to answer it. The opening sentence to paragraph two contains the needed information. That sentence states *Every drug would prove effective if special steps were not taken to neutralize the placebo effect*. So the answer is (C).

Choice (D) illustrates why you must refer directly to the passage to answer a description question: unless you have a remarkable memory, you would be unsure whether the statement was that **all** or **most** drugs would prove effective.

4. It can be inferred from the passage that the author might
   (F) believe that the benefits of a placebo treatment program which leads patients to believe they were getting a real drug would outweigh the moral issue of lying.
   (G) support legislation outlawing the use of placebos.
   (H) open up a medical clinic that would treat patients exclusively through placebo methods.
   (J) believe that factors other than faith are responsible for the curative power of the placebo.

This is an extension question.

The answer is (F). One of the first clues to the author's view on this issue is contained in the pivotal clause *yet the patient . . . effective drug* (fourth paragraph). Later, in paragraph six, the author nearly advocates that the patient should not be told that he or she might be receiving a placebo. Finally, the closing line of the passage cinches it. There, the author implies that certain principles *can be* sacrificed for the greater good of the patients.

5. Which one of the following best describes the organization of the material presented in the passage?
   (A) A general proposition is stated; then evidence for its support is given.
   (B) Two types of drug treatment—placebo and non-placebo—are compared and contrasted.
   (C) A result is stated, its cause is explained, and an application is suggested.
   (D) A series of examples is presented; then a conclusion is drawn from them.

This is a writing technique question.

In the first paragraph the author claims that placebos can cure everything from dandruff to leprosy—this is a result. Then in paragraphs two, three, four, and five, he explains the causes of the result. Finally, he alludes to an application—the placebo treatment centers. The answer is (C).

6. Which one of the following most accurately characterizes the author's attitude toward placebo treatment?
   (F) reserved advocacy
   (G) feigned objectivity
   (H) summary dismissal
   (J) perplexed by its effectiveness

This is a tone question.

This question is a little tricky. Only choices (F) and (G) have any real merit. Although the passage has a detached, third-person style, the author *does* present his opinions—namely that placebos work and that their use should be expanded. However, that advocacy is reserved, so the answer is (F).

The other choices can be quickly eliminated:
- (H) *Summary dismissal* is not supported by the passage. Besides, a scholar would never summarily dismiss something; he would consider it carefully—or at least give the impression that he has—before rejecting it. This eliminates (H).
- (J) Given the human ego, we are unlikely to admit that we don't understand the subject we are writing about. This eliminates (J).

Points to Remember

THE THREE-STEP METHOD
1. (Optional) Preview the first sentence of each paragraph.

2. Read the passage at a faster than usual pace (but not to the point that comprehension suffers), being alert to places from which any of the six questions might be drawn:
    a. Main Idea
    b. Description
    c. Writing Technique
    d. Extension
    e. Application
    f. Tone

3. Annotate the passage and circle any pivotal words. Then use these as reference points for answering the questions. Following are some common annotation marks (you may want to add to this list):

   A = **A**uthor's Attitude
   C = **C**omplex point
   ? = **Q**uestion? I don't understand this part (you can bet that this area will be important to *at least* one question)
   SP = **S**ignificant **p**oint
   ! = **E**xclamation! Strong opinion
   W = **W**eak, questionable or unsupported argument or premise

One final word: Try to enjoy the passages. Although it may seem like a chore, some of the reading material on the ACT is very interesting. If you go into a passage with a positive outlook rather than a negative one, you might be surprised how much easier the material will be to read.

Mentored Exercise

> Directions: This passage is followed by a group of questions to be answered based on what is stated or implied in the passage. Choose the best answer; the one that most accurately and completely answers the question.

Following the Three-Step Method, we preview the first sentence of each paragraph in the passage: (The body of the passage will be presented later.)

The enigmatic opening sentence *"Many readers, I suspect, will take the title of this article [Women, Fire, and Dangerous Things] as suggesting that women, fire, and dangerous things have something in common—say, that women are fiery and dangerous"* does not give us much of a clue to what the passage is about.

The sentence *"The classical view that categories are based on shared properties is not entirely wrong"* is more helpful. It tells us the passage is about categorization and that there are at least two theories about it: the classical view, which has merit, and the modern view, which is apparently superior.

The sentence *"Categorization is not a matter to be taken lightly"* merely confirms the subject of the passage.

Although only one sentence was helpful, previewing did reveal a lot about the passage's subject matter—categorization. Now we read the passage, circling pivotal words, annotating, and noting likely places from which any of the six questions might be drawn. After each paragraph, we will stop to analyze and interpret what the author has presented:

> Many readers, I suspect, will take the title of this article [*Women, Fire, and Dangerous Things*] as suggesting that women, fire, and dangerous things have something in common—say, that women are fiery and dangerous. Most feminists I've mentioned it to have loved the title for that reason, though some have hated it for the same reason. But the chain of inference—from conjunction to categorization to commonality—is the norm. The inference is based on the common idea of what it means to be in the same category: things are categorized together on the basis of what they have in common. The idea that categories are defined by common properties is not only our everyday folk theory of what a category is, it is also the principle technical theory—one that has been with us for more than two thousand years.

In this paragraph, the author introduces the subject matter of the passage—categorization. And the pivotal sentence, introduced by "but," explains the classical theory of categorization, albeit rather obtusely. Namely, like things are placed in the same category.

> Now we consider the second paragraph:
>
> The classical view that categories are based on shared properties is not entirely wrong. We often do categorize things on that basis. But that is only a small part of the story. In recent years it has become clear that categorization is far more complex than that. A new theory of categorization, called *prototype theory*, has emerged. It shows that human categorization is based on principles that extend far beyond those envisioned in the classical theory. One of our goals is to survey the complexities of the way people really categorize. For example, the title of this book was inspired by the Australian aboriginal language Dyirbal, which has a category, *balan*, that actually includes women, fire, and dangerous things. It also includes birds that are *not* dangerous, as well as exceptional animals, such as the platypus, bandicoot, and echidna. This is not simply a matter of categorization by common properties.

In this paragraph, the second pivotal word—but—is crucial. It introduces the main idea of the passage—the prototype theory of categorization. Now everything that is introduced should be attributed to the prototype theory, <u>not</u> to the classical theory. Wrong answer-choices are likely to be baited with just the opposite.

The author states that the prototype theory goes "far beyond" the classical theory. Although he does not tell us what the prototype theory *is*, he does tell us that it *is not* merely categorization by common properties.

Now we turn to the third paragraph:

> Categorization is not a matter to be taken lightly. There is nothing more basic than categorization to our thought, perception, action and speech. Every time we see something as a *kind* of thing, for example, a tree, we are categorizing. Whenever we reason about *kinds* of things—chairs, nations, illnesses, emotions, any kind of thing at all—we are employing categories. Whenever we intentionally perform any *kind* of action, say something as mundane as writing with a pencil, hammering with a hammer, or ironing clothes, we are using categories. The particular action we perform on that occasion is a *kind* of motor activity, that is, it is in a particular category of motor actions. They are never done in exactly the same way, yet despite the differences in particular movements, they are all movements of a kind, and we know how to make movements of that kind. And any time we either produce or understand any utterance of any reasonable length, we are employing dozens if not hundreds of categories: categories of speech sounds, of words, of phrases and clauses, as well as conceptual categories. Without the ability to categorize, we could not function at all, either in the physical world or in our social and intellectual lives.

Though the author does not explicitly state it, this paragraph defines the theory of prototypes. Notice the author likes to use an indirect, even cryptic, method of introducing or switching topics, which makes this a classic ACT type passage. The ACT writers have many opportunities here to test whether you are following the author's train of thought.

Now we attack the questions.

1. The author probably chose *Women, Fire, and Dangerous Things* as the title of the article because
   I. he thought that since the Dyirbal placed all three items in the same category, women, fire, and dangerous things necessarily had something in common.
   II. he was hoping to draw attention to the fact that because items have been placed in the same category doesn't mean that they necessarily have anything in common.
   III. he wanted to use the Dyirbal classification system as an example of how primitive classifications are not as functional as contemporary Western classification systems.

   (A) I only
   (B) II only
   (C) III only
   (D) II and III only

This is an extension question. The second paragraph contains the information needed to answer it. There the author states that women, fire, and dangerous things belong to a category called *balan* in an Australian aboriginal language, which is not simply based on common properties. This eliminates Statement I and confirms Statement II.

The answer is (B).

2. According to the author,
   I. categorizing is a fundamental activity of people.
   II. whenever a word refers to a kind of thing, it signifies a category.
   III. one has to be able to categorize in order to function in our culture.
   (A) I only
   (B) II only
   (C) I and II only
   (D) I, II, and III

This is a description question, so we must find the points in the passage from which the statements were drawn.

Remember, the answer to a description question will not directly quote a statement from the passage, but it will be closely related to one—often a paraphrase.

The needed references for Statements I, II, and III are all contained in the closing paragraph.

The answer is (D).

3. Which one of the following facts would most weaken the significance of the author's title?
   (A) The discovery that all the birds and animals classified as *balan* in Dyirbal are female
   (B) The discovery that the male Dyirbal culture considers females to be both fiery and dangerous
   (C) The discovery that all items in the *balan* category are considered female
   (D) The discovery that neither fire nor women are considered dangerous

To weaken an argument, attack one or more of its premises. Now the implication of the title is that *women*, *fire*, and *dangerous things* do not have anything in common. To weaken this implication, the answer should state that all things in the *balan* category have something in common.

The answer is (C).

3. To weaken an argument, attack one or more of its premises. Now the implication of the title is that *women*, *fire*, and *dangerous things* do not have anything in common. To weaken this implication, the answer should state that all things in the *balan* category have something in common.

The answer is (C).

4. If linguistic experts cannot perceive how women, fire, and dangerous things in the category *balan* have at least one thing in common, it follows that

   (A) there probably is something other than shared properties that led to all items in *balan* being placed in that category.
   (B) the anthropologists simply weren't able to perceive what the items had in common.
   (C) the anthropologists might not have been able to see what the items had in common.
   (D) the items do not have anything in common.

This is an extension question; we are asked to draw a conclusion based on the passage.

Hint: The thrust of the passage is that commonality is not the only way to categorize things.

The answer is (A).

5. Which one of the following sentences would best complete the last paragraph of the passage?

   (A) An understanding of how we categorize is central to any understanding of how we think and how we function, and therefore central to an understanding of what makes us human.
   (B) The prototype theory is only the latest in a series of new and improved theories of categorization; undoubtedly even better theories will replace it.
   (C) The prototype theory of categories has not only unified a major branch of linguistics, but it has applications to mathematics and physics as well.
   (D) An understanding of how the prototype theory of categorization evolved from the classical theory is essential to any understanding of how we think and how we function in society.

This is an application question; we are asked to complete a thought for the author.

Most of the third paragraph is introducing the prototype theory of categorization. But in the last sentence the author changes direction somewhat—without any notice, as is typical of his style. Now he is discussing the importance of the ability to categorize. The clause *"Without the ability to categorize, we could not function at all"* indicates that this ability is fundamental to our very being.

Be careful not to choose (D). Although it is probably true, it is too specific: in the final sentence the author is discussing categorization in general.

The answer is (A).

Solo Exercise

> Directions: This passage is followed by a group of questions to be answered based on what is stated or implied in the passage. Choose the best answer; the one that most accurately and completely answers the question.

Global strategies to control infectious disease have historically included the erection of barriers to international travel and immigration. Keeping people with infectious diseases outside national borders has reemerged as an important public health policy in the human immunodeficiency virus (HIV) epidemic. Between 29 and 50 countries are reported to have introduced border restrictions on HIV-positive foreigners, usually those planning an extended stay in the country, such as students, workers, or seamen.

Travel restrictions have been established primarily by countries in the western Pacific and Mediterranean regions, where HIV seroprevalence is relatively low. However, the country with the broadest policy of testing and excluding foreigners is the United States. From December 1, 1987, when HIV infection was first classified in the United States as a contagious disease, through September 30, 1989, more than 3 million people seeking permanent residence in this country were tested for HIV antibodies. The U.S. policy has been sharply criticized by national and international organizations as being contrary to public health goals and human-rights principles. Many of these organizations are boycotting international meetings in the United States that are vital for the study of prevention, education, and treatment of HIV infection.

The Immigration and Nationality Act requires the Public Health Service to list "dangerous contagious diseases" for which aliens can be excluded from the United States. By 1987 there were seven designated diseases—five of them sexually transmitted (chancroid, gonorrhea, granuloma inguinale, lymphogranuloma venereum, and infectious syphilis) and two non-venereal (active tuberculosis and infectious leprosy). On June 8, 1987, in response to a Congressional direction in the Helms Amendment, the Public Health Service added HIV infection to the list of dangerous contagious diseases.

A just and efficacious travel and immigration policy would not exclude people because of their serologic status unless they posed a danger to the community through casual transmission. U.S. regulations should list only active tuberculosis as a contagious infectious disease. We support well-funded programs to protect the health of travelers infected with HIV through appropriate immunizations and prophylactic treatment and to reduce behaviors that may transmit infection.

We recognize that treating patients infected with HIV who immigrate to the United States will incur costs for the public sector. It is inequitable, however, to use cost as a reason to exclude people infected with HIV, for there are no similar exclusionary policies for those with other costly chronic diseases, such as heart disease or cancer.

Rather than arbitrarily restrict the movement of a subgroup of infected people, we must dedicate ourselves to the principles of justice, scientific cooperation, and a global response to the HIV pandemic.

1. According to the passage, countries in the western Pacific have

    (A) a very high frequency of HIV-positive immigrants and have a greater reason to be concerned over this issue than other countries.
    (B) opposed efforts on the part of Mediterranean states to establish travel restrictions on HIV-positive residents.
    (C) a low HIV seroprevalence and, in tandem with Mediterranean regions, have established travel restrictions on HIV-positive foreigners.
    (D) continued to obstruct efforts to unify policy concerning immigrant screening.

2. The authors of the passage conclude that

   (A) it is unjust to exclude people based on their serological status without the knowledge that they pose a danger to the public.
   (B) U.S. regulations should require more stringent testing to be implemented at all major border crossings.
   (C) it is the responsibility of the public sector to absorb costs incurred by treatment of immigrants infected with HIV.
   (D) the HIV pandemic is largely overstated and that, based on new epidemiological data, screening immigrants is not indicated.

3. It can be inferred from the passage that

   (A) more than 3 million HIV-positive people have sought permanent residence in the United States.
   (B) countries with a low seroprevalence of HIV have a disproportionate and unjustified concern over the spread of AIDS by immigration.
   (C) the United States is more concerned with controlling the number of HIV-positive immigrants than with avoiding criticism from outside its borders.
   (D) current law is meeting the demand for prudent handling of a potentially hazardous international issue.

4. Before the Helms Amendment in 1987, seven designated diseases were listed as being cause for denying immigration. We can conclude from the passage that

   (A) the authors agree fully with this policy but disagree with adding HIV to the list.
   (B) the authors believe that sexual diseases are appropriate reasons for denying immigration but not non-venereal diseases.
   (C) the authors disagree with the amendment.
   (D) the authors believe that non-venereal diseases are justifiable reasons for exclusion, but not sexually transmitted diseases.

5. In referring to the "costs" incurred by the public (opening of the fifth paragraph), the authors apparently mean

   (A) financial costs.
   (B) costs to the public health.
   (C) costs in manpower.
   (D) costs in international reputation.

ACT Verbal Prep Course

Answers and Solutions to Exercise

Previewing the first sentence of each paragraph shows that the passage is about restricting travel of HIV-positive persons and that the authors feel there should be no restrictions. There are two pivotal words: "however" (second sentence of the second paragraph), and "Rather than" (opening of the last paragraph), which introduces the concluding paragraph.

1. This is a description question, so we must find the point in the passage from which the question is drawn. It is the opening sentence to paragraph two. There it is stated that countries in the western Pacific and Mediterranean regions have a low incidence of HIV infection and have introduced border restrictions. The answer, therefore, is (C).

2. This is another description question. The answer is (A). This is directly supported by the opening sentence of paragraph four. Note that (A) is a paraphrase of that sentence.

Be careful with (C). Although this is hinted at in paragraph five, it is never directly stated that the public sector is <u>responsible</u> for these costs, only that it would in fact pick up these costs. Remember: A description question must be answered from what is directly stated in the passage, not from what it implies.

3. This is an extension question. The second paragraph states *"U.S. policy has been sharply criticized by national and international organizations."* Given that this criticism has not caused the United States to change its policies, it must be more concerned with controlling the number of HIV-positive immigrants than with avoiding criticism. The answer, therefore, is (C).

Don't be tempted by (A); it's a same language trap. Every word in it is taken from the passage. However, the passage states that over 3 million people were tested for HIV antibodies (second paragraph), <u>not</u> that they were tested "positive" for HIV antibodies.

4. This is another extension question. At the end of the fourth paragraph, the authors state that only active tuberculosis should be listed as a dangerous contagious disease. We expect that they would oppose adding HIV to the list. The answer is (C).

5. Although governments have ostensibly restricted the immigration of HIV-positive persons out of fear that they may spread the disease, the authors apparently are referring to financial costs, not costs to public health. This is indicated by the end of the fifth paragraph, where they describe heart disease and cancer as non-contagious and costly, yet still admissible. The answer, therefore, is (A).

Practice Reading Test

On the actual ACT, you will read four full-length (around 750 words each) passages. Each passage will then be followed by ten questions. However, to help ease you into it all, this practice test will only ask you a few questions on each of the following passages. And, unlike the ACT, there is no time limit. So feel free to take your time. Remember: preview topic sentences, circle pivotal words, annotate the passage, and have fun!

> Directions: Each passage in this group is followed by questions based on its content. After reading a passage, choose the best answer to each question. Answer all questions following a passage on the basis of what is stated or implied in that passage.

Passage 1:

Most students arrive at [college] using "discrete, concrete, and absolute categories to understand people, knowledge, and values." These students live with a *dualistic* view, seeing "the world in polar terms of we-right-good vs. other-wrong-bad." These students cannot acknowledge the existence of more than one point of view toward any issue. There is one "right" way. And because these absolutes are assumed by or imposed on the individual from external authority, they cannot be personally substantiated or authenticated by experience. These students are slaves to the generalizations of their authorities. An eye for an eye! Capital punishment is apt justice for murder. The Bible says so.

Most students break through the dualistic stage to another equally frustrating stage—*multiplicity*. Within this stage, students see a variety of ways to deal with any given topic or problem. However, while these students accept multiple points of view, they are unable to evaluate or justify them. To have an opinion is everyone's right. While students in the dualistic stage are unable to produce evidence to support what they consider to be self-evident absolutes, students in the multiplistic stage are unable to connect instances into coherent generalizations. Every assertion, every point, is valid. In their democracy they are directionless. Capital punishment? What sense is there in answering one murder with another?

The third stage of development finds students living in a world of *relativism*. Knowledge is relative: right and wrong depend on the context. No longer recognizing the validity of each individual idea or action, relativists examine everything to find its place in an overall framework. While the multiplist views the world as unconnected, almost random, the relativist seeks always to place phenomena into coherent larger patterns. Students in this stage view the world analytically. They appreciate authority for its expertise, using it to defend their own generalizations. In addition, they accept or reject ostensible authority *after systematically* evaluating its validity. In this stage, however, students resist decision making. Suffering the ambivalence of finding several consistent and acceptable alternatives, they are almost overwhelmed by diversity and need means for managing it. Capital punishment is appropriate justice—in some instances.

In the final stage students manage diversity through individual *commitment*. Students do not deny relativism. Rather they assert an identity by forming commitments and assuming responsibility for them. They gather personal experience into a coherent framework, abstract principles to guide their actions, and use these principles to discipline and govern their thoughts and actions. The individual has chosen to join a particular community and agrees to live by its tenets. The accused has had the benefit of due process to guard his civil rights, a jury of peers has found him guilty, and the state has the right to end his life. This is a principle my community and I endorse.

1. It can be inferred from the passage that the author would consider which of the following to be good examples of dualistic thinking?
   I. People who think there is a right way and a wrong way to do things
   II. Teenagers who assume they know more about the real world than adults do
   III. People who back our country, right or wrong, when it goes to war
   (A) I only
   (B) III only
   (C) I and II only
   (D) I and III only

2. Students who are dualistic thinkers may not be able to support their beliefs convincingly because
   (F) most of their beliefs *cannot* be supported by arguments.
   (G) they have accepted their truths simply because authorities have said these things are true.
   (H) they half-believe and half-disbelieve just about everything.
   (J) they are enslaved by their authorities.

3. Which one of the following assertions is supported by the passage?
   (A) *Committed* thinkers are not very sure of their positions.
   (B) *Relativistic* thinkers have learned how to make sense out of the world and have chosen their own positions in it.
   (C) *Multiplicity* thinkers have difficulty understanding the relationships between different points of view.
   (D) *Dualistic* thinkers have thought out the reasons for taking their positions.

4. In paragraph two, the author states that in their democracy students in the *multiplicity* stage are directionless. The writer describes *multiplicity* students as being in a democracy because
   (F) there are so many different kinds of people in a democracy.
   (G) in an ideal democracy, all people are considered equal; by extension, so are their opinions.
   (H) Democrats generally do not have a good sense of direction.
   (J) although democracies may grant freedom, they are generally acknowledged to be less efficient than more authoritarian forms of government.

5. Which one of the following kinds of thinking is NOT described in the passage?
   (A) People who assume that there is no right or wrong in any issue
   (B) People who believe that right or wrong depends on the situation
   (C) People who commit themselves to a particular point of view after having considered several alternative concepts
   (D) People who think that all behavior can be accounted for by cause and effect relationships

6. Which one of the following best describes the organization of the passage?
   (F) Four methods of thought are compared and contrasted.
   (G) Four methods of thought are presented, and each is shown to complement the other.
   (H) The evolution of thought from simplistic and provincial through considered and cosmopolitan is illustrated by four stages.
   (J) The evolution of thought through four stages is presented, and each stage is illustrated by how it views capital punishment.

Passage 2:
A growing taste for shark steaks and shark-fin soup has for the first time in 400 million years put the scourge of the sea at the wrong end of the food chain. Commercial landings of this toothsome fish have doubled every year since 1986, and shark populations are plunging. It is hardly a case of good riddance. Sharks do for gentler fish what lions do for the wildebeest: they check populations by feeding on the weak. Also, sharks apparently do not get cancer and may therefore harbor clues to the nature of that disease.

Finally, there is the issue of motherhood. Sharks are viviparous. That is, they bear their young alive and swimming (not sealed in eggs), after gestation periods lasting from nine months to two years. Shark mothers generally give birth to litters of from eight to twelve pups and bear only one litter every other year.

This is why sharks have one of the lowest fecundity rates in the ocean. The female cod, for example, spawns annually and lays a few million eggs at a time. If three quarters of the cod were to be fished this year, they could be back in full force in a few years. But if humans took that big of a bite out of the sharks, the population would not recover for 15 years.

So, late this summer, if all goes according to plan, the shark will join the bald eagle and the buffalo on the list of managed species. The federal government will cap the U.S. commercial catch at 5,800 metric tons, about half of the 1989 level, and limit sportsmen to two sharks per boat. Another provision discourages finning, the harvesting of shark fins alone, by limiting the weight of fins to 7 percent of that of all the carcasses.

Finning got under the skin of environmentalists, and the resulting anger helped to mobilize support for the new regulations. Finning itself is a fairly recent innovation. Shark fins contain noodle-like cartilaginous tissues that Chinese chefs have traditionally used to thicken and flavor soup. Over the past few years rising demand in Hong Kong has made the fins as valuable as the rest of the fish. Long strands are prized, so unusually large fins can be worth considerably more to the fisherman than the average price of about $10 a pound.

But can U.S. quotas save shark species that wander the whole Atlantic? The blue shark, for example, migrates into the waters of something like 23 countries. John G. Casey, a biologist with the National Marine Fisheries Service Research Center in Narragansett, R.I., admits that international co-ordination will eventually be necessary. But he supports U.S. quotas as a first step in mobilizing other nations. Meanwhile the commercial fishermen are not waiting for the new rules to take effect. "There's a pre-quota rush on sharks," Casey says, "and it's going on as we speak."

7. According to the passage, shark populations are at greater risk than cod populations because
   (A) sharks are now being eaten more than cod.
   (B) the shark reproduction rate is lower than that of the cod.
   (C) sharks are quickly becoming fewer in number.
   (D) sharks are now as scarce as bald eagles and buffalo.

8. According to the passage, a decrease in shark populations
   I. *might cause some fish populations to go unchecked.*
   II. *would hamper cancer research.*
   III. *to one-quarter the current level would take over a decade to recover from.*
   (A) II only
   (B) III only
   (C) I and III only
   (D) I and II only

9. If the species Homo logicus was determined to be viviparous and to have extremely low fecundity rates on land, we might expect that
   (A) *Homo logicus* could overpopulate its niche and should be controlled.
   (B) *Homo logicus* might be declared an endangered species.
   (C) *Homo logicus* would pose no danger to other species and would itself be in no danger.
   (D) None of these events would be expected with certainty.

10. Which one of the following best describes the author's attitude toward the efforts to protect shark populations?
    (A) strong advocate
    (B) impartial observer
    (C) opposed
    (D) resigned to their ineffectiveness

11. It can be inferred from the passage that
    I. *research efforts on cancer will be hindered if shark populations are threatened.*
    II. *U.S. quotas on shark fishing will have limited effectiveness in protecting certain species.*
    III. *some practices of Chinese chefs have angered environmentalists.*
    (F) I only
    (G) II only
    (H) I and II only
    (J) II and III only

12. An irony resulting from the announcement that sharks will be placed on the managed list is
    (A) we will now find out less about cancer, so by saving the sharks, we are hurting ourselves.
    (B) sharks are far more dangerous to other fish than we are to them.
    (C) more chefs are now using the cartilaginous tissues found in shark fins.
    (D) more sharks are being killed now than before the announcement.

Passage 3:
"A writer's job is to tell the truth," said Hemingway in 1942. No other writer of our time had so fiercely asserted, so pugnaciously defended or so consistently exemplified the writer's obligation to speak truly. His standard of truth-telling remained, moreover, so high and so rigorous that he was ordinarily unwilling to admit secondary evidence, whether literary evidence or evidence picked up from other sources than his own experience. "I only know what I have seen," was a statement which came often to his lips and pen. What he had personally done, or what he knew unforgettably by having gone through one version of it, was what he was interested in telling about. This is not to say that he refused to invent freely, but that he always made it a sacrosanct point to invent in terms of what he actually knew of.

The primary intent of his writing, from first to last, was to seize and project for the reader what he often called "the way it was." This is a characteristically simple phrase for a concept of extraordinary complexity, and Hemingway's conception of its meaning subtly changed several times in the course of his career—always in the direction of greater complexity. At the core of the concept, however, one can invariably discern the operation of three aesthetic instruments: the sense of place, the sense of fact, and the sense of scene.

The first of these, obviously a strong passion with Hemingway, is the sense of place. "Unless you have geography, background," he once told George Antheil, "you have nothing." You have, that is to say, a dramatic vacuum. Few writers have been more place-conscious. Few have so carefully charted out the geographical ground work of their novels while managing to keep background so conspicuously unobtrusive. Few, accordingly, have been able to record more economically and graphically the way it is when you walk through the streets of Paris in search of breakfast at a corner café . . . Or when, at around six o'clock of a Spanish dawn, you watch the bulls running from the corrals at the Puerta Rochapea through the streets of Pamplona towards the bullring.

"When I woke it was the sound of the rocket exploding that announced the release of the bulls from the corrals at the edge of town. Down below the narrow street was empty. All the balconies were crowded with people. Suddenly a crowd came down the street. They were all running, packed close together. They passed along and up the street toward the bullring and behind them came more men running faster, and then some stragglers who were really running. Behind them was a little bare space, and then the bulls, galloping, tossing their heads up and down. It all went out of sight around the corner. One man fell, rolled to the gutter, and lay quiet. But the bulls went right on and did not notice him. They were all running together."

This landscape is as morning-fresh as a design in India ink on clean white paper. First is the bare white street, seen from above, quiet and empty. Then one sees the first packed clot of runners. Behind these are the thinner ranks of those who move faster because they are closer to the bulls. Then the almost comic stragglers, who are "really running." Brilliantly behind these shines the "little bare space," a desperate margin for error. Then the clot of running bulls—closing the design, except of course for the man in the gutter making himself, like the designer's initials, as inconspicuous as possible.

13. From the author's comments and the example of the bulls (paragraph 4), what was the most likely reason that Hemingway took care to include details of place?
    (F) He felt that geography in some way illuminated other, more important events.
    (G) He thought readers generally did not have enough imagination to visualize the scenes for themselves.
    (H) He had no other recourse since he was avoiding the use of other literary sources.
    (J) He thought that landscapes were more important than characters to convey "the way it was."

14. One might infer from the passage that Hemingway preferred which one of the following sources for his novels and short stories?
    (A) Stories that he had heard from friends or chance acquaintances
    (B) Stories that he had read about in newspapers or other secondary sources
    (C) Stories that came to him in periods of meditation or in dreams
    (D) Stories that he had lived rather than read about

15. It has been suggested that part of Hemingway's genius lies in the way in which he removes himself from his stories in order to let readers experience the stories for themselves. Which of the following elements of the passage support this suggestion?
    I. The comparison of the designer's initials to the man who fell and lay in the gutter (fourth paragraph) during the running of the bulls
    II. Hemingway's stated intent to project for the reader "the way it was" (opening of the second paragraph)
    III. Hemingway's ability to invent fascinating tales from his own experience
    (F) I only
    (G) II only
    (H) I and II only
    (J) I and III only

16. From the passage, one can assume that which of the following statements would best describe Hemingway's attitude toward knowledge?
    (A) One can learn about life only by living it fully.
    (B) A wise person will read widely in order to learn about life.
    (C) Knowledge is a powerful tool that should be reserved only for those who know how to use it.
    (D) Experience is a poor teacher.

17. The author calls "the way it was" a characteristically simple phrase for a concept of extraordinary complexity (opening of the second paragraph) because
    (F) the phrase reflects Hemingway's talent for obscuring ordinary events.
    (G) the relationship between simplicity and complexity reflected the relationship between the style and content of Hemingway's writing.
    (H) Hemingway became increasingly confused about "the way it was" throughout the course of his career.
    (J) Hemingway's obsession for geographic details progressively overshadowed the dramatic element of his stories.

Passage 4:

Imagine that we stand on any ordinary seaside pier, and watch the waves rolling in and striking against the iron columns of the pier. Large waves pay very little attention to the columns—they divide right and left and re-unite after passing each column, much as a regiment of soldiers would if a tree stood in their way; it is almost as though the columns had not been there. But the short waves and ripples find the columns of the pier a much more formidable obstacle. When the short waves impinge on the columns, they are reflected back and spread as new ripples in all directions. To use the technical term, they are scattered. The obstacle provided by the iron columns hardly affects the long waves at all, but scatters the short ripples.

We have been watching a working model of the way in which sunlight struggles through the earth's atmosphere. Between us on earth and outer space the atmosphere interposes innumerable obstacles in the form of molecules of air, tiny droplets of water, and small particles of dust. They are represented by the columns of the pier.

The waves of the sea represent the sunlight. We know that sunlight is a blend of lights of many colors—as we can prove for ourselves by passing it through a prism, or even through a jug of water, or as Nature demonstrates to us when she passes it through the raindrops of a summer shower and produces a rainbow. We also know that light consists of waves, and that the different colors of light are produced by waves of different lengths, red light by long waves and blue light by short waves. The mixture of waves which constitutes sunlight has to struggle through the obstacles it meets in the atmosphere, just as the mixture of waves at the seaside has to struggle past the columns of the pier. And these obstacles treat the light waves much as the columns of the pier treat the sea-waves. The long waves which constitute red light are hardly affected, but the short waves which constitute blue light are scattered in all directions.

Thus, the different constituents of sunlight are treated in different ways as they struggle through the earth's atmosphere. A wave of blue light may be scattered by a dust particle, and turned out of its course. After a time a second dust particle again turns it out of its course, and so on, until finally it enters our eyes by a path as zigzag as that of a flash of lightning. Consequently, the blue waves of the sunlight enter our eyes from all directions. And that is why the sky looks blue.

18. We know from experience that if we look directly at the sun, we will see red light near the sun. This observation is supported by the passage for which one of the following reasons?

    (A) It seems reasonable to assume that red light would surround the sun because the sun is basically a large fireball.
    (B) It seems reasonable to assume that the other colors of light would either cancel each other or combine to produce red.
    (C) It seems reasonable to assume that red light would not be disturbed by the atmospheric particles and would consequently reach us by a relatively direct path from the sun to our eyes.
    (D) It is not supported by the passage. The author does not say what color of light should be near the sun, and he provides no reasons that would allow us to assume that the light would be red.

19. Scientists have observed that shorter wavelength light has more energy than longer wavelength light. From this we can conclude that

    (A) red light will exert more energy when it hits the surface of the earth than will blue light.
    (B) lightning is caused by the collision of blue light with particles in the air.
    (C) red light will travel faster than blue light.
    (D) blue light has more energy than red light.

20. A scientist makes new observations and learns that water waves of shorter wavelengths spread in all directions not only because they scatter off piers but also because they interact with previously scattered short water waves. Drawing upon the analogy between water waves and light waves, we might hypothesize which of the following?
    (A) Blue light waves act like ripples that other blue light waves meet and scatter from.
    (B) Red light waves will be scattered by blue light waves like incoming long water waves are scattered by outgoing ripples.
    (C) Red light waves can scatter blue light waves, but blue light waves cannot scatter red.
    (D) The analogy between water and light waves cannot be extended to include the way in which short water waves become ripples and scatter one another.

21. Which one of the following is a reason for assuming that sunlight is constituted of waves of many colors?
    (A) The mixture of waves that make up sunlight has to struggle through a variety of obstacles in the atmosphere.
    (B) When passing through water in the atmosphere, sunlight is sometimes broken down into an array of colors.
    (C) Many different wavelengths of light enter our eyes from all directions.
    (D) The mere fact that light waves can be scattered is a reason for assuming that sunlight is constituted of waves of different colors.

22. From the information presented in the passage, what can we conclude about the color of the sky on a day with a large quantity of dust in the air?
    (A) The sky would be even bluer
    (B) The sky would be redder
    (C) The sky would not change colors
    (D) We do not have enough information to determine a change in color

23. We all know that when there is a clear sky, the western sky appears red as the sun sets. From the information presented in the passage, this phenomenon would seem to be explained by which of the following?
    I. Light meets more obstacles when passing parallel to the earth's surface than when traveling perpendicular. Consequently, even red light is diffused.
    II. The blue light may not make it through the denser pathway of the evening sky, leaving only the long light waves of red.
    III. The short red light waves have more energy and are the only waves that can make it through the thick atmosphere of the evening sky.
    (A) I only
    (B) II only
    (C) I and II only
    (D) II and III only

24. Which one of the following does the author seem to imply?
    (A) Waves of light and waves of water are identical.
    (B) Waves of light have the same physical shape as waves of water.
    (C) Waves of light and waves of water do not have very much in common.
    (D) Waves of water are only models of waves of light.

Practice Reading Test

Answers and Solutions

1. D	7. B	13. F	19. D
2. G	8. C	14. D	20. D
3. C	9. D	15. H	21. B
4. G	10. B	16. A	22. D
5. D	11. G	17. G	23. C
6. J	12. D	18. C	24. D

1. This is an extension question. Statement I is true. This is the essential characteristic of dualistic (right/wrong) thinkers (opening lines of the first paragraph). This eliminates (B). Statement II is false. Dualistic thinkers grant authority (right thinking) to adults and adult figures. This is clear from the sentence, "These students are slaves to the generalizations of their authorities." This eliminates (C). Unfortunately, we have to check Statement III. It is true since Dualistic thinkers believe their group is right and the other group is wrong. (Again, see the opening lines of the first paragraph.) The answer, therefore is (D).

2. This is another extension question. Dualistic thinkers probably cannot give cogent arguments for their beliefs since they have adopted them unquestioningly from authority figures; dualistic thinkers do not know - or have never thought of - the reasons for which their beliefs are right or wrong. Hence the answer is (G).

3. This is a description question. Choice (A) is false. After carefully thinking through their reasons, committed thinkers are reasonably sure of their position. Choice (B) is also false. Relativistic thinkers make sense of the world, but they have not chosen their position. Choice (C) is true. Multiplicity thinkers see the world as randomly organized; they can't see the relationships that connect different positions. (See the first pivotal word, *however* [second paragraph].)

4. This is an extension question. Multiplicity students view all opinions as equally valid. They have yet to learn how to rank opinions (truths)—all votes (thoughts) count equally. The answer is (G). Note, (H) is offered to humor Republicans. The test-makers sometimes run out of tempting wrong choices. Don't dwell on such humorous nonsense.

5. This is another description question. Don't confuse (A) and (B). Multiplists acknowledge no right or wrong; whereas, Relativists acknowledge a morality, but one that is context dependent. The answer is (D).

6. This is a writing technique question. In each paragraph the author shows how a stage of thought evolved from a previous stage—except the dualistic stage, which starts the analysis. Furthermore, the thought process in each stage is illustrated by how it views capital punishment. So the answer is (J). Be careful not to choose (H). Although dualistic thinking certainly is simplistic and provincial, and committed thinking seems to be considered and cosmopolitan, neither of these judgments is stated nor implied by the passage.

7. This is a description question. Paragraph 3 contains the information needed to answer it. There it is stated that the cod population can replenish itself in a few years, but the shark population would take 15 years. Hence the answer is (B).

Don't make the mistake of choosing (C). Although it is certainly supported by the passage, it does not state how this relates to cod—they too may be decreasing in number. (C) uses the true-but-irrelevant ploy.

8. This is a description question. Statement I is true. It is supported by the analogy drawn between lions and sharks (first paragraph). This eliminates (A) and (B). Statement II is false. It is too strong an inference to draw from the information at the end of the first paragraph. If sharks were on the verge of extinction, this "could hamper" research. But given that the author does not claim or imply that sharks are near extinction, "would hamper" is too strong. Besides, the author does not state that sharks are being used in research, just that they may be useful in that regard. This eliminates (D). Hence, by process of elimination, we have learned the answer is (C).

9. This is an application question; we are asked to apply what we have learned in the passage to a hypothetical situation. A review of the passage shows that only (B) and (D) have any real merit. But sharks have survived for 400 million years with an extremely low fecundity rate. This eliminates (B). Hence the answer is (D).

10. This is a rather easy tone question. The passage has a matter-of-fact or journalistic tone to it, so the answer is (B).

11. This is an extension question. Statement I is incorrect: it overstates. Statement II is correct: we know that some species of sharks migrate into the waters of over 20 countries. U.S. quotas alone cannot protect these sharks, even if the quotas reduce the rate of killing in U.S. waters. Statement III is incorrect: the environmentalists are angry at the finning fishermen who are over-fishing the waters, but there is nothing in the passage to suggest that this anger is also directed towards the chefs. The answer is (G).

12. By announcing the impending classification, the federal government ironically encourages fishermen to kill as many sharks as they can before the regulations go into effect—stimulating the opposite of what was intended, i.e., the saving of sharks. The answer is (D).

13. This is an extension question. In the opening of the third paragraph, Hemingway effectively equates geography with background, and says that without them you have nothing. Later in third paragraph, the author refers to the geographical groundwork of Hemingway's novels. Both of these statements imply that details of place set the stage for other, more important events. Hence the answer is (F). Don't try to draw a distinction between geography, background, and landscape. The author uses them interchangeably when referring to details of place. Such latitude with labels is often mimicked by the Question-Writers.

14. Hemingway's primary intent was to project for the reader the way it was, as seen through his eyes. The answer is (D).

15. This is an extension question. Statement I is true: the last line of the passage states that the designer's initials (i.e., the writer's presence) are made as inconspicuous as possible. Statement II is also true: readers cannot see the way it was if they are looking through another medium (the author). Hemingway appears to say, in effect: *"I'm striving to report exactly what happened (and not my opinions about it). The readers must draw their own conclusions." S*tatement III is false: in fact, a good case could be made that writing only from personal experience would tend to increase, not decrease, the presence of the writer in his writings. The answer is (H).

16. This is an application question; we are asked to put ourselves in Hemingway's mind. From Hemingway's statement "I only know what I have seen" and from the author's assertion that Hemingway refused to honor secondary sources, we can infer that he believed one can know only through experience. The answer is (A).

17. This is an extension question. The answer is (G). *Phrase* (in the passage) corresponds to *style* (in the answer-choice), and *concept* corresponds to *content*.

18. This is an extension question. According to the passage, red light would not be significantly deflected and consequently would pass through a relatively direct route from the sun to our eyes. Hence the answer is (C).

19. This is another extension question. Since the passage is a science selection, we should expect a lot of extension questions.
(A): No, if anything, blue light would exert more energy.
(B): No. We cannot infer this. The collision of blue light with particles in the air is the reason for a blue sky, not for lightning.
(C): No. Speed of light is not mentioned in the passage.
(D): Yes. Blue light has a shorter wavelength, consequently it has more energy than red light.

20. This is an application question since it introduces new information about water waves and asks us to conclude how the behavior of light waves might be similarly affected. Given this information, however, we can justify no conclusion about whether light waves imitate water waves in this new regard. The analogy might hold or it might break down. We don't yet know. (To find out we would have to do an experiment using light.) The answer is (D).

21. (A): No. We do not know anything about a "variety" of obstacles; even if we did, we would have no reason to assume that light is constituted of different colors.
(B): Yes. See the first part of the third paragraph. Rainbows occur because light is constituted of many colors.
(C): No. This is a distortion of the final lines of the passage, and it sounds illogical to boot.
(D): No. This gives no reason to assume that light is constituted of many colors.

22. (A): No. Although dust is mentioned as one of the three important obstacles (second paragraph), we simply do not have enough information to conclude how dust density would change sky color.
(B): No. While this idea may fit with the common lore that a lot of dust in the air creates great, red sunsets, the passage itself gives no basis to any conclusion regarding color change.
(C): No. Same reason as in (A) and (B).
(D): Yes. There is not enough information in the passage to determine a relationship between color change and dust density. The dust may give off a certain color of its own—we can't say for certain.

23. Statement I is true. There are obviously more particles on a horizontal than a vertical path. The glowing red sky is reasonable evidence for some diffusion. Note that Question 24 asks "what can we *conclude*" while this question asks what seems *plausible* (what "would seem to be explained"). So, while we are attempting to make very similar inferences in both questions, what we can do with the data depends, among other things, on the degree of certainty requested. Statement II is true. The path of evening light probably has a greater average density, since it spends more time passing through a zone of thicker atmosphere. It is reasonable to assume this significantly greater density, or the absolute number of particles, might present an obstacle to blue light. Statement III is false. There are two things wrong with this answer: (1) red light waves are not short, relative to blue; (2) we do not know that waves with more energy will more readily pass through obstacles. The passage, in fact, implies just the opposite. The answer is (C).

24. (A): No. Water waves offer only a model for light waves. As a model, they are identical in some ways but not in others.
(B): No. This is not implied by the passage. What they have in common is the way they act when they impinge on obstacles.
(C): No. Waves of water are used as a model because they have much in common with waves of light.
(D): Yes. See explanation for (A).

Part Three
WRITING TEST

- **INTRODUCTION**

- **THE ESSAY**

    - **Re-Cap**
        - Structure
        - Style

    - **Presenting a Perspective on an Issue**
        - Patterns of Development
        - Writing Your Essay
        - Sample Prompts & Essays
        - Practice

- **SAMPLE ESSAYS**

Introduction

Format of the Writing Section

The Writing Test is 30 minutes long and consists of one prompt from which to write an essay. And, although the Writing Test is optional, three-quarters of colleges and universities require this section of the ACT. So it's probably a good idea to buckle down and take it. If you take it and your university *doesn't* require it, then you have nothing to lose. But if you don't take it and your university *does* require it, then you have everything to lose. Again, it's probably in your best interest to take the darn test.

How to Get a Top-Half Score

Since critical and creative skills will be tested and evaluated in a subjective manner, writing essays often raises anxieties in even the best test takers. This is known as performance anxiety. From having a difficult time understanding exactly what is being asked to having debilitating uncertainties about how to begin an answer, *Performance anxiety* can lead to a host of problems.

The best way to reduce such anxieties, and therefore increase your chance of obtaining a top-half score, is through *rehearsal*, which encompasses four activities that need to take place before taking the ACT:
1) understanding the writing tasks
2) knowing what the evaluators expect to find in top-half essays
3) anticipating an organizational scheme for the essay
4) practicing by writing an essay in response to at least one practice question in this book

After you can complete these four steps, you will be in an excellent position to approach the writing test with confidence and competency.

Scoring

The writing test asks you to present your perspective on a given issue. In addition, you are required to provide solid evidence to support your position. You will be given an essay prompt, along with an assignment, and you will have 30 minutes to plan and write your essay. Following is the grading scale for the essay.

6 OUTSTANDING

A 6 essay presents a cogent, well-articulated discussion of the issue and demonstrates mastery of the elements of effective writing.

A typical paper in this category

— explores ideas and develops a position on the issue with insightful reasons and/or persuasive examples
— sustains a well-focused, well-organized discussion of the subject
— expresses ideas with language that is clear and precise
— varies sentence structure and vocabulary appropriate to the subject
— demonstrates superior facility with the conventions (grammar, usage, and mechanics) of standard written English but may have minor flaws

5 EFFECTIVE

A 5 essay presents a well-developed discussion of the issue and demonstrates a strong control of the elements of effective writing.

A typical paper in this category

— develops a position on the issue with well-chosen reasons and/or examples
— is focused and generally well organized
— uses language fluently, with varied sentence structure and appropriate vocabulary
— demonstrates facility with the conventions of standard written English but may have minor flaws

4 COMPETENT

A 4 essay presents a competent discussion of the issue and demonstrates adequate control of the elements of writing.

A typical paper in this category

— develops a position on the issue with relevant reasons and/or examples
— is adequately organized
— expresses ideas clearly
— demonstrates adequate control of language, including diction and syntax, but may lack sentence variety
— demonstrates adequate control of the conventions of standard written English but may have some flaws

3   INADEQUATE

A 3 essay presents some competence in its discussion of the issue and in its control of the elements of writing but is clearly flawed.

A typical paper in this category exhibits <u>one or more</u> of the following characteristics:

— is vague or limited in developing a position on the issue
— is poorly focused and/or poorly organized
— is weak in the use of relevant reasons and/or examples
— has problems expressing ideas clearly
— has problems in fluency, with poorly formed sentences or inappropriate vocabulary
— has occasional major errors or frequent minor errors in grammar, usage, and mechanics

---

2   SERIOUSLY LIMITED

A 2 essay presents a weak discussion of the issue and demonstrates little control of the elements of writing.

A typical paper in this category exhibits <u>one or more</u> of the following characteristics:

— is unclear or seriously limited in presenting and developing a position on the issue
— is unfocused and/or disorganized
— provides few, if any, relevant reasons or examples
— has serious and frequent problems in the use of language and sentence structure
— contains frequent errors in grammar, usage, or mechanics that interfere with meaning

---

1   FUNDAMENTALLY LACKING

A 1 essay is seriously deficient in basic writing skills.

A typical paper in this category exhibits <u>one or more</u> of the following characteristics:

— provides little evidence of the ability to organize or develop a coherent response on the issue
— has severe and persistent errors in language and sentence structure
— contains a pervasive pattern of errors in grammar, usage, and mechanics that interfere with meaning

---

0   Any paper that is blank, totally illegible, or obviously not written on the assigned topic receives a score of zero.

The Essay

Structure

Learning the rules that govern written English is one thing; putting your knowledge to use is another. We will discuss some specific tips that pertain to the type of essay you will be required to write, but for now, let's look at some general techniques to make your essay the best it can be.

➢ **Introduction** - The introduction should serve two structural purposes: It should restate the topic so that the reader need not review the given question, and it should offer a clear thesis so the reader knows what your purpose is. Simply defined, a *thesis* states the main idea of your essay.

In other words, your reader should be able to ascertain the issue or argument without reading the given topic. Suppose the ACT gives you this topic and assignment:

Prompt:
The new writing section was recently added to the ACT with the idea that such a section would encourage more teaching of writing. In turn, students would be more mature writers by graduation time.

Assignment:
Do you think that the added writing section will indeed improve writing skills? Plan and write an essay that depicts your point of view on this subject. Provide support on your position by pulling examples from your own experiences.

Your initial reaction to this assignment may be to begin your essay with a direct response such as *I agree with this assumption...* However, this introductory sentence does not provide adequate information because it does not specify *which* assumption and therefore it would leave the reader confused. Following is the beginning of an introduction that does give adequate information to the reader:

"Does the new ACT really help improve the writing skills of high school graduates? The impetus behind the development of the new writing section is to prompt more in-depth teaching of writing. Added writing curriculum should turn out more mature writers. This is a valid assumption because..."

Not only should you restate the topic, but you should also do so in a way that will spark interest. It may seem like a tall order to restate your topic, create a thesis, AND make it captivating, but if you don't grab your reader's attention in the introduction, it doesn't matter how interesting the body of your essay is because readers won't feel compelled to read on. Think of your introduction as the worm on a fishhook, just dangling there enticing the fish to bite. There are several techniques you can employ to get your reader to bite and read on.

- Begin your introduction with a question. Naturally, when a question is posed to your reader, he or she will want to keep reading to find out the answer.
- Begin your introduction with a quote. Because you will not have time to research your topic for the ACT test, this may not be as feasible as, say, on a term paper for a college class; however, if you can remember a specific quote pertinent to your topic, use it.
- Begin with an anecdote. An anecdote is entertaining and will thus draw in the reader.
- Begin with an illustration or a hypothetical example based on the topic you are going to discuss.
- Begin with a true-to-life example.
- Begin with vivid description of something pertaining to your topic.

It is particularly important that, in the context of the ACT, you make a concerted effort to create a captivating introduction. Keep in mind that the scorers of your essays are the scorers of everyone else's essays. They read hundreds of responses to the same issues and arguments. You must make your essay stand out. What better way to make it stand out than to make it exceptional from the beginning?

> **Conclusion -** The conclusion of your essay is just as important as the introduction because it wraps up your thoughts and evidence. It should leave your reader satisfied that a convincing discussion has just taken place. Your conclusion should include a restatement of your thesis and then end with a more general statement, perhaps a warning or a call for action.

Tip: If time is running out and you get stuck trying to formulate a conclusion, try beginning with *In conclusion* or *In summary*. Then continue by restating your thesis.

Style

How does a writer make a piece of writing his own? And how does a writer add interest to his essays? The way a writer uses words and phrases to add personality to his writing is called *style*.

Although we talked about style earlier, let's briefly re-cap.

> **Transitions**—Transitional phrases are an important element of formal writing because they create coherence. They guide the reader from point A to point B. Look at the lists below for some examples of transitional words and phrases that help achieve cohesiveness.

> **Agreement:** *also, plus, in addition, further, furthermore, moreover, additionally, to add to that, next, in accordance with, accordingly, in agreement, finally, for instance, for example, in exemplification, exemplifying that, in fact, factually speaking, in terms of, and so forth, in coordination with, along those lines, collectively speaking, generally speaking, indeed, undoubtedly, obviously, to be sure, equally*

> **Contrast:** *however, in contrast, on the contrary, on the other hand, from a different angle, nonetheless, nevertheless, but, yet, a catch to this is, sadly enough, as a hindrance, oddly enough, instead, in direct opposition, still, rather*

Result: *as a result, as a consequence, consequently, thus, therefore, hence, thereby, resulting in, ultimately, in the end, finally, in the overall analysis, in hindsight, in retrospect, retrospectively, vicariously, the long term effect, as a short term result, significantly, as a major effect, effectively, heretofore, hereafter, thereafter, in short, generally, over all, concluding*

✓ Check your work

Transitional words and phrases are helpful not only in linking ideas between sentences, but also in providing cohesiveness from paragraph to paragraph. Without this clarity, an essay will likely be choppy and difficult to read and understand. A word of caution, though: Be careful not to overuse transitional words and phrases. Overuse can make you sound like a pedantic writer rather than an intelligent one.

➢ **Varying Sentences**—No matter how well an essay flows, the reader will easily get bored if it consists only of sentences that contain the same words and follow the same structure.

Example:
Dogs help blind people. Dogs also help epileptic people. Dogs can sense when an epileptic person is about to have a seizure. Dogs are also used in rescue work. They help rescue skiers. They also help in catastrophic events. They rescue people after earthquakes.

There are several things wrong with this paragraph:
- Almost every sentence is the same length.
- The structure in each sentence is almost identical: Subject + Verb + Direct Object.
- The same words are used over and over: *dogs, they, rescue, help, people.*
- No description is used to further illustrate the writer's points.

✓ Check your work

To add more interest, try varying sentence length and structure. Try different sentence styles, employ a variety of words and use these words to paint a vivid picture of the subject. For example, you could begin your sentence with a subject and a predicate and then build on them using various words and phrases.

Cumulative sentence:
The energetic children played hard, chasing each other in all directions, occasionally falling and then scrambling to their feet, giggling at each other's antics and never stopping for even a moment to catch their breath.

Periodic sentence:
With flour in her hair, dough in between her fingers and sauce all over her face, she attempted to make a gourmet pizza.

Both of the above sentences not only add variety, but also bring rhythm and cadence to the writing. This rhythm creates interest and is pleasant to read. Additionally, descriptive words paint a clear picture for the reader.

> **Figurative Language**—Another excellent way to paint a vivid picture is to use figures of speech. Figures of speech—like similes, metaphors, analogies, personification, hyperbole, irony, and allusion—when used correctly, add extra flair to writing. They add an extra element that takes writing from ordinary to extraordinary.

> *Similes* show a marked comparison between two things by using the phrases *like*, *as*, or, *as if:*

> The cat stood poised and *still as a statue*, waiting for the opportune moment to pounce.

> *Metaphors* show absolute comparison by omitting *like*, *as*, or, *as if:*

> She is Mother Theresa when it comes to her generosity and compassion.

Here the comparison is absolute because the writer states that this person *is* Mother Theresa, even though she is not actually Mother Theresa.

> *Analogies* compare the similar features of two dissimilar things, and they often bring clarity to writing by showing the reader another way of seeing something. Analogies are not limited to a sentence; sometimes an analogy streams its way through an entire piece of writing.

> **Example:**
> Office cooperation is like a soccer game. Each employee has a position on the playing field, and each position dictates an employee's function. Working together, the office completes passes by communicating well within each department. Shots on goal are taken when employees meet with prospective clients to pitch ideas, and the whole office triumphs when a goal is scored and a prospect becomes a client.

Although an office and a soccer team are two very unrelated things, the writer sees similarities between the two and uses these similarities to clearly show how an office works.

> *Personification* gives human characteristics to animals, inanimate objects and ideas in order to make them more real and understandable:

> The rusty car groaned, coughed, then gave one last sputter and died.

The car in this sentence comes to life even as it "dies" because of the human characteristics it is given.

> *Hyperbole* uses deliberate exaggeration or overstatement to show special emphasis or create humor.

> **Example:**
> Fat-free foods have become so popular that soon all vendors will want to sell them. Before you know it, Kentucky Fried Chicken will have fat-free fried chicken. Big Macs will contain 0 grams of fat. And the amount of fat in a Pizza Hut cheese pizza? You guessed it—none!

In order to show how excessive people's obsession with fat-free foods has become, this description purposefully exaggerates a world where the most unlikely things are fat-free.

Irony uses language to make a suggestion that directly contrasts with the literal word or idea. It can offer humor to writing, or a bitter tone when it is used in sarcasm.

Example:
Scientists have worked hard to develop ways to decrease infant mortality rates and increase longevity. As a result, more people are living longer and scientists will soon have to develop some methods with which to control overpopulation.

This sentence uses irony by predicting that, because scientists have now discovered ways to increase a person's life span, they will soon have to deal with another problem—overpopulation.

Allusion makes indirect reference to known cultural works, people or events. The familiarity allusions bring to writing helps the writer make connections with the reader:

I have so much to do today, I feel like David must have felt as he approached Goliath.

David must have felt a bit intimidated when facing the giant, Goliath—a feeling this writer alludes to when thinking about everything that needs to be done.

➢ **Tone -** The words you choose will greatly affect the tone of your essay. Likewise, the tone you wish to achieve will depend on your audience. On the ACT, you know your audience will consist of men and women who will be quickly reading your essay and then assigning a score based on their impression and how well you handled the topic. Knowing this, you will want to use a professional, formal tone, the kind you will probably use in most of your college work. Using a formal tone means that you will want to keep some distance between you, the writer, and your audience, the scorer. Be courteous and polite but avoid being chummy or intimate in any way. Furthermore, you should avoid all colloquialisms and slang.

➢ **Diction -** While tone defines the overall language you use, diction deals with the specific kinds of words and phrases you choose for your essay. Since you have already determined your audience and thus ascertained that you need to portray a formal tone in your essay, you must be consistent with your diction, or word choice. Diction may be classified as technical (*homo sapien* rather than *human*), formal (*Please inform me when you are ready to depart.*), informal or colloquial (*Give me a buzz when you're ready to go.*), or slang (*She's a real couch potato and watches the tube from early morning 'til the cows come home.*) Knowing that your audience dictates a formal tone, you must also be consistent in maintaining formal diction. Look at the following example of inconsistent diction:

Violence in schools has become an epidemic problem. School shootings occur regularly, and fights erupt daily in the nation's classrooms. Even with the addition of metal detectors at school entrances, violence will never be eradicated because the jocks are always ganging up on the geeks. If only we could just all get along.

This example begins with a formal tone and formal diction; however, it takes a quick turn when the writer uses slang words like *jocks* and *geeks*. The paragraph is concluded informally with *If only we could just all get along*.

As you write your essay, and later, when you proofread it, you should make sure that you preserve the formality your audience requires.

> **Person** - It is important to maintain consistency in person. For example, if you begin your essay in second person (*you*) do not shift to third person (*he*, *she*, *it*, *one*, or *they*). Let's look at a couple of examples illustrating a shift in person:

>> **Example:**
>> One can get excellent grades in school if you study hard.

The switch from *one* to *you* is confusing and awkward.

>> **Example:**
>> Off the coast of Puerto Rico, on the island of Vieques, is an old French mansion turned hotel. Here one can enjoy spacious guest rooms and a cozy library. One can lounge around the pool and indulge in the honorary pool bar. Because the hotel is not far from the ocean, you can also take a leisurely walk down to the white sandy beach where one can spend a lazy day basking in the sun.

The switch from *one* to *you* is confusing in this paragraph and detracts from the imagery. Decide from the beginning of your essay what person you wish to employ and make a conscious effort to stick to it.

✓ Check your work

Your goal as a writer is to create interest and coherence through your unique writing style. Using figures of speech and maintaining consistent use of tone, diction, and person are effective ways to create interest. Using transitional words help to create coherence. Remember, though, that part of creating coherence is being concise. Use only the details that are necessary to support your topic and avoid tedious descriptions. This isn't to say that you should avoid vivid imagery, but only that you should take care to ensure that the above methods add to your writing rather than detract from it.

The most important aspect to remember is that style can only develop through practice. Practice your writing and proofread, proofread, proofread. If you do all of these things, you'll be well on your way to becoming an effective, skillful writer.

The Essay

Warm-Up Drills

> Directions: Read each paragraph in the following essay and rewrite it, making necessary changes in order to enhance the effectiveness of the essay. Pay close attention to all of the elements you learned about writing style.

Prompt:
It is more beneficial to complete independent study than to attend college.

Assignment:
Do you think that a student can benefit more from completing independent study than from attending college? Plan and develop an essay in which you provide detailed and persuasive support for your opinion.

1. This opinion is not valid and is clearly not based on any evidence that would prove its validity. One can't gain more knowledge by completing independent study instead of attending college. It is necessary to look at some evidence to prove this.

2. Some people think that there are too many distractions at college because there are so many other students who take up class time. Interaction with other students can provide valuable insight into topics you study in college. Other people's backgrounds and experience add differences in perspectives and, in some cases, valuable expertise. Professors add expertise as well since they are the experts in the areas they are teaching. When a student studies on his own, he is dependent only on what he knows. He is also dependent on what he can read about. He is also dependent on his own background and experiences. This is very limiting to the value he can obtain from his education.

3. Some people think that students can learn more discipline by studying independently at home instead of going to college. College students learn a lot of discipline. They are held accountable by their college professors. They are held accountable by fellow students too. They depend upon them to contribute to the class. Students who study on their own are only accountable to themselves. Many times, studies get set aside when life gets too busy. Studies get the boot when a student encounters a subject they're not too excited about.

4. Studying at home independently is not as beneficial as attending college because the degree you get, if you get a degree at all, will not carry as much weight with potential employers as will a college degree from an accredited college or university. Employers place more weight on someone whose expertise they can depend on. Employers feel they can depend more on the expertise of someone who has been trained at a college or university.

5. People should go to college. You can't depend on your own motivation to finish your studies at home. A student gains a lot more from the interaction they receive between other students and professors in college. Students who get a degree from a college may have a better chance of getting a good job after college.

Solutions to Warm-Up Drills

1. The opening sentence in this paragraph does not make an effective introduction. It does not restate the topic but rather makes a direct address to the topic question. A good introduction should not require the reader to read the topic. The second sentence of the paragraph gives a concise thesis statement but should be elaborated on a bit. Also, the contraction *can't* does not fit with the formal tone of the essay. The last sentence serves as a transition to the next paragraph, but it does not show much sophistication or subtlety.

   Better:
   Should a student give up a college education in order to complete an independent study at home? Although the financial savings of independent study may be substantial, one can gain more benefits by obtaining a college or university education. Studying at a college or university can give a student a broader education, can help him learn discipline through accountability, and can pay off in the long run.

   This introduction begins with a question, which is more effective than directly addressing the question/topic. The thesis statement concisely lists three reasons a formal education is better than independent study; this sentence gives the reader a clear idea of what the essay will be about.

2. The first sentence serves as a topic sentence for the paragraph; however, it should be reworded to act as a better transitional sentence, one that would tie in with the last sentence of the preceding paragraph. The second sentence would function better with a transitional phrase like *On the contrary* to introduce it. Also in this sentence, the use of second person *you* is inconsistent with the rest of the essay. The fourth sentence uses the same two words *add* and *expertise* that were used in the preceding sentence. These should be changed to add some variety. The next three sentences are repetitive and should be combined.

   Better:
   Some people think that distractions at college from other students who take up class time results in a narrow education. On the contrary, interaction with other students can provide valuable insight into the topics one studies in college. Other people's backgrounds and experience add different perspectives and, in some cases, valuable expertise. Professors offer much value as well since they are the experts in the areas they are teaching. When a student studies on his own, he is dependent only on what he knows or can read about and on his own background and experiences. This severely limits the value he can obtain from his education.

   The first sentence works as a transition because it uses the word *narrow*, which contrasts with the word *broader* from the thesis statement in the preceding paragraph.

3. The first sentence works well as a topic sentence, but it uses the same wording as the topic sentence for the preceding paragraph. In the fifth sentence, the use of *they* and *them* is confusing because it is unclear whether the pronoun reference is to the student or fellow students. The remaining sentences are all the same length and therefore choppy. The last sentence strays from the formal tone of the essay. In addition, the word *they* does not agree in person with *a student*.

   Better:
   One valuable lesson students can learn at college is discipline. College students learn a lot of discipline because they are held accountable by their professors. Moreover, they are often held accountable by fellow students who depend upon them to contribute to the class. Students who study on their own are accountable only to themselves. Many times, studies get set aside when life gets too busy or when a student encounters a subject for which he is not enthusiastic.

   The word *valuable* ties in well with the word *value* in the last sentence of the preceding paragraph. Thus, this sentence serves not only as a topic sentence but also as a transitional sentence.

4. Again, the first sentence provides a good topic sentence but not a good transition from the preceding paragraph. The second sentence unnecessarily repeats the word *weight* from the first sentence. In the third sentence, the text shifts to second person *you*. The last sentence repeats the word *depend* from the preceding sentence.

   Better:
   Studying at a college or university may not make every topic seem scintillating; however, when a student is held accountable, he is more driven. As he is driven to succeed, he will eventually earn a degree. Studying at home independently is not as beneficial as attending college because the degree a student gets, if he gets a degree at all, will not carry as much weight with potential employers as will a degree from an accredited college or university. Employers place more confidence in someone whose expertise they can rely on. Employers feel they can depend more on the expertise of someone who has been trained at a college or university.

   The topic sentence in this paragraph provides transition because it refers to the preceding paragraph by relating *scintillating* courses to being *enthusiastic* about subjects.

5. The first sentence does not act as a thorough topic sentence, nor does it provide a good transition. The second sentence uses *you* and *your*, which is an inconsistent use of person. In addition, the contraction *can't* takes away from the formal tone of the essay. Overall, this last paragraph is not effective; it has short, choppy sentences and does not adequately conclude the subject by restating the topic and giving final remarks.

   Better:
   Whether one is trained at a university or opts to stay home to study independently, an education is extremely important; however, it is clear that a student can benefit more from a formal education than from independent study. Students should not depend on their own motivation to finish their studies, nor should they miss out on the opportunity to benefit from the interaction they will receive from other students and professors in college. Despite any financial savings a student may earn by studying independently, the rewards of a college education will pay off in the long run.

   The transition here works well because the first sentence uses the word *trained*, which is used in the sentence before it. This final paragraph functions effectively as a conclusion because it restates the topic. It also brings the writing full circle by once again mentioning the monetary aspect of education, which, as you recall, was mentioned in the introductory paragraph.

Presenting a Perspective on an Issue

If you are the typical high school student, you are more than likely wriggling in you seat, waiting to ask the all important question: *How long does my essay have to be?* A good rule of thumb to follow is the five-paragraph essay. In a five-paragraph essay, your first paragraph introduces your topic, three body paragraphs support your topic, and the last paragraph acts as your concluding paragraph.

Writing five paragraphs on one topic may seem like a daunting task; however, there are tricks to developing your topic and organizing your thoughts into paragraphs.

Patterns of Development

Just as there is no universal answer to every question, there are many different strategies used to write an essay. These strategies, or methods, are called *patterns of development*. The type of pattern you choose to employ is dependent upon the question or prompt to which you are responding. Usually, an essay question will contain certain clues, which enable you to determine which pattern of development to use. Utilizing these patterns will help you to develop a clear, concise thesis, which, in turn, will affect the way you organize your essay.

Compare & Contrast - When an essay prompt uses words that suggest similarity or difference, or if an essay prompt seeks to persuade you that one item is superior to another, chances are that the writers of the ACT are trying to tell you something. They're looking for a Compare & Contrast essay.

Example:
American cars are better than foreign cars.

Here, the author uses the word *than* to compare the two cars, and he seeks to persuade the reader that an American car is a wiser choice than a foreign one.

To write a compare and contrast essay, you will need to portray similarities and differences between two given items (here, cars) to prove which one is superior, either in agreement or disagreement with the prompt.

Cause & Effect - If an essay prompt uses an "If...then" statement or lacks an effect, then the writer's of the ACT are again trying to tell you what type of essay they want to see. A Cause & Effect essay.

Example (if...then):
<u>If</u> college and university faculty spent time outside the academic world working in professions relevant to the courses they teach, <u>then</u> the overall quality of higher education would greatly increase.

The author is arguing that if faculty spent time outside the academic world, in professions relevant to their courses, a desirable effect is achieved. So, in your essay, you must prove that the prompt's cause actually does result in the overall quality of education increasing. Either that, or you must prove that the prompt is wrong by introducing a negative effect based on the original cause, which was teachers working in professions relevant to the courses they teach.

Example (lack of effect):
More restrictions should be set on teenage drivers.

In this call to action statement, the author offers no effects that will result if the action is taken. However, it is implied that, if the author feels the action should be taken, he assumes something positive will result.

To write an essay off a *lack of effect* prompt, you will need to support a position in agreement with the above statement or against it, thus proving or disproving the implied effect.

<u>Definition</u> - Sometimes an essay prompt will attempt to show that a particular idea or concept is of great value. When this happens, prompts can be quite difficult to decipher. While it's easy to recognize a great value prompt, it becomes harder when these prompts only show a limited definition of a particular idea or concept.

Example (limited definition):
A person's generosity can be determined by examining what he or she has given to charity.

In this example, the author seeks to provide a very limited definition of a generosity, when, in fact, generosity can be defined by much more than a person's wallet and the amount that they've given to charity. After reading this prompt, your job would then be to either support the author's definition with evidence or show that the definition is much broader, maybe even wrong.

Let's look at another example.

Example (great value):
Patriotism breaks down the walls of division.

The author believes that patriotism can do great things. Whether or not you agree or disagree, it would be your job to define patriotism and show that, because of its attributes and qualities, it has value or it lacks value.

Presenting a Perspective on an Issue

Planning & Writing

Now that you're familiar with the different methods you can employ to write an essay, let's get down to the nitty gritty. Remember, you're aiming for a 6 essay, one that presents clear, concise evidence to support a view. Writing a 6 essay doesn't have to be a difficult task. All you have to do is follow seven simple steps.

(Although some of the following steps may include specific formulas, you won't need to enter complete, descriptive sentences into the formulas; simple notes and phrases should be enough.)

➢ **Step 1 – Understand the Issue -** In order to properly present your perspective on an issue, you must first understand the issue you are being asked to discuss. Understanding the issue allows you to fully develop your position, presenting your evidence in a way that is most effective and appropriate for the topic. There are two steps that will help you understand the issue.

First, take a couple of minutes to read the given question carefully. Second, ask yourself the following questions about the prompt:
- What does the statement mean?
- What is the issue at hand?
- What is implied by the statement?
- What is the writer's opinion of the issue?
- What, if any, evidence does the writer use to support his position?
- What, specifically, is the assignment?

➢ **Step 2 – Choose A Pattern of Development -** Keeping in mind our discussion about the three patterns of development, look for the necessary criteria in the prompt. If you think the question requires more than one method, choose the one you think works the best. Although, on a timed writing assignment, your essay will be fairly short and therefore you cannot adequately utilize two methods.

➢ **Step 3 – Develop Your Thesis -** The next and most important step is to develop your thesis. Your thesis states the purpose of your essay. Without a thesis statement, your reader does not know what you are setting out to prove. And without a thesis statement, it would be very difficult to organize your essay with clarity and coherence. Don't be intimidated by the task of formulating what is to be the crux of your essay. It can be quite simple.

THESIS FOR A COMPARE & CONTRAST ESSAY *(formula 1-1)*:
I believe that Item A, _____, is better than Item B, _____, because
1) _____, 2) _____, 3) _____.

THESIS FOR A CAUSE & EFFECT ESSAY *(formula 1-2)*:
If _____, then _____, because
1) _____, 2) _____, 3) _____.

THESIS FOR A DEFINITION ESSAY *(formula 1-3)*:
By definition, _____ possess(es) these qualities: 1) _____,
2) _____, 3) _____ which have a positive effect because
A) _____, B) _____, C) _____.

- **Step 4 – Understand Counter Arguments -** Have you ever been in an argument and found that you're covering zero ground? This could be because you are failing to see things from the other person's point of view. Being able to see the other side of a coin can go a long way in proving your point and disarming your opponent's objections. By showing that you are aware, though perhaps not understanding, of the opposing side you are adding credibility to your argument because it is clear that you have viewed the issue from all angles. To write an effective essay, you must show that you have considered the other side of the argument.

    COMPARISON & CONTRAST COUNTER CLAIM *(formula 2-1)*:
    Others may think Item B is better than Item A because 1) _____,
    2) _____, 3) _____.
    (Note that these three points should contrast directly with the three points of your thesis.)(see *formula 1-1*)

    CAUSE & EFFECT COUNTER CLAIM *(formula 2-2)*:
    Some may feel that _____ would cause _____ based on _____.
    (Note that this point should contrast directly with point #1 of your thesis.)
    (see *formula 1-2*)

    DEFINITION *(formula 2-3)*:
    By definition some may feel that _____ exhibits or is defined by _____ which could be positive / negative.
    (Note that this point should contrast directly with point #1 of your thesis.)
    (see *formula 1-3*)

- **Step 5 – Organize Your Thoughts -** Each of the following formulas will prompt you to plug in your thesis and counter argument points. In addition, there are spaces in the formula for you to insert 1 or 2 pieces of supporting evidence. Don't be intimidated, though. The formulas are meant to be a skeleton for organizing your essay. If you practice writing essays using the sample prompts in this book, you'll soon get accustomed to using the outlines, and they will seem much less imposing.

    COMPARISON & CONTRAST ESSAY OUTLINE *(formula 3-1)*:
    I. Introduction – Paragraph 1
        A. Restate your topic
        B. Thesis statement *(formula 1-1)*
    II. Support – Paragraph 2
        A. Counter Claim point #1 *(formula 2-1)*
        B. Thesis point #1 *(formula 1-1)*
            1. Support for thesis point #1
            2. Support for thesis point #1
    III. Support – Paragraph 3
        A. Counter Claim point #2 *(formula 2-1)*
        B. Thesis point #2 *(formula 1-1)*
            1. Support for thesis point #2
            2. Support for thesis point #2
    IV. Support – Paragraph 4
        A. Counter Claim point #3 *(formula 2-1)*
        B. Thesis point #3 *(formula 1-1)*

        1. Support for thesis point #3
        2. Support for thesis point #3
V. Conclusion – Paragraph 5
    A. Restate thesis
    B. Issue a warning or a call to action

CAUSE & EFFECT ESSAY OUTLINE *(formula 3-2)*:
I. Introduction – Paragraph 1
    A. Restate your topic
    B. Thesis statement *(formula 1-2)*
II. Support – Paragraph 2
    A. Counter Claim *(formula 2-2)*
    B. Thesis point #1 *(formula 1-2)*
        1. Support for thesis point #1
        2. Support for thesis point #1
III. Support – Paragraph 3 – Thesis point #2 *(formula 1-2)*
    A. Support for thesis point #2
    B. Support for thesis point #2
IV. Support – Paragraph 4 – Thesis point #3 *(formula 1-2)*
    A. Support for thesis point #3
    B. Support for thesis point #3
V. Conclusion – Paragraph 5
    A. Restate thesis
    B. Issue a warning or a call to action

DEFINITION ESSAY FORMULA *(formula 3-3)*:
I. Introduction – Paragraph 1
    A. Restate your topic
    B. Thesis statement *(formula 1-3)*
II. Support – Paragraph 2
    A. Counter Claim *(formula 2-3)*
    B. Thesis point #1 *(formula 1-3)*
        1. Support by using thesis point A *(formula 1-3)*
        2. Support by using thesis point A *(formula 1-3)*
III. Support – Paragraph 3 – Thesis point #2 *(formula 1-3)*
    A. Support by using point B *(formula 1-3)*
    B. Support by using point B *(formula 1-3)*
IV. Support – Paragraph 4 – Thesis point #3 *(formula 1-3)*
    A. Support by using point C *(formula 1-3)*
    B. Support by using point C *(formula 1-3)*
V. Conclusion – Paragraph 5
    A. Restate thesis
    B. Issue a warning or a call for action

➤ **Step 6 – Write Your Essay -** Now that you have organized your thought, it's time to write! The best strategy under the pressure of a time restraint is to just begin writing—as quickly as you can while still being careful. (You should allow yourself about 20 minutes for writing.) Organization should not be difficult with the help of your formulas and outlines, but don't forget to add transitional words, phrases and sentences to help give your essay coherence. As you write, remember the mechanical rules you learned earlier and keep in mind the techniques we discussed in the section *The Essay*. The key to successful, timed writing is to reserve a bit of time at the end so that you can go back and proofread. You'll need this time to add finishing touch that will better you essay and help your idea flow more smoothly.

➤ **Step 7 – Revise Your Essay -** Because you have written quickly, you must spend some time, about 5 minutes, at the end to review your essay, making necessary changes to enhance the clarity, coherence and grammatical accuracy of your writing. You must look for misspellings and mechanical errors while at the same time keeping in mind the following questions:
- Is my introduction captivating?
- Is my thesis statement concise?
- Do my body paragraphs clearly support my thesis?
- Have I used logical transitions that help the text flow smoothly between sentences and between paragraphs?
- Have I maintained a formal tone and proper diction throughout my essay?
- Have I maintained consistent use of person (i.e., first, second, third)?
- Is there a word, or are there words, which I have employed too often throughout the essay?
- Do my sentences vary in length and structure?

As you ask yourself these questions, make the necessary changes. If you still have time left after you have completed the initial revision, go back and read your essay again. A writer makes many, many revisions to his manuscript before it is ready to be published, so you can never proofread too many times!

Sample Prompts & Essays

Now let's apply the 7 steps to three examples.

➢ **Example 1: Comparison & Contrast Essay**

   Prompt:
   A new custom home is a much better purchase than an older, run-down home.

   Assignment:
   Is it more wise to purchase an older, run-down home than a new custom home? Based on your own experiences in your family, plan and write an essay in which you develop your opinion on the better choice between new and old homes. Provide effective support for your opinion.

➢ Step 1 – Understand the Issue

- What does the statement mean? *If you are in the market to buy a house, a new home would be a better value.*
- What is the issue at hand? *What kind of home is the best to buy?*
- What is implied by the statement? *That one who purchases an old home is not making a wise choice. Also implied is that an older home is run-down.*
- What is the writer's stand on the issue? *He believes a new home is superior to an old one.*
- What, if any, evidence does the writer use to support his position? *Old houses are run-down, new homes can be custom built.*
- What, specifically, is the assignment? *To give my opinion about which home I think would make a wiser choice—a new home or an old home. To give support to persuasively develop my opinion.*

➢ Step 2 – Choose A Pattern of Development

This prompt requires me to employ the Comparison & Contrast pattern of development because the statement uses the word *than*, a contrasting word. The author is also trying to convince me that it is better to buy a new home than an old one.

➢ Step 3 – Develop Your Thesis

THESIS FOR A COMPARISON & CONTRAST ESSAY *(formula 1-1)*:
I believe that Item A, <u>an old home</u>, is better than Item B, <u>a new home</u>, because 1) <u>an old home exemplifies old-style motifs that are unique in today's market</u>, 2) <u>foundations are stronger in older homes</u>, 3) <u>can remodel an old home in any way</u>.

➢ Step 4 – Understand Counter Arguments

COMPARISON & CONTRAST COUNTER CLAIM *(formula 2-1)*:
Others may think Item B is better than Item A because 1) <u>you can "keep up with the Joneses" with your modern décor</u>, 2) <u>new homes may be built quickly for easy occupancy</u>, 3) <u>new homes can be custom-built</u>. (Note that these three points should contrast directly with the three points of your thesis.) (see *formula 1-1*)

➢ Step 5 – Organize Your Thoughts

COMPARISON & CONTRAST ESSAY FORMULA *(formula 3-1)*:
I. Introduction – Paragraph 1
   A. Some people feel that the purchase of a new home is a smarter investment choice than the purchase of an older home.
   B. For anyone who puts stock in the aged and unique, the traditional home may be the choice of a lifetime with its old-fashioned motifs, its strong foundations, and its versatility to become the house its owner designs.
II. Support – Paragraph 2
   A. keeping up with the Joneses – modern décor
   B. bring back old-time motifs
      1. More choices – can choose from different time periods
      2. More unique versus "cookie cutter" homes of today
III. Support – Paragraph 3
   A. Homes can be built quicker
   B. As a result, foundations not as strong in new homes
      1. Mass production of homes – builder doesn't establish good foundation
      2. Older homes in better condition over long period of time because built more solidly
IV. Support – Paragraph 4
   A. Custom-built
   B. Can remodel any way owner wants
      1. No allowance restrictions placed on owner by builder
V. Conclusion – Paragraph 5
   A. Modern homes just don't offer the old-fashioned charm an older well-built, unique home can offer.
   B. When it comes to such an important decision as purchasing a home, the choice is clear: an older home has much more to offer and will last for many years to come.

➢ Step 6 – Write Your Essay

Modern-day housing developments are springing up everywhere, dotting hills and filling in every open space available. Characterized by "cookie cutter" homes, houses all cut from the same mold, the look of these communities lacks distinctiveness. For anyone who puts stock in the aged and unique rather than the new and ordinary, the traditional house may be the choice of a lifetime, with its old-fashioned motifs, its strong foundations, and its versatility to become the home of its owner's design.

Many homeowners do not feel the need to be the designer behind their home. Rather, they strive to "keep up with the Joneses" by filling their houses with the same modern décor that fills the homes of their neighbors. On the flip side, when seeking to invest in a traditional home, the buyer has a plethora of options because older homes offer so much uniqueness. This uniqueness can be seen in the motifs of style, which are almost non-existent in today's market of prefabricated homes but are powerful reminders of the past in older structures. These are the structures that offer a homeowner an admirable individuality.

Clearly, modern-day homes, which lack individuality, are built more quickly than homes of the past, a fact that seems to fit today's hurried society. But what does a homeowner have to show for this efficiency years down the road? There is much value added to a home constructed by a builder who takes time and pays attention to detail instead of putting up as many homes as possible in the shortest amount of time possible.

For example, in the past when builders did take extra time and care, the foundations and overall structures were, and still are, much stronger. This is because many builders today, eager to make a quick buck, do not give homes ample time to settle on their foundation before continuing with the construction. Overall, older houses are in better condition, even over the course of time, because they were more solidly built.

Many prospective buyers today overlook the quality of a home's structure and are compelled to purchase by the alluring idea of custom building their house. These homebuyers enjoy the process of choosing paint colors, fixtures and floor coverings. Consider an older home, however. Here the possibilities are endless, and traditional buyers may even negotiate remodeling into the price of the house. What is more, there are no spending restrictions which contemporary builders often impose on their buyers.

Spending restrictions represent just one of many ways that freedom is limited when purchasing a new home instead of an older home. Whether one prefers an elegant, plantation-style mansion or a peaceful, rustic country getaway, the distinctive older home has much more to offer than the commonplace modern home set in communities of houses that all look the same. Simply put, it comes down to whether the prospective buyer is willing to trade quality and originality for expediency.

➢ Step 7 – Revise Your Essay

When critiquing other essays, you can often learn a lot about the strengths and weaknesses in your own writing. So here's an assignment: Complete the task required for each of the following questions.

- Is the introduction captivating? Why or why not? Do you recognize a certain method the author employed to make the introduction interesting?
- Is the thesis statement concise? Does it clearly show the purpose of the essay?

- Do the body paragraphs clearly support each point made in the thesis? If not, where does the essay lack necessary support?

- Are there logical transitions that make the text flow smoothly between sentences and between paragraphs? Underline each word, phrase or sentence that acts as a transition.

- Is the tone and diction consistent throughout the essay? If not, point out the places where consistency breaks down.

- Is the use of person consistent? If not, point out the places where consistency is not maintained.

- Is there a word, or are there words, which have been used too often in the essay? List these words. Also list the words that have been used to provide variety in the essay.

- Do the sentences vary in length and structure?

ACT Verbal Prep Course

> **Example 2: Cause & Effect Essay**

>> **Prompt:**
>> *Students should not be required to take courses outside their field of study.*

>> **Assignment:**
>> Do you think that college students should be required to take a well-rounded selection of courses even if they do not pertain to their major? Plan and write a well-developed essay in which you discuss your opinion on this topic. Support your opinion with persuasive details.

> Step 1 – Understand the Issue

- What does the statement mean? *Colleges should not make students take courses, like General Education courses, if they do not pertain to their area of study.*
- What is the issue at hand? *Whether or not students benefit from taking college courses that don't pertain to their major.*
- What is implied by the statement? *That a student will be adequately prepared for the "real world" without taking a wide range of classes.*
- What is the writer's stand on the issue? *That students should not be required to take these classes.*
- What, if any, evidence does the writer use to support his position? *The writer does not give any evidence to support his view.*
- What, specifically, is the assignment? *To show my perspective on whether college students should have to take classes that do not have anything to do with their major. I need to give support that will persuade the reader that the college student will benefit based on my opinion.*

> Step 2 – Choose A Pattern of Development

This prompt is a call to action statement, and, although no effect is discussed, the writer implies that his recommended course of action would result in a positive effect.

> Step 3 – Develop Your Thesis

THESIS FOR CAUSE & EFFECT ESSAY *(formula 1-2)*:
If <u>students are not required to take courses outside their field of study</u>, then <u>they will not be prepared</u>, because 1) <u>they will be ill-prepared if they fail to get a job in their field</u>, 2) <u>they will be lacking in important skills – communication or thinking/reasoning skills</u>, 3) <u>they will be close-minded and ignorant to things happening in the world around them</u>.

> Step 4 – Understand Counter Arguments

CAUSE & EFFECT COUNTER CLAIM *(formula 2-2)*:
Some may feel that <u>requiring students to take courses only in their field of study</u> would cause <u>students to be more knowledgeable in their field</u> because <u>they would have more thoroughly studied this area</u>.
(Note that this point should contrast directly with point #1 of your thesis.)
(see *formula 1-2*)

➢ Step 5 – Organize Your Thoughts

CAUSE & EFFECT ESSAY FORMULA *(formula 3-2)*:
I. Introduction – Paragraph 1
   A. Some feel students should not be required to take courses outside their field of study.
   B. If students are not required to take courses outside their field of study, they will be ill-prepared should they fail to get a job in their field, they will lack important skills, and they will be close-minded and ignorant to things happening in the world around them.
II. Support – Paragraph 2
   A. Some may feel that requiring students to take courses only in their field of study would cause students to be more knowledgeable in their field because they would have more thoroughly studied this area.
   B. Many people are unable to get a job in their field after they graduate.
      1. Without some knowledge of other fields, these highly trained people will be stuck working menial jobs.
III. They will be lacking in important skills.
   A. Students studying the sciences will lack communication skills.
   B. Students studying the arts will lack critical thinking and reasoning skills.
IV. They will be close-minded and ignorant of things happening in the world around them.
   A. Lack of familiarity with certain fields promotes disinterest in these topics as they pertain to current events (politics, scientific research).
   B. This disinterest promotes apathy in participating in or supporting causes that result from these current events.
V. Conclusion – Paragraph 5
   A. Students must take a well-rounded schedule of classes in order to be prepared for work outside their field and so they will have adequate skills to use toward a common interest in society.
   B. Students should welcome an opportunity to learn about all areas of study.

➢ Step 6 – Write Your Essay

Colleges and universities require students, regardless of their majors, to complete General Education courses, basic courses that cover general subject areas. These classes include basic literature and writing courses, basic science and math courses, and basic arts classes like music and drama. Some feel students should not be required to take these General Education classes. However, if students are not required to take courses outside their major, they will be ill-prepared should they fail to get a job in their field, they will lack important skills, and they will be close-minded and ignorant of things happening in the world around them.

Many opponents of General Education classes are themselves unaware of the advantages of a well-rounded education. They focus only on the theory that students will be more fully prepared to enter their field as a result of more extensive study in their area. What they fail to see, however, is that many graduates are not able to find jobs in their field of expertise. So, without a broad range of knowledge, these highly trained graduates would be stuck in menial jobs.

Even if graduates do get jobs within their field, such a wide range of skills are required in the workplace in order to be successful that, without a diverse educational background, a graduate will not be fully competent in any job. For example, when a graduate begins looking for a job, she will discover that excellent communication skills are invaluable in the workplace, both in dealing with customers and with colleagues. Without some base of communication knowledge, such as a student would receive in a basic English class, the candidate will be overlooked for someone who does show strength in communication. Moreover, most jobs require strong problem-solving skills, skills that develop from learning how to think and reason critically. These skills are reinforced in math and science classes.

Lack of familiarity in certain educational arenas, like math and science, results in a provincial attitude. This lack of familiarity leads to disinterest in the areas where a student has not gained knowledge. Likewise, this disinterest leads to apathy in participating or supporting any causes that are linked to these fields of study. For example, a student who has not studied science will be indifferent to scientific ideas, ideas which could become theories and could help all of mankind. A student who does not study politics and government will likely be apathetic toward participating in important political events such as elections.

It is important that a country's citizens take part in supporting causes and concepts that generate a common interest in society. Without a well-rounded schedule of classes in college, however, the citizen base will soon be filled with people who are unprepared and indifferent to anything that does not directly pertain to their area of interest. Instead of complaining about an opportunity to gain a broad range of knowledge, students should consider it a privilege and an asset.

➢ Step 7 – Revise Your Essay

Read over the essay above and then answer the following questions.

- Is the introduction captivating? Why or why not? Do you recognize a certain method the author employed to make the introduction interesting?

- Is the thesis statement concise? Does it clearly show the purpose of the essay?

- Do the body paragraphs clearly support each point made in the thesis? If not, where does the essay lack necessary support?

- Are there logical transitions that make the text flow smoothly between sentences and between paragraphs? Underline each word, phrase or sentence that acts as a transition.

- Is the tone and diction consistent throughout the essay? If not, point out the places where consistency breaks down.

- Is the use of person consistent? If not, point out the places where consistency is not maintained.

- Is there a word, or are there words, which have been used too often in the essay? List these words. Also list the words that have been used to provide variety in the essay.

- Do the sentences vary in length and structure?

➢ **Example 3: Definition Essay**

Prompt:
The positive effects of competition in a society far outweigh the negative effects.

Assignment:
Do you think that competition has a positive or negative effect on a community? Write an essay in which you develop your opinion. Support your perspective by drawing from personal experience and knowledge you have gained in your life. Make sure your support is specific and persuasive.

➢ Step 1 – Understand the Issue

- What does the statement mean? *Competition affects society in a good way, not a bad way.*
- What is the issue at hand? *Whether or not competition is good for society.*
- What is implied by the statement? *That a society benefits from competition among its members.*
- What is the writer's stand on the issue? *That competition is good and provides benefits.*
- What, if any, evidence does the writer use to support his position? *The writer does not give any evidence to support his view.*
- What, specifically, is the assignment? *To persuasively discuss with the reader my perspective on the effects of competition in society. I can use personal experience to make my points clear.*

➢ Step 2 – Choose A Pattern of Development

Although the comparison between a society driven by competition and one where competition plays little or no role seems to hint that the Compare & Contrast method should be used, the Definition pattern of development is a better fit because it is necessary to look at the qualities of competition that make it a positive influence rather than a negative one.

➢ Step 3 – Develop Your Thesis

THESIS FOR DEFINITION ESSAY *(formula 1-3)*:
By definition, <u>competition</u> possesses these qualities: 1) <u>gives everyone the same chance at the beginning</u>, 2) <u>drives people to succeed</u>, 3) <u>provides a way to recognize people who advance</u> which have a positive effect because A) <u>no one can use the excuse that they didn't have the same opportunities; everyone has a chance to succeed</u>, B) <u>people want to be the best, and gives everyone their "place" in life</u>, C) <u>gives self-worth to those who are recognized for their accomplishments</u>.

➢ Step 4 – Understand Counter Arguments

DEFINITION *(formula 2-3)*:
By definition, some may feel that <u>competition helps only a few/pushing only a few to the top, leaving others feeling left out or insignificant</u> which could be positive or **negative**.
(Note that this point should contrast directly with point #1 of your thesis.)
(see *formula 1-3*)

➢ Step 5 – Organize Your Thoughts

DEFINITION ESSAY FORMULA *(formula 3-3)*:
I. Introduction – Paragraph 1
   A. Competition benefits a society.
   B. Everyone is given a chance to succeed in a society where competition drives people to be the best and recognizes the accomplishments of the many who advance.
II. Support – Paragraph 2
   A. Some feel that competition helps only a few, leaving others feeling left out or insignificant. There is a push to eliminate salutatorian/valedictorian recognition speeches at graduation.
   B. Competition gives everyone the same chance at the beginning.
      1. Just like a marathon – everyone begins at the same starting line.
      2. No one has an excuse – it is up to each individual to decide how to run the race. Some want to work harder than others and therefore deserve recognition.
III. Competition drives people to be their best
   A. Everyone's "best" is different.
   B. Gives everyone their place in life – if no competition, we'd have a world full of custodians, no CEO's or vice versa.
IV. With competition comes the chance to recognize winners.
   A. Gives self-worth to those recognized, causing them to set even greater goals.
   B. Encourages those who were not recognized to try harder so that they too may be recognized.
V. Conclusion – Paragraph 5
   A. Competition is vital to a growing and thriving society.
   B. How will you run the race? Will you strive to be the best?

➤ Step 6 – Write Your Essay

On your mark! All the runners are at the starting line. *Get set!* The runners are poised, in position. *Go!* The runners take off. The spirit of competition is the driving force behind these runners' desire to win. And, as an integral part of society, competition brings many benefits. Everyone is given a chance to succeed in a society where competition drives people to be their best, and competition recognizes the accomplishments of those who advance.

Some feel that, although competition recognizes winners, there are so few winners that many are left feeling insignificant and alienated. This attitude has, for example, lead to a movement to eliminate salutatorian and valedictorian recognition and speeches at graduation ceremonies. Those in the movement claim that acknowledging salutatorian and valedictorian students for their scholastic achievements causes other students to feel slighted. This is a misguided assumption. Government gives everyone equal opportunity to attend school and to excel. Some students work harder than others and deserve special honors at graduation. Just like in a race, everyone begins at the same starting line and therefore has the same chance to succeed. Each person makes his own decision about how he will run the race. No one has an excuse, then, for not trying his best to succeed.

Competition drives people to achieve a goal. For most, this goal represents a person's best. Since everyone's concept of "best" is different, achievement differs for each person. Therefore, when an individual reaches his goal, this gives him a certain status. This status is different for each person, depending on the goal that was attained. This is extremely important because if competition did not place people at different positions in life, the resulting equality would be stultifying to society. For example, the work force would consist of only custodians and no CEO's or vice versa.

CEO's get to where they are only through competition. As an employee works hard and competes within a company, he is rewarded for his accomplishments with promotions. Not only does competition award people through tangible benefits like promotions, but competition also gives long-lasting psychological awards such as a feeling of self-worth or pride. This recognition encourages people who succeed to raise their personal goals even higher. Recognition also drives those who were not recognized to do better so that they too may be rewarded.

Because competition results in rewards, both tangible and emotional, it is essential for a growing and thriving society. Everyone begins at the same starting line and is given the same chance to succeed. When the starting gun fires, it is up to each runner to decide how he will run the race. This decision will ultimately determine who will become the winners. Driven by competition, these winners, along with the losers, comprise a successful society.

➤ Step 7 – Revise Your Essay

Read over the essay previous and then answer the following questions:

- Is the introduction captivating? Why or why not? Do you recognize a certain method the author employed to make the introduction interesting?

- Is the thesis statement concise? Does it clearly show the purpose of the essay?

- Do the body paragraphs clearly support each point made in the thesis? If not, where does the essay lack necessary support?

- Are there logical transitions that make the text flow smoothly between sentences and between paragraphs? Underline each word, phrase or sentence that acts as a transition.

- Is the tone and diction consistent throughout the essay? If not, point out the places where consistency breaks down.

- Is the use of person consistent? If not, point out the places where consistency is not maintained.

- Is there a word, or are there words, which have been used too often in the essay? List these words. Also list the words that have been used to provide variety in the essay.

- Do the sentences vary in length and structure?

ACT Verbal Prep Course

Practice

Now it's your turn to practice some essays. Consider the five prompts and assignments below and write an essay, using the 7 steps that we've talked about in this section. Remember: the only way to become better at writing is through practice, practice, practice.

Prompt:
Museums should have the liberty to exhibit whatever displays they want without the interference of government censorship.

Assignment:
Do you think the government should impose censorship on controversial museum displays, or should museums be permitted to display whatever they choose? Plan and write an essay in which you discuss your perspective on this type of censorship. Support your opinion with clear and persuasive evidence.

Prompt:
When people work in teams, they are more productive than when they work individually.

Assignment:
Do you think that people work more effectively in teams or by themselves? Explain your opinion in a well-developed essay. Support your perspective by drawing from personal experience and knowledge you have gained.

Prompt:
If everyone would closely examine their past, they would realize that only a few individuals have played a role in shaping their behavior and their way of thinking.

Assignment:
Do you think your behavior and way of thinking was shaped by merely a few people, or were you impacted by many others? Thinking about your own personal experiences, plan and write an essay in which you discuss your perspective on the shaping of behavior.

Prompt:
Success is easily obtained but difficult to maintain.

Assignment:
In your opinion, is it easy or difficult to obtain success? Along the same lines, do you think that, once obtained, success is easy or difficult to maintain? Plan and write an essay in which you develop your opinion about success. Support your perspective by providing concise evidence.

Prompt:
Society is governed by two types of laws, just and unjust. People must obey just laws but are at liberty to defy those laws which they determine are frivolous or unjust.

Assignment:
Do you agree that some laws are just while others are unjust? Moreover, if you do agree with this statement, do you feel that people need only obey those laws which they deem just? Discuss your opinion about the justice of laws. Provide concrete and persuasive support for your opinion.

Sample Essays

Prompt:
There is little need for books today because one can learn just as much or more from television.

Assignment:
Do you think that television is a good replacement for books? Plan and write an essay in which you discuss your opinion on the relevance of books in today's world. Make sure you support your opinion by drawing on your experiences and knowledge.

When I was little, I would line up my stuffed animals and "read" to them. Although I was not old enough to know the letters formed words and the words formed sentences, I knew there was a story to tell, and I knew there was an audience who would be interested in hearing the story. Now I watch my two-year-old daughter do the same thing. In this media age, books often take a back seat to television, which is unfortunate because books offer so much more. Books are a better tool with which to build imagination. Moreover, readers can gain much more knowledge from the wide variety of books that are available.

Satellite dishes and improved cable offer hundreds of channels, a variety that some TV viewers argue is sufficient to replace reading. However, libraries and bookstores offer thousands, not hundreds, of titles from which to choose. Among these choices, a reader can find books on any theme he chooses, from topics of today to stories of every era in the past. Television, unfortunately, is controlled mostly by popular trends. Aside from a handful of specialty channels like *The History Channel*, there is little on TV about historical events. Furthermore, TV viewers' choices are limited since the television broadcasting companies choose what they will offer on each channel.

A limited choice of TV channels results in limited knowledge. The written word offers much more detail than television. Most TV shows are limited to two hours or less, and because of this time restriction, fewer details can be included in shows like movies and documentaries. For example, a TV documentary on orangutans would most likely be a one hour program which would offer some basic knowledge about orangutans, their habitat and their way of life. A book about orangutans, on the other hand, would educate the reader far beyond the basic knowledge he would gain from watching a television program.

In addition to offering more information on a greater number of subjects, the added description included in books helps readers improve vocabulary. In books, readers see unfamiliar words in context, enabling them to decipher the meaning. For TV viewers, unfamiliar words in conversation usually go unnoticed. In fact, many people watch TV simply to "veg," or, in other words, to sit and do nothing but be vaguely aware of the images flickering across the screen. Watching television requires little of the concentration that is required for reading books; consequently the viewer overlooks many details.

Because watching TV does not require active participation, the imagination suffers. Television programs take the viewer quickly from one scene to the next, prohibiting the viewer from taking notice of the details of the setting. Books inspire imagination, allowing the reader to picture for herself the setting and characters of the story. A book's character may be described as tall, dark complected, and wearing a bright purple robe; it is up to the reader to imagine exactly what the character looks like. Is the character Italian or perhaps Native American? Is the bright purple robe rather gaudy looking, or does it give the character an air of sophistication? Television makes those decisions for the viewer by placing in the program a specific actor in garb chosen by costume designers, thus leaving little room for imagination.

Imagination is the key to forward thinking, thinking that brings a person success in what he does. Without imagination, problems go unsolved and new and inventive ideas never make it to the drawing board. Imagination produces creativity, which inspires dreamers. I hope my daughter will continue to be a dreamer, allowing her imagination to blossom. And when the letters, then words, then sentences take form for her, she will have the added benefit of gaining boundless knowledge from books.

Prompt:
Many of today's technological conveniences were developed to save time. Ironically, these developments have created an even more hurried, fast-paced society, where people actually have less leisure time.

Assignment:
Do you think modern technological advances have resulted in a less relaxed society? Develop an essay in which you give your perspective on the effects of modern conveniences on today's society. Pull from your own experiences to persuasively support your opinion.

Ah, the good ol' days! When people sat on their front porch talking and watching the world go by instead of finishing up last-minute work on their laptops. When letters took a week to spread the latest news instead of a few seconds through e-mail. In a world of pagers, faxes, cell phones, and computers, a very hurried society is characterized by impatient workaholics whose nerves are on edge and whose lives are unknowingly empty.

Many of today's conveniences were developed to meet growing impatience with the speed it took to spread information. Through the development of such things as faxes, cell phones and e-mail, however, a new impatience was born. This new impatience is characterized by frustration with the sophistication and complexity of modern technology. Office workers grit their teeth in frustration when an e-mail takes too long to download. In annoyance, they may shut down their computer assuming there is something wrong with the machine. This wastes even more time while restarting the computer and finally retrieving the culprit e-mail. Overnight delivery services emerged to meet this all-consuming impatience as well. Oftentimes, however, even this speedy service is not expedient enough. Some find it necessary to rush a package to the airport so that it may arrive at its destination just a few hours earlier.

This annoyance with our more efficient world has thrown society into a frenzy where even the most technologically advanced equipment is unsatisfactorily slow. The resulting annoyance and impatience can turn into rage in the office and on the highway, with stressed out employees who "go postal," losing all rationale and even causing injury to colleagues. Preventable injuries occur on highways as road rage consumes drivers who are eager to get to their next destination.

In a world where people are eager to pass information ever more quickly and get to their next destination ever more quickly, this has truly become a society of workaholics. Because the transfer of information is so much more efficient with modern technologies, workers find they can accomplish much more in a given day. Driven by this fact, they work more hours. There is always time to make that last call or send a quick e-mail at the end of the day. And portable conveniences like laptops and palm pilots make it possible for people to work essentially anywhere; work is no longer confined to the office and is often completed at home.

Perhaps the most detrimental aspect of our more hurried society lies at home. Because many people spend more time working, and because work is transportable, many spouses discover that their partners spend more time with their computers and cell phones than with their family. Additionally, other conveniences like microwave meals encourage quick meals on-the-go. Rushed families rarely spend quality time together around the dinner table. Rather, they all go their separate ways to eat in front of the TV, at the computer, or at a desk reviewing reports.

At home, in the office and on the streets, a fast-paced society continues to become more hurried as technology continues to match a perpetually growing impatience. Is all of this annoyance, frustration, and rage worth the added convenience that technology has brought to our society? It hardly seems so. In fact, in looking back at the good 'ol days, it seems that in a world with far less vexation and anger, there was more happiness.

Prompt:
Character is created in a crisis.

Assignment:
Do you think character is created in a crisis or merely manifested? Plan and write an essay in which you define your opinion. Make sure you provide clear support for your answer.

In 1992, Hurricane Andrew slammed into Florida causing millions of dollars of damage. Many residents lost everything, including their homes. Those houses that had the strongest foundations withstood the storm most favorably. Additionally, the homes that had been adequately prepared to face the storm fared better than those whose windows were not boarded. Character is like a house. If your character has a strong foundation and displays traits of preparedness, you can weather a storm well. In this light, it is clear that character is not born from crisis, but rather, it merely emerges during difficult times.

It is not adversity but the small moments of life that create character. Poor decisions, regardless of how insignificant, break down your character. Anytime you are inconsistent in following your principles, no matter how small the compromise, cracks in your foundation undoubtedly weaken your character. On the positive side, though, you can learn a lot from your mistakes. In fact, lessons learned from failures are indispensable in building character. To discern the lesson to be learned, however, takes conscious effort. If you are unwilling to put effort into developing character, you will continue to repeat your mistakes, and your life will stagnate.

Part of building character and thus avoiding stagnation is building on your strengths. Taking what is good and making it exceptional is what character building is all about. Continued improvement in life makes you stronger. This too takes a conscious effort in using strengths to positively affect others around you. Channeling the positive to help others results in personal growth, which in turn builds character.

Only when you are willing to learn from your mistakes and make a conscious effort to grow can you face a crisis successfully. It is during this adversity that character comes to light. If you have learned from past failures, you will have the strength to face a crisis head on. You will have adequate problem-solving skills to overcome obstacles set before you. If you have made the conscious effort to build on your positive traits, you will have the means with which to get through the crisis positively with the will to move ahead.

The will and ability to move forward from crisis is the defining moment of your character. As you move forward, though, you should never stop working to improve, because the stronger your foundation is, the better it will weather any type of storm. What kind of storm can the foundation of your character withstand?

Prompt:
People should pursue careers that provide financial security even if they do not enjoy the work.

Assignment:
Should people make financial gain their main criteria for a career choice, or should personal satisfaction play a large role as well? Develop an essay in which you discuss your perspective about choosing a career. Make sure you support your answer with strong evidence.

"I want to be a fireman when I grow up!" A simple dream from a young child in response to the question every youngster faces at one point or another: What do you want to be when you grow up? The innocence of a child, however, protects him from the world of finances, something everyone is forced to face later on in life. And when that realization hits, what path is best for a person to take: the path that leads to a career with large financial promises, or the one that leads to a career that provides more personal satisfaction? Because contentment has so many rewards, it is better for a person to choose the job that will provide happiness even if it does not pay as well as other jobs.

Some people find it necessary to get the best paying job to make financial ends meet. Often someone in financial dire straits will stick with a good paying job just long enough to get ahead and then, because they are unhappy at the job, they quit to find work elsewhere. This has several negative effects. First, the transition to a new job is difficult, and it can be made worse for a new employee if they are followed by negativity. Company officers are reluctant to invest training time and money in employees only to have them leave after a short time and therefore may not be willing to provide favorable references. Second, workers who leave jobs after short periods of time are not with a company long enough to advance within the company. These workers may find that they would have done just as well to begin in a job that they like even if it did not pay as well, because by the time they start all over, they could have already been promoted. The increase in salary that comes with most promotions could equal the wages they were earning at the job they did not enjoy.

The potential for promotion should be a major consideration when deciding between the high paying job and the job that provides satisfaction. Employees in positions they do not enjoy often work with a poor attitude. This promotes laziness and apathy. Managers quickly pick up on this and likely pass up these types of employees for promotions. On the other hand, workers who enjoy their job greet each workday with enthusiasm, fresh creativity and perseverance. Bosses commend this type of work ethic and reward such employees with promotions.

Careers that offer promotions and, most importantly, job satisfaction stimulate self-respect and pride. These characteristics are priceless and have an enormously positive impact on a person and their job performance. The employee who has pride in what he does takes ownership. He is empowered to take charge of the position he holds and give it 110 percent. This attitude has a domino effect and soon colleagues begin to take more pride in their work as well. Managers notice this natural leadership and reward it with promotions.

Taking pride in a job leads to success, not just monetarily, but also personally. Personal success and satisfaction far outweigh monetary gain. So if the little boy still wants to be a fireman when he grows up, he should be a fireman, even if it means he will live in a modest home instead of a mansion. He will never regret the happiness and contentment he will feel by following his dream instead of following the green.

Prompt:
Public figures should expect their private lives to be scrutinized.

Assignment:
Do you think public figures like actors and politicians should expect their personal lives to be exposed? Why do you think there is so much interest in the private lives of the rich and famous? Discuss your opinion on this subject. Support your answer. You may provide some support by using examples from current or past events.

Television shows, newspapers, books, magazines and tabloids delve into the lives of singers, actors, athletes and politicians on a daily basis. Should these public figures expect to lose some of their privacy? Whether they want to or not, people who are in positions that will sometimes place them in the spotlight open themselves to scrutiny from their audience, because people have a natural curiosity and interest in those who have achieved fame.

Although public figures should expect some scrutiny in their lives, there is a point where it can become dangerous. For example, it was reported in 1997 that the driver of Princess Diana's car was driving recklessly to get away from aggressive Paparazzi. As a result, the car spun out of control killing Diana. Other similar stories report stalkers and "Peeping Toms" who take too much liberty in examining the private lives of stars, athletes and politicians. While these are extreme cases of obsession, public figures must realize that there is a natural human desire to more intimately know the familiar faces on TV or on the sports field. This is especially true of actors and actresses. Television and movie viewers get to know their favorite characters on screen and therefore have a desire to "get to know" the actors behind these characters.

Not only do people want to get to know those whom they look up to, but they also strive to be like their favorite stars. Ads on TV encourage viewers to "Be like Mike [Michael Jordan]." On Halloween, teenage girls can emulate their favorite pop singer by obtaining a Britney Spears costume. Although many people admittedly would not choose a life of glamour and fame, there is something alluring about the lifestyle, and therefore admirers of people in the limelight are driven to discover personal facts about those whom they admire. Knowing these intimate details makes a famous person seem more down-to-earth and thus allows the ordinary person to feel like they have something in common with the rich and famous.

The media makes a concerted effort to give viewers a chance to become acquainted with public figures. They splash familiar stars' faces on the cover of magazines. Channels like *E!* and *VH1* feature behind the scenes stories about singers and actors, their highs and lows and how they became famous. Tabloids are a huge business supported by readers who hungrily devour the latest gossip about their favorite star. Even the news capitalizes on human interest stories that feature public figures. For example, although long and drawn-out, OJ Simpson's murder trial dominated the news, yet no one seemed to complain.

The news often highlights human interest stories that uncover the blunders of politicians. Former President Clinton's escapades with Monica Lewinsky, for example, made headlines for months. Many public figures, especially politicians, anticipate the scrutinizing eye under which they will find themselves and proactively confess to past mistakes. This takes some of the media pressure off them. Sadly, others find themselves on the front cover of every magazine and newspaper and in every headline when marital infidelity or an encounter with drugs is exposed.

Politicians are of deep interest to the public because they are the nation's leaders. Since people must place some trust in political figures to run the country effectively, politicians should expect their private lives to be examined. Not only should they expect ordinary citizens to dig into their lives, but they should also anticipate other political figures to look closely at their lives. Political campaigns, unfortunately, often focus on tearing apart the opponent. To do this, a politician must find a way to attack his opponent, which requires investigating the personal life of the candidate. This comes with the territory. If a would-be politician cannot stomach having some negative aspect of his life exposed, he should not enter the world of politics.

Although many people work hard to achieve the fame of a popular singer, actor, athlete, or politician, some become bitterly disenchanted with the lifestyle when they realize they may lose much of their privacy. This should certainly be a matter of consideration before pursuing any career that places a person in the spotlight. It is, after all, natural that admirers will be interested in the details of the life of public figures. Public figures should consider this admiration flattery rather than an intrusion on their privacy.

Prompt:
It is necessary for a leader to compromise his principles if compromising them is favorable to a greater number of people.

Assignment:
In order to be in step with the majority, do you think a leader must sometimes compromise his principles? Discuss your perspective on leadership, pulling from your personal experience and knowledge for support.

This nation has seen many outstanding leaders, like George Washington and Abraham Lincoln. Have you ever wondered what separates great leaders from ineffective leaders? Contrary to popular belief, great leaders are not born. Rather, if you want to be an effective leader, you must realize that it takes a lot of work and perseverance. Furthermore, of all the character traits that can be cultivated to make a good leader, the ability to stick to your principles is the most important; to be a great leader, you should never compromise your principles, no matter how high the price.

As a leader, you may sometimes pay a price by losing favor with the majority because of a decision you have made. At these times, it may be tempting for you to give in to the demands of your followers. However, remember that, regardless of the capacity in which you lead, you are in a position of leadership because there are people who thought your ideas were good, and therefore they made a conscious decision to follow you. Knowing this, you should be encouraged to stick to your decisions since, in the end, even if your followers still disagree with your decision, they will respect you for standing firm on your principles. If you possess honor in your word, your followers will entrust you with more responsibility knowing that, since you did not compromise your beliefs in one decision, you are not likely to go back on your word in other situations.

As followers take note that you refuse to give in by compromising your principles, they will come to the realization that they made an excellent choice in a leader, and they will gain a deeper respect for you as their leader. As people gain new respect for you, they will be more willing to follow you in all of your decisions, even if they do not fully agree with all of them. This type of respect is important for your leadership because it creates an atmosphere conducive to cooperation and teamwork. In this cooperative environment, your followers will be willing to step up and take on some of the responsibility if they believe in you and what you stand for.

With you as their guide, your team's confidence will grow. As their confidence grows, your self-confidence will flourish. A confident leader is much more effective than one who is unsure of himself. If you do not portray confidence in what you do, others will not feel confident in your decisions either. Moreover, if you lack confidence in your ability as a leader, you will likely at some point give in to others' wishes over your own principles. Your followers will perceive you as weak and will recede from your leadership. If you believe in yourself, however, you will benefit from lifelong supporters who respect your confidence and the consistency of your principles.

Unwillingness to compromise principles breeds the stalwart leader within you. Becoming an effective leader requires this confidence in the actions that you take and the decisions that you make. The respect you will earn by standing firm in what you believe will take your leadership farther than you ever thought possible.

Prompt:
Parents must be involved in their children's education in order to make them successful.

Assignment:
How integral is parental involvement in a child's education? Plan and write an essay in which you discuss the effects of a parent's involvement in his or her child's education. Make sure you provide ample support for your opinion.

Sally is a Sophomore in high school. Although she is a bright girl and has the potential to excel in school, she lacks the ability to apply herself and therefore is not doing well. As a result, she does not enjoy school and often cuts classes to hang out at the mall with friends who share her same ethic. Sally enjoys athletics and earned a spot on the Girls' Softball team. She competed in six matches, but when progress reports were issued, she was forced to leave the team because her grades were not up to par. Sally's father is a lawyer and often works so late, the family rarely sees him. Sally's mother works in an office, but after work, she enjoys going out with her colleagues. Often, Sally is on her own when she gets home and must prepare dinner for herself and her 12-year-old sister. Sally's parents have missed countless parent-teacher conferences and have yet to meet most of her teachers. They are aware of only one instance of Sally's truancy; usually she gets home in time to erase the school's message from the answering machine. When her parents heard about her "first" unexcused absence from school, they did nothing but tell her not to do it again.

Tommy is also a Sophomore. He is intelligent and works hard to obtain near-perfect grades. He enjoys school and enthusiastically participates in all of his classes. Tommy is the goalie on the Boys' Soccer team and can be depended upon to maintain his important position on the team. Tommy's parents are divorced, and Tommy and his twin 10-year-old brothers live with their mother. She works in an office and gets home promptly by 5:30. Although she must rely on Tommy to watch the twins after school, she always prepares dinner when she gets home. After dinner, Tommy and his brothers must finish their homework before they are permitted to do anything else. Tommy's mom checks everyone's homework when they are done and helps them with work they do not understand. Although Tommy's father lives an hour away, he often meets Tommy's mother for parent-teacher conferences, and he consistently makes it to Tommy's games. Tommy has never considered skipping school because he knows the consequences at home would be great.

Two students, two very different results at school and two opposite attitudes about life. The difference? Parental involvement. Although teachers can equip a student with the tools he needs to succeed in life, it is up to parents to instill in their children the motivation and determination to use these tools to be successful.

To do this, parents must be willing to be involved in every aspect of their children's lives, particularly in their education. It is unfair for parents to expect teachers and school administrators to take sole re

Some parents feel inadequate to help their children in school because they are unfamiliar with their children's school subjects, or because they did not do well in school themselves. No matter how little academic knowledge parents have, however, they can play an integral part in her child's education. For example, there are many opportunities to volunteer in schools. Parents can become a part of the school's Parent-Teacher Association or Parent-Teacher-Student Organization. Parents can help with sports' teams or at the very least, make an effort to support the athletes by coming to the games. If parents' jobs hinder them from attending school functions, they can play an important role at home by keeping their children accountable in school matters like homework. They can help their children with things the children do not understand or get a tutor if they do not understand it either.

Although parents cannot always help a child scholastically, they can teach their children lifelong lessons in motivation and determination. If a man wants to learn how to fish, he can obtain a net and a boat and learn how to cast the net. But he is not a fisherman simply because he has the right tools and knowledge. Someone must instill in him the motivation and determination to sit on a boat day after day performing the tedious task of casting a net that does not always produce a big catch. In the same way, a teacher can give their students the book knowledge they need to be experts in various fields; however, it is the parents who must empower their children to use the knowledge to be successful. This requires parents to teach their children the value of education and thus inspire motivation; parents must teach their children never to give up and thus inspire determination.

Only motivated learners have the determination to gain the knowledge and responsibility that will enable them to succeed in life. It is the responsibility of parents to instill in their children these qualities. One of the most effective ways parents can teach their children the importance of such qualities is by modeling them in their own lives. Parents should make an effort to model responsibility through motivation and determination in their own lives. Such examples provide the best lessons a student will ever learn.

Part Four
Vocabulary

- **INTRODUCTION**
  Techniques for Learning New Vocabulary
  Setting Goals
  When You Don't Know the Word

- **ETYMOLOGY**
  A Biography of English
  The Birth of a Word
  The Life of a Word
  The Death of a Word

- **THE UBIQUITOUS 400**

- **VOCABULARY 4000**

Introduction

Many students write off questions on the ACT that contain words they don't recognize. This is a mistake. As promised earlier, the following chapter will be dedicated to numerous techniques for decoding unfamiliar words. Armed with these techniques, you will soon be able to squeeze out enough meaning from an unfamiliar word to answer one of the many vocabulary questions that plague the ACT Verbal Section.

Techniques for Learning New Vocabulary

- **Write the Definition in Your Own Words -** The first technique for learning new words is to put the definition in your own words, condensing the definition to only one or two words. For example, take the word

    Heinous - The definition of *heinous* is "abominable, vile." However, you may find it much easier to remember by the word *horrible*.

Often the dictionary definition of a word can be simplified by condensing the definition into one word. Take, for example, the word

    Expiate - The dictionary definition is "to put an end to; to extinguish guilt, to make amends for." This definition may be summed up by one word, *Atone*.

Putting definitions in your own words makes them more familiar and therefore easier to remember.

- **Write Down the Words -** Many people are visual learners and do not fully benefit from a mere review of words and their definitions. For these learners, writing the words and their definitions could cause a dramatic difference in retaining the words and their meanings. For many, it may take several times of writing the word down along with its definition before it all sinks in. If you think this method can work for you, get a notebook and start writing.

- **Use Flashcards -** Cut heavyweight paper into a size that you feel is manageable. Then, simply write the words on one side of a flashcard and write the definition on the other side.

- **Create a Word Picture -** In grade school, you may remember learning the difference between the word *principal* and *principle*. Your teacher probably told you that *principal* refers to the leader of an educational institution and the word ends with *pal*. Your school principal wants to be your pal, so this is easy to remember (after all, you always wanted to be best friends with your principal, right?). Your teacher gave you a mental word picture.

Let's take another word: *sovereign*. *Sovereign* means "monarch." The word itself contains the word *reign*. What do you think of when you think of *reign*? You probably think of a king—or a monarch. So, picture a king when you are trying to recall the meaning of *sovereign*, and it should be easy to remember.

How about *pestilence*. *Pestilence* means "disease." The word *pest* is in the word. Pests are common in a garden, and, unfortunately, they often cause diseases among the plants in a garden. So when you see this word, picture a garden and then picture all of the pests that bring diseases to your garden.

If you're using flashcards, it may help to draw a small reminder on the flashcard of your mental word picture to further ingrain the word in your memory. Creating mental word pictures helps you retain the meanings of new words and clarifies your thinking when you get to the test.

Setting Goals

Whatever technique you use, it is necessary to set goals if you plan to learn the following word lists. To do this, first look ahead to your intended test date. Next, determine how many days you have before that date. Finally, divide the list so you have a preset goal each day of how many words to study. This will make the task much less formidable because you will be able to measure your accomplishments each day rather than trying to attack in one sitting.

When You Don't Know the Word

You can't possibly memorize the whole dictionary, and, while you can learn the words that occur most frequently on the ACT, there will inevitably still be some that you do not know. Don't be discouraged. There are some very effective techniques that can be applied when a word does not look familiar to you.

➤ **Put the Word in Context -** In our daily speech, we combine words into phrases and sentences; rarely do we use a single word by itself. For example, take the word *whet*. Most people don't recognize it in isolation, yet most people understand it in the following phrase: *To whet your appetite*. *Whet* means to stimulate.

If you don't recognize the meaning of a word, think of a phrase in which you have heard it used.

➤ **Change the Word Into a More Common Form -** Most words are built from other words. Although you may not know a given word, you may spot the root word from which it is derived and thereby deduce the meaning of the original word.

      Example:
      PERTURBATION

You may not know how to pronounce PERTURBATION let alone know its meaning. However, changing its ending yields the more common form of the word *perturbed*, which means "upset, agitated."

      Example:
      TEMPESTUOUS

TEMPESTUOUS is a hard word. However, if we drop the ending *stuous* and add the letter *r* we get the common word *temper*.

➤ **Test Words for Positive or Negative Connotations -** Testing words for positive and negative connotations is a very effective technique. Surprisingly, you can often solve a problem knowing only that a given word has a negative connotation.

Example:
REPUDIATE

You may not know what *repudiate* means, but you probably sense that it has a negative connotation. Since we will probably looking for a word whose meaning is opposite of *repudiate*, we can eliminate any answer-choices that are also negative.

General Connotation Rules:
- Any ACT word that starts with *DE, DIS,* or *ANTI* will almost certainly be negative.

    Examples: Degradation, Discrepancy, Discriminating, Debase, Antipathy

- Any ACT word that includes the notion of "going up" will almost certainly be positive, and any ACT word that includes the notion of "going down" will almost certainly be negative.

    Examples (positive): Elevate, Ascendancy, Lofty
    Examples (negative): Decline, Subjugate, Suborn (to encourage false witness)

➢ <u>**Be Alert to Secondary Meanings**</u> - ACT writers often use common words, but they use their uncommon meanings.

Example:
CHAMPION

The common meaning of *champion* is winner. But *champion* also means to support or fight for someone else.

Example:
AIR

AIR is commonly used as a noun—indicating that which we breathe. A secondary meaning for AIR is to discuss publicly. So beware of tricky, second meanings.

➢ <u>**Use Your Past Knowledge**</u> - Since you are studying for the ACT, you have probably completed, or almost completed, your high school studies. Therefore, you have a wealth of knowledge from which to draw when it comes to examining the words that will appear on the test. In your classes, you studied history and probably one or more foreign language. You may have even taken a Latin class. Because the English language has borrowed so many words from other languages, especially Latin and French, these classes give you valuable clues to the meanings of many of the words you may come across.

Example:
NARCISSISTIC

You may remember Narcissus from one of your literature or Greek mythology classes. Narcissus was a man who fell in love with his own reflection in a pool. Because of his requited love, he dies. As a man in love with his own reflection, he portrays self-love to the ultimate degree. A man like this is pretentious.

Example:
VERDANT

In Spanish *verde* means green, and in French *vert* means green as well. *Verdant*, which also means green, can refer to being green in experience or judgment. Or inexperienced.

Points to Remember

Techniques To Learn New Words
- Put the definition in your own words
- Write down the words
- Use flashcards
- Create a word picture
- Set goals

When You Don't Know The Word
- Put the word in context
- Change the word into a more common form
- Test words for positive and negative connotation
- Be alert to secondary (often rare) meanings of words
- Use your past education/knowledge

Tips
- If the word starts with *De*, *Dis*, or *Anti*, the word most likely has a negative connotation.
- If the word contains the notion of going up, it will most likely have a positive connotation.
- If the word contains the notion of going down, it will most likely have a negative connotation.

Etymology

Etymology is the study of the development of words and their forms. Many of the words in the English language have fascinating histories; familiarity with these stories and the development of the words can help you remember the meanings of some words and can help you decipher the meanings of other words.

A Biography of English

English, a language less than 2000 years old, has made its way to almost every corner of the world, making it the one true global language. Knowing something about the history of the language as well as its present qualities should not only intrigue you, but also give you more facility to acquire new vocabulary and use it well in your writing.

It has been said that English came to Britain "on the edge of a sword." In 449 AD, Britain, at the time settled by the Celts, became the target of several invasions. The first group of people to invade, the Anglo-Saxons, drove the Celtic-Britons westward, settled into the fertile land, and began farming their new property. The Anglo-Saxons were an agricultural people; everyday words like *sheep*, *shepherd*, *ox*, *earth*, *dog*, *wood*, *field*, and *work* come from the Anglo-Saxon Old English. It is also nearly impossible to write a modern English sentence without using Anglo-Saxon words like *the*, *is*, *you*, *here*, and *there*.

The Vikings built on the Anglo-Saxon vocabulary with their merciless invasions. During the time of the Viking invasions, Anglo-Saxon writing reflected a bitter, negative tone. Themes like transience of life, heroism, and keeping dignity in the face of defeat permeated their writings about the cruel sea, ruined cities, war, and exile. One notable example of Old English writing is the heroic epic poem *Beowulf*. Lines 20-25 of the Prologue in Old English read:

> Swa sceal geong guma gode gewyrcean,
> fromum feohgiftum on fæder bearme,
> þæt hine on ylde eft gewunigen
> wilgesipas, ponne wig cume,
> leode gelæsten; lofdædum sceal
> in mægpa gehwære man gepeon.

These lines are translated as follows:

> So becomes it a youth to quit him well
> with his father's friends, by fee and gift,
> that to aid him, aged, in after days,
> come warriors willing, should war draw nigh,
> liegemen loyal; by lauded deeds
> shall an earl have honor in every clan.

Most likely, you found it impossible to interpret even one word of the poem as it was originally written; Old English was certainly very different from English as we know it today.

It would take yet another invasion to add just a bit of present-day normalcy to English. This invasion came in 1066 and became known as the Norman Conquest. It transformed the English language, marking a turning point in the language's history from Old English to Middle English. When the Normans invaded Britain from present-day Normandy, France, and William the conqueror took the throne, English began its transformation into the melting pot of all languages.

When the Normans arrived in Britain, they found a people governed by what they considered to be inferior moral and cultural standards. Consequently, French was the language of the aristocrats, the well-bred—the language of the civilized. However, English survived for a number of reasons. First and foremost, it was too established to disappear. In addition, there was intermarriage between the French-speaking Normans and the English-speaking Anglos, and, in instances where an Anglo woman married a Norman, the children were more likely to speak their mother's language, thus carrying the language to the next generation.

Other events had an effect on the strength of English as well. The Hundred Years War caused French to lose its prestige while it bolstered nationalism for English. During the war, the Black Plague took so many lives that labor was scarce, forcing the rise of the English working man. The disease had the same effect in churches and monasteries.

Through the survival of English came many changes to its vocabulary and to its written form. The biggest change was the addition of many borrowed words, especially from French and Latin. Although English borrowed many words from French, French had little impact on the grammatical structure of the language, though there were notable changes to its form. For example, pronunciations and spelling changed as regional dialects formed. In addition, word order began to change. Through all the changes, English began to take on more of the look that we recognize today, although there were still marked differences. Following is an excerpt from the Prologue of Chaucer's *Canterbury Tales*. Try deciphering it for yourself without referring to the translation.

**Here bygynneth the Book
of the tales of Caunterbury**
Whan that aprill with his shoures soote
The droghte of march hath perced to the roote,
And bathed every veyne in swich licour
Of which vertu engendred is the flour;
Whan zephirus eek with his sweete breeth
Inspired hath in every holt and heeth
Tendre croppes, and the yonge sonne
Hath in the ram his halve cours yronne,
And smale foweles maken melodye,
That slepen al the nyght with open ye
(so priketh hem nature in hir corages);
Thanne longen folk to goon on pilgrimages,
And palmeres for to seken straunge strondes,
To ferne halwes, kowthe in sondry londes;
And specially from every shires ende
Of engelond to caunterbury they wende,
The hooly blisful martir for to seke,
That hem hath holpen whan that they were seeke.

**Here begins the Book
of the Tales of Canterbury**

When April with his showers sweet with fruit
The drought of March has pierced unto the root
And bathed each vein with liquor that has power
To generate therein and sire the flower;
When Zephyr also has, with his sweet breath,
Quickened again, in every holt and heath,
The tender shoots and buds, and the young sun
Into the Ram one half his course has run,
And many little birds make melody
That sleep through all the night with open eye
(So Nature pricks them on to ramp and rage);
Then do folk long to go on pilgrimage,
And palmers to go seeking out strange strands,
To distant shrines well known in sundry lands.
And specially from every shire's end
Of England they to Canterbury wend,
The holy blessed martyr there to seek
Who helped them when they lay so ill and weak

Canterbury Tales is far easier to decipher than *Beowulf*, even in its original form. Clearer still is the following well-known excerpt from William Shakespeare's *Romeo and Juliet*:

> O Romeo, Romeo, wherefore art thou Romeo?
> Deny thy father and refuse thy name!
> Or, if thou wilt not, be but sworn my love,
> And I'll no longer be a Capulet. *(2.2.33-36)*

William Shakespeare along with King James marked the change from Middle English to Modern English although their writing reflected a use of word order that still sounds awkward in our present-day English. For example, the King James version of the Bible uses such phrases as *follow thou me*, *speak ye unto me*, *cake unleavened*, *things eternal*, *they knew him not*. Although these authors' writings may seem antiquated to us today, they both have left a lasting impression. Many present-day phrases came from Shakespeare: *good riddance*, *lie low*, *the long and the short of it*, *a fool's paradise*, *sleep a wink*, *green-eyed jealousy*, and *love at first sight*. King James contributed many of today's idioms: *the root of the matter*, *wolf in sheep's clothing*, *lambs to the slaughter*, *an eye for an eye*, and *straight and narrow*.

In comparison, English as Shakespeare and King James knew it and English as we know it is quite different. English is a changing language. And, although it seems to have already had a very full life, there is no reason to assume that it will not continue to pass through new and different stages of its life.

The Birth of a Word

Just as the English language was born and has lived a life of change, so too a word has a life. From its birth, a word can undergo changes or remain static throughout its life; it may be immortal, or it may die. Words have ancestors; they have relatives. Words also have friends (*synonyms*) and enemies (*antonyms*). Studying the life of words is fascinating and gives you an upper hand at understanding and using words and deciphering unfamiliar words you may find on the ACT.

A word's ancestor is called a *cognate*. Cognates are ancient words that bare a close resemblance to modern words. For example, in ancient Indo-European Sanskrit the word *father* is "pitar;" in Latin, "pater;" in French, "père;" in Spanish "padre." In Sanskrit, *mother* is "matar;" in Latin, "mater;" in French, "mère;" in Spanish, "madre." Sir William Jones, a British judge, was the first to point out the close relationship between languages despite the passage of time. His theory, a theory shared by many today, was that the languages of 1/3 of the human race have a common source in this Indo-European language.

This common source found in cognates should not be confused with borrowed words. Borrowing is one way that words are given birth in the English language. English has borrowed more words than any other language, especially from French and Latin—a direct result from the Norman Conquest. Borrowed words sometimes keep their original form. For example, the French word *laissez-faire* is commonly used in English and refers to the "policy of non-interference, especially as pertaining to government." In other instances, however, words change form to fit the accepted rules and pronunciation that govern the English language. For example, the word *adroit* means "right, justice." The word is from the French *à*, which means "to" and *droit* (pronounced *dwa*), which means "right." Through their transition to English, the words changed spelling to become one word, the English version lost the accent mark, and the pronunciation changed. Following are some examples of other borrowed words:

ABERRATION
Present meaning: departure from what is normal
Derived from: Latin *aberrare*, to wander away from
Details of origin: Originally a psychological term describing a person who mentally deviates from the norm.

ABOMINATE
Present meaning: loathe
Derived from: Latin *abominor*, "I pray that the event predicted by the omen may be averted"
Details of origin: A superstitious word the Romans uttered to ward off evil spirits when anyone said something unlucky.

ALOOF
Present meaning: distant (as pertaining to emotion)
Derived from: Dutch *te loef*, to windward; also used as a sailor's term *a loof*, to the luff or windward direction
Details of origin: Present meaning suggests that the use of the term to mean "keeping a ship's head to the wind and away from the shore" developed into our meaning of "distance."

EBULLIENT
Present meaning: high-spirited; exuberant
Derived from: Latin *ebullire*, to boil over
Details of origin: Much as a pot boils over, one who is ebullient "boils over" with enthusiasm.

EXPUNGE
Present meaning: erase; remove
Derived from: Latin *expungere*, to prick through or mark off
Details of origin: In ancient Rome, when a soldier would retire, a series of dots and points were placed under his name on service lists.

GREGARIOUS
Present meaning: sociable
Derived from: Latin *gregarius* and *grex*, flock or herd
Details of origin: From the idea that animals stayed in flocks or herds because they were sociable came our present-day meaning.

LETHARGY
Present meaning: drowsiness; sluggishness
Derived from: Greek *lethargia* or *lethe*, forgetfulness
Details of origin: Because of the Greeks belief in afterlife, legend had it that the dead crossed the river Lethe, which took them through Hades. Anyone who drank from the river would forget his past. This idea of forgetfulness lead to our meaning of sluggishness.

While some words are borrowed directly from another language, others are adopted from interesting people and events in history. For example, you have probably at one time or another made a *Freudian slip*, an unintentional comment based on some subconscious feeling. And did you know that a *bootlegger* was originally someone who smuggled illegal alcoholic liquor in the tops of his boots? Here are some other words with fascinating histories:

AMALGAM
Present meaning: mixture, combination
Derived from: Latin *amalgama*, alloy of mercury; Greek *malagma*, softening substance
Details of origin: Evolved to present meaning in 1775.

BOWDLERIZE
Present meaning: to remove offensive words from a book
Derived from: Scottish physician Dr. Thomas Bowdler
Details of origin: Dr. Bowdler published an edition of Shakespeare's works, omitting certain words which he deemed offensive.

CHAUVINISM
Present meaning: exaggerated patriotism
Derived from: one of Napoleon's soldiers, Nicolas Chauvin
Details of origin: After retiring from the army, Chauvin spoke so highly of himself and his feats while in battle that he became a joke and thus the term was coined.

CYNOSURE
Present meaning: center of attention or admiration
Derived from: Greek mythology *Cynosura*, dog's tail
Details of origin: The Greek god Zeus honored a nymph by placing her as a constellation in the sky. One star in the constellation in particular stood out. To many, the constellation looked like a dog's tail because of the one bright star.

DESULTORY
Present meaning: lacking in consistency; disconnected
Derived from: Romans *desultor*, a leaper
Details of origin: Often Roman soldiers would go into battle with two horses so that when one horse tired, the soldier could leap to the second horse striding alongside. This person became known as a *desultor*, or leaper. The term evolved since this leaper only stayed on one horse for a short amount of time before becoming disconnected and jumping to the other horse.

FIASCO
Present meaning: humiliating failure or breakdown
Derived from: Italian *fiasco*, flask or bottle
Details of origin: Venetian glassblowers set aside fine glass with flaws to use in making ordinary bottles. The term resulted from the fact that something fine should be turned into something ordinary.

GAMUT
Present meaning: whole series or range of something
Derived from: medieval musician Guido of Arezzo
Details of origin: Arezzo was the first to use the lines of the musical staff, and he assigned the Greek letter "gamma" for the lowest tone. This note was called "gamma ut" and thus "gamut" evolved into our present meaning.

INTRANSIGENT
Present meaning: uncompromising
Derived from: Spanish *intransigente*, not compromising
Details of origin: In 1873, Amadeus was forced to give up the throne of Spain. After this occurred, a group of people attempted to form a political party of their own. This group was known as *los intransigentes* because they would not conform to the policies of any other groups.

JOVIAL
Present meaning: merry
Derived from: Latin *Jovialis*, of Jupiter; *Jovius*, Jupiter
Details of origin: Astrologers believed that those born under the sign of Jupiter were characterized by a merry disposition.

MESMERIZE
Present meaning: fascinate; spellbind
Derived from: Austrian doctor Friedrich Anton Mesmer
Details of origin: Doctor Mesmer was the first to successfully use hypnotism. Although the term is still used today to relate to the technique of hypnotism, its meaning has broadened to encompass a general idea of fascination.

OSTRACIZE
Present meaning: to exclude from a society as by general consent
Derived from: Greek *ostrakon*, tile, shell
Details of origin: In ancient Greece, if a man was considered dangerous to society, judges would cast their votes regarding banishment by writing their names on a tile and dropping them in an urn.

QUARANTINE
Present meaning: isolation to prevent contagion
Derived from: Latin *quadraginta*, forty and *quattuor*, four; *quarantina*, space of forty days
Details of origin: This word has a rich history, originally referring to the period of time that a widow in the 1500's could live in her dead husband's house. It was also used to reference the period of 40 days during which Christ fasted in the wilderness. In the 1600's, the Venetians kept ships at bay for 40 days if their voyage originated in a disease-stricken country. Since then, the term has broadened to encompass any period of isolation.

QUISLING
Present meaning: traitor
Derived from: Norweigan army officer Vidkun Quisling
Details of origin: Although the term loosely refers to a traitor, more specifically it describes a traitor who betrays his country to serve a dictatorial government. Officer Quisling was one such traitor who betrayed Norway to join arms with the Nazis in World War II.

SYCOPHANT
Present meaning: self-seeking flatterer
Derived from: Greek *sykon*, fig; *phantes*, one who shows
Details of origin: Originally, a sycophant referred to an informer. Etymologists speculate that the term "fig-shower" was used in this context because ancient Greeks, or sycophants, would act as informers against merchants who were unlawfully exporting figs.

The process by which a word comes into being is called *neologism* or *coinage*. A new word is coined when it is used by a large number of people for a significant amount of time. Though not a very specific and measurable process, it is clearer when we look at three main reasons people begin using new words. First, new words are created when two words are combined into one. For example, the word *breakfast* evolved from the two words *break* and *fast*. Breakfast breaks the fast your body undergoes during the night. Other words like *roommate*, *housewife*, *stay-at-home*, and *doorbell* were coined by the same process of combining multiple words to form one.

The opposite process also forms new words. For example, the word *ref* is short for *referee*; *gym* is short for *gymnasium*; and *exam* is short for *examination*. It is easy to imagine how shortened words become coined—as a society, we are always looking for shortcuts, and clipping words is a convenient shortcut.

New words are also coined to avoid confusion, most often between languages. For example, have you ever wondered exactly where the tennis term *love* came from? It seems a strange term to use for scoring. Tennis is originally a French game, and since a zero is egg-shaped, the French referred to it as *l'œuf*. This term was confused in translation and only the pronunciation was adopted; English-speakers heard love and it stuck. Another example of confusion is the word *maudlin*, which means "tearfully sentimental." The word evolved from the British English pronunciation of Mary Magdalene. During the Middle Ages, one of the popular plays depicted the life of the Bible's Mary Magdalene. Because the character was usually tearful in every scene and, because the British pronunciation was Maudlin, the term picked up this meaning.

The Life of a Word

Whatever the birth story, some words live exciting lives of change while others retain their original meaning. Words can undergo changes by being clipped as mentioned above or by being combined with other words to form completely new ones. Some words become more powerful. For example, the words *filth* and *foul* were originally used to mean plain old dirt. Originally, you might wipe down your kitchen counter at the end of the day because it was *filthy* or *foul*. Today *filthy* and *foul* have taken on a more powerful meaning so that you probably only associate *filth* and *foul* with the nearest garbage dump. Another example of a word that has gained force is *disaster*. At one time, the word simply referred to an unlucky event. Today, we hear the word used in reference to disaster areas resulting from earthquakes, floods, and tornadoes. There is much more power associated with the word now.

Words can also lose power. Take the word *mortify*, for example. It originally meant "to make dead." Now it can simply refer to a moment of humiliation: He was *mortified* when he realized that his zipper was down during his important speech. Other words have powerful meanings, even as depicted in the dictionary, but in everyday speech they are used rather casually. For example, the word *atrocious* by definition refers to something that is "extremely savage or wicked." But you've probably heard the word in reference to someone's taste in style: Did you see that *atrocious* purple and green striped dress she was wearing?

Words gain power and they lose power. Words can also gain or lose a bad reputation. The word *lewd* has gained a negative connotation over the years from its original reference to all laymen. From there it evolved to present-day where it now encompasses things that are "indecent or obscene." On the other hand, *marshal* once referred to a person who took care of horses. Over the years, the position gained more respect and now not only refers to the person who controls parades, but also refers to someone in a high-ranking position such as a sheriff.

In both the example of *lewd* and the example of *marshal*, not only did the meanings change from positive to negative and vice versa, but they also changed in scope. *Lewd* became more narrow in its meaning, *marshal* more broad. *Butcher* is another example of a word that has broadened in scope. A butcher was originally a man who killed goats. Nowadays, you can expect to find a vast array of meats in a butcher shop. By contrast, the original meaning of *disease* was "ill at ease." The word has narrowed its scope over the years so that now it refers to specific ailments and maladies.

What a boring language we would speak if words did not change in so many different ways! And how mundane our speech would be if it were not colored with such flourishes as slang and colloquialisms.

How Words Die

Although certain words are seemingly immortal like *and*, *the*, and *is*, others do meet their death. When a word meets its death, it becomes *obsolete*. The King James version of the Bible as well as any one of Shakespeare's plays contains a vast sum of words that, today, are obsolete. Slang words and colloquialisms are also quick to become obsolete. This is because slang and colloquialisms generally come into existence through trends. Speaking trends fade in and fade out just as quickly as the latest fashion trends.

Some words do not fade away, but their meaning does. A well-known example of such a phenomenon is the word *gay*, which at one time meant "happy." Today the word is used in reference to homosexuality. And did you know that *nice* originally referred to something that was "silly" or "foolish"? Other meanings of words are surely on their way out as technology advances. For example, very few people actually dial a number into their phone because there are few rotary phones still in use. Along the same lines, singers no longer put out albums because we now have compact discs rather than records. It is probably just a matter of time until these meanings die.

When you study the life of a word, it is easy to see that English is truly a unique language. Studying its history, its life, and its patterns is both fascinating and helpful in learning to communicate effectively.

The Ubiquitous 400

The ACT tests a surprisingly limited number of words. In the following lists, you will find words that occur frequently on the ACT. Granted, memorizing a list of words is rather dry, but it is probably the most effective way to improve your performance on the reading test.

As you read through the lists, mark any words that you do not know with a check mark. Then, when you read through the list again, mark any that you do not remember with two checks. Continue in this manner until you have learned the words.

The first list, The Ubiquitous 400, contains words that have appeared frequently on the ACT over the years. Our second list, Vocabulary 4000, has been an invaluable tool for students who have both the time and the determination to wade through it. It's chocked-full of words that are prime candidates for the ACT.

abash humiliate, embarrass
abdicate relinquish power or position
aberrant abnormal
abet aid, encourage (typically of crime)
abeyance postponement
aboriginal indigenous
abridge shorten
abstemious moderate
acclimate accustom oneself to a climate
accost to approach and speak to someone
acquiesce agree passively
acumen insight
adamant insistent
admonish warn gently
adulterate contaminate, corrupt
adversity hardship
aegis that which protects
aesthetic pleasing to the senses, beautiful
affable friendly

affinity fondness
aggregate total, collect
aghast horrified
alacrity swiftness
alienate estrange, antagonize
alleviate lessen, assuage
altruism benevolence, generosity
amalgamation mixture
ambiguous unclear
ambivalence conflicting emotions
amenable agreeable
amorphous shapeless
anachronistic out of historical order
analogous similar
anarchy absence of government
anathema curse
animus hate
anomalous abnormal
antipathy repulsion, hatred
antipodal exactly opposite
antiquated outdated, obsolete

apathy indifference
appease pacify
approbation approval
artless naive, simple
ascetic self-denying
assiduous hard-working
assimilate absorb
audacity boldness
auspicious favorable
austere harsh, Spartan
autonomous self-governing
avarice greed
axiom self-evident truth
banal trite
belie misrepresent
belittle disparage
bellicose warlike
benefactor patron
boisterous noisy
boor vulgar person
bourgeois middle class
bucolic rustic
buttress support
cachet prestige

cacophony dissonance, harsh noise
callow inexperienced
canon rule
capacious spacious
capitulate surrender
castigate criticize
cathartic purgative, purifying
catholic universal, worldly
caustic scathing (of speech)
censure condemn
chagrin embarrassment
charlatan quack
chary cautious
coagulate thicken
coda concluding passage
cogent well-put, convincing
collusion conspiracy
commensurate proportionate
commiserate empathize
compensatory redeeming
compliant submissive
conciliatory reconciling
condone overlook wrong doing
conducive helping
connoisseur an expert, gourmet
consensus general agreement
contentious argumentative
conundrum puzzle, enigma
convoluted twisted, complicated
covenant agreement, pact
covert secret
credence belief
credulous believing
cynical scornful of the motives of others
dauntless courageous
dearth scarcity
defamation (noun) slander
deference courteously yielding to another
deleterious harmful
delineate draw a line around, describe
demur take exception

denigrate defame
deprecate belittle
desiccate dehydrate
despot tyrant
destitute poor
desultory without direction in life
deterrent hindrance
devoid empty
devout pious
diatribe long denunciation
dichotomy a division into two parts
didactic instructional
diffident shy
digress ramble
disabuse correct a misconception
discerning observant
discord lack of harmony
discrete separate
discretion prudence
disingenuous deceptive
disparate various
disseminate distribute
dissent disagree
dissolution disintegration
dissonance discord
distend swell
divest strip, deprive
divulge disclose
dogmatic certain, unchanging in opinion
dormant asleep
eclectic from many sources
efficacy effectiveness
effigy likeness, mannequin
effloresce to bloom
effrontery insolence
elicit provoke
eloquent well-spoken
emancipate liberate
embellish exaggerate
endemic peculiar to a particular region
enervate weaken
engender generate
ennui boredom

enumerate count
esoteric known by only a few
esthetic artistic
euphemism genteel expression
euphoria elation
evanescent fleeting, very brief
exacerbate worsen
exasperate irritate
exhibitionist one who draws attention to himself
exonerate free from blame
expedite hasten
extemporize improvise
extol praise highly
facetious joking, sarcastic
facilitate make easier
fallacy false belief
fathom understand
fervor intensity
fickle always changing one's mind
filibuster long speech
fledgling just beginning, struggling
flout to show disregard for the law or rules
foment instigate
forsake abandon
fortuitous lucky
foster encourage
frugal thrifty
fulminate denounce, menace
furtive stealthy
gainsay contradict
germane relevant
glib insincere manner
gratuitous unwarranted, uncalled for
gregarious sociable
halcyon serene
hamper obstruct
harangue tirade
harry harass
hedonism excessive pursuit of pleasure in life
hegemony authority, domination
histrionic overly dramatic

homogeneous uniform
hyperbole exaggeration
hypocritical deceiving, two-faced
iconoclast one who rails against sacred institutions
idiosyncrasy peculiarity
imminent about to happen
impecunious indigent
imperative vital, pressing
imperturbable calm
impervious impenetrable
impetuous impulsive
implicit implied
impolitic unwise
impulsive to act suddenly
impunity exemption from harm
inadvertent unintentional
incendiary inflammatory
incipient beginning
incontrovertible indisputable
incorrigible unreformable
indifferent unconcerned
indigent poor
indolent lazy
indomitable invincible
ineffable inexpressible
inert inactive
inherent innate, inborn
inhibit restrain
inimical adverse, hostile
insatiable gluttonous
insidious treacherous
insipid flat, dull
insufferable unbearable
insular narrow-minded
intangible not perceptible by touch
internecine mutually destructive
intractable unmanageable
intrepid fearless
inundate flood
inure accustom, habituate, harden
invective verbal insult
inveigle lure

irascible irritable
irresolute hesitant, uncertain
itinerary route
judicious prudent
laconic brief, terse
lassitude lethargy
laudatory commendable
levity frivolity
lucid clearly understood
lurid ghastly
Machiavellian politically crafty, cunning
magnanimous generous, kindhearted
magnate a powerful, successful person
malevolence bad intent, malice
malinger shirk
malleable moldable, tractable
misanthrope hater of mankind
miscreant evildoer
mitigate lessen the severity
mundane ordinary
nadir lowest point
narcissism self-love
nascent incipient
neologism newly coined expression
nonplus confound
noxious toxic
obfuscate bewilder, muddle
obtuse stupid
obviate make unnecessary
odious despicable
officious forward, obtrusive
omnipotent all-powerful
onerous burdensome
opprobrium disgrace
oscillate waver
paean a song of praise
paradigm a model
paragon standard of excellence
parody imitation, ridicule
parsimonious stingy
paucity scarcity
pedagogical pertaining to teaching

pedantic bookish
penchant inclination
penury poverty
pernicious destructive
perpetuity eternity
perspicacious keen
pervade permeate
philanthropic charitable
phlegmatic sluggish
piety devoutness
pious devout, holy
piquant tart-tasting, spicy
pithy concise
platitude trite remark
platonic nonsexual
plethora overabundance
polemic a controversy
posthumous after death
pragmatic practical
precarious dangerous, risky
precipitate cause
precursor forerunner
preponderance predominance
presumptuous assuming
pretentious affected, inflated
pretext excuse
prevaricate lie
probity integrity
problematic uncertain
prodigal wasteful
prodigious marvelous, enormous
prodigy a person with extraordinary ability or talent
profligate licentious, prodigal
profound deep, knowledgeable
profusion overabundance
prolific fruitful, productive
propensity inclination
proportionate commensurate
propriety decorum
prosaic uninspired, flat
proscribe prohibit
protuberance bulge
pundit politically astute person
pungent sharp smell or taste

qualms misgivings
quash put down, suppress
querulous complaining
quixotic impractical, romantic
raconteur story teller
recalcitrant stubborn
recant retract
redoubtable formidable, steadfast
refractory obstinate
relegate assign to an inferior position
renege break a promise
renounce disown
reprehensible blameworthy
reproach blame
reprobate miscreant
repudiate disavow
requisite necessary
rescind revoke
resolute determined
reticent reserved
retribution reprisal
reverent respectful
rhapsody ecstasy
rhetoric elocution, grandiloquence
sanctimonious self-righteous
sanction approval
sanguinary gory, murderous
satiate satisfy fully
satire ridicule
schism rift
secular worldly, nonreligious
sedulous diligent
severance division
skeptical doubtful
solicitous considerate, concerned
solvent financially sound
sophistry specious reasoning
specious false but plausible
spurious false, counterfeit
squander waste
stolid impassive
stupefy deaden, dumfound
stymie hinder, thwart
sullen sulky, sour
supercilious arrogant
superfluous overabundant
surfeit overabundance
synthesis combination
tacit understood without being spoken
temerity boldness
tenuous thin, insubstantial
terse concise
torpid lethargic, inactive
tractable docile, manageable
transient fleeting, temporary
trenchant incisive, penetrating
truculent fierce, savage
ubiquitous omnipresent, pervasive
ulterior hidden, covert
untenable cannot be achieved
untoward perverse
urbane refined, worldly
vacillate waver
venerable revered
veracity truthfulness
verbose wordy
vernacular common speech
vex annoy
viable capable of surviving
vilify defame
virulent deadly, poisonous
vitriolic scathing
vituperative abusive
vivacious lively
volatile unstable
voluminous bulky, extensive
voracious hungry
xenophobia fear of foreigners
zealot fanatic

Vocabulary 4000

A

a cappella without accompaniment
à la carte priced separately
a priori reasoning based on general principles
aback unexpected
abacus counting device
abandon desert, forsake
abase degrade
abash humiliate, embarrass
abate lessen
abatement alleviation
abbey monastery
abbreviate shorten
abdicate relinquish power or position
abdomen belly
abduct kidnap
aberrant abnormal
abet aid, encourage (typically of crime)
abeyance postponement
abhor detest
abide submit, endure
abject wretched
abjure renounce
ablate cut away
ablution cleansing
abode home
abolish annul
abominable detestable
aboriginal indigenous
abortive unsuccessful
abound be plentiful
abreast side-by-side
abridge shorten
abroad overseas
abrogate cancel
abrupt ending suddenly

abscess infected and inflamed tissue
abscond to run away (secretly)
absolve acquit
abstain refrain
abstract theoretical, intangible
abstruse difficult to understand
abut touch, border on
abysmal deficient, sub par
abyss chasm
academy school
accede yield
accentuate emphasize
accession attainment of rank
accessory attachment
acclaim recognition, fame
acclimate accustom oneself to a climate
acclivity ascent, incline
accolade applause
accommodate adapt
accomplice one who aids a lawbreaker
accord agreement
accost to approach and speak to someone
accouter equip
accredit authorize
accrete grow larger
accrue accumulate
accumulate amass
acerbic caustic (of speech)
acme summit
acolyte assistant
acoustic pertaining to sound
acquaint familiarize
acquiesce agree passively
acquit free from blame
acrid pungent, caustic
acrimonious caustic, bitter
acrophobia fear of heights

225

actuate induce, start
acumen insight
acute sharp, intense
ad nauseam to a ridiculous degree
ad-lib improvise
adage proverb
adamant insistent
adapt adjust to changing conditions
adaptable pliable
addendum appendix
adduce offer as example
adept skillful
adhere stick to
adherent supporter
adieu farewell
adipose fatty
adjacent next to
adjourn discontinue
adjudicate judge
adjunct addition
administer manage
admissible allowable
admonish warn gently
ado fuss
Adonis beautiful man
adroit skillful
adulation applause
adulterate contaminate, corrupt
adumbration overshadow
advent arrival
adventitious accidental
adversary opponent
adverse unfavorable
adversity hardship
advise give counsel
advocate urge
aegis that which protects
aerial pertaining to the air
aerobics exercise
aesthetic pleasing to the senses, beautiful
affable friendly
affect influence
affectation pretense
affidavit sworn written statement
affiliate associate
affiliation connection
affinity fondness
affix fasten

affliction illness
affluent abundant, wealthy
affray brawl
affront insult
aficionado devotee, ardent follower
afoul entangled
aft rear
aftermath consequence
agape wonder
agenda plan, timetable
agent provocateur agitator
aggrandize exaggerate
aggravate worsen
aggregate total, collect
aggressor attacker
aggrieve mistreat
aggrieved unjustly injured
aghast horrified
agile nimble
agitate stir up
agnate related on the father's side
agnostic not knowing whether God exists
agrarian pertaining to farming
agronomy science of crop production
air discuss, broadcast
airs pretension
akimbo with hands on hips
akin related
al fresco outdoors
alacrity swiftness
albatross large sea bird
albino lacking pigmentation
alcove recess, niche
alfresco outdoors
alias assumed name
alibi excuse
alienate estrange, antagonize
alight land, descend
allay to reassure
allege assert without proof
allegiance loyalty

Quiz 1 (Matching)

Match each word in the first column with its definition in the second column.

1. ABASE
2. ABSTAIN
3. ACOLYTE
4. ABEYANCE
5. ABRIDGE
6. ACCOLADE
7. ACRIMONIOUS
8. ADDUCE
9. ADULATION
10. AEROBICS

A. applause
B. caustic
C. shorten
D. applause
E. assistant
F. postponement
G. refrain
H. exercise
I. degrade
J. offer as example

allegory fable
allegro fast
alleviate lessen, assuage
alliteration repetition of the same sound
allocate distribute
allot allocate
allude refer to indirectly
ally unite for a purpose
almanac calendar with additional information
alms charity
aloof arrogant
altercation argument
altitude height
alto low female voice
altruism benevolence, generosity
amalgamation mixture
amass collect
ambient surrounding, environment
ambiguous unclear
ambivalence conflicting emotions
ambulatory able to walk
ameliorate improve
amenable agreeable
amend correct
amenities courtesies, comforts
amenity pleasantness
amiable friendly
amid among
amiss wrong, out of place
amity friendship
amnesty pardon
amoral without morals
amorous loving, sexual
amorphous shapeless

amortize pay by installments
amphibious able to operate in water and land
amphitheater oval-shaped theater
amuck murderous frenzy
amulet charm, talisman
amuse entertain
anachronistic out of historical order
anaerobic without oxygen
anagram a word formed by rearranging the letters of another word
analgesic pain-soother
analogous similar
analogy point by point comparison
anarchist terrorist
anarchy absence of government
anathema curse
anecdote story
aneurysm bulging in a blood vessel
angst anxiety, dread
animadversion critical remark
animated exuberant
animosity dislike
animus hate
annals historical records
annex to attach
annihilate destroy
annotate to add explanatory notes
annul cancel
annular ring-shaped
anodyne pain soothing
anoint consecrate
anomalous abnormal
anonymity state of being anonymous
antagonistic hostile

antagonize harass
antechamber waiting room
antediluvian ancient, obsolete
anthology collection
anthrax disease
antic caper, prank
antipathy repulsion, hated
antipodal exactly opposite
antiquated outdated, obsolete
antiquity ancient times
antithesis direct opposite
apartheid racial segregation
apathetic unconcerned
apathy indifference
ape mimic
aperture opening
apex highest point
aphasia speechless
aphorism maxim
aplomb poise
apocalyptic ominous, doomed
apocryphal of doubtful authenticity
apoplexy stroke
apostate one who abandons one's faith
apotheosis deification
appall horrify
apparition phantom
appease pacify
appellation title
append affix
apposite apt
apprehensive anxious
apprise inform
approbation approval
apropos appropriate
apt suitable
aptitude ability
aquatic pertaining to water
arbiter judge
arbitrament final judgment
arbitrary tyrannical, capricious
arcane secret
archaic antiquated
archetype original model
archipelago group of island
archives public records
ardent passionate
ardor passion

arduous hard
argonauts gold-seekers, adventurers
argot specialized vocabulary
aria operatic song
arid dry, dull
aristocrat nobleman
armada fleet of ships
armistice truce
arraign indict
array arrangement
arrears in debt
arrogate seize without right
arroyo gully
arsenal supply
artful skillful, cunning
articulate well-spoken
artifice trick
artless naive, simple
ascend rise
ascendancy powerful state
ascertain discover
ascetic self-denying
ascribe to attribute
aseptic sterile
ashen pale
asinine stupid
askance to view with suspicion
askew crooked
aspersion slander
asphyxiate suffocate
aspirant contestant
aspiration ambition
assail attack
assassin murderer
assent agree
assert affirm
assess appraise
assiduous hard-working
assimilate absorb
assonance partial rhyme
assuage lessen (pain)
astral pertaining to stars
astringent causing contraction, severe
astute wise
asunder apart
asylum place of refuge
asymmetric uneven

atavistic exhibiting the characteristics of one's forebears
atelier workshop
atoll reef
atomize vaporize
atone make amends
atrophy the wasting away of muscle
attenuate weaken
attest testify
attire dress
attribute ascribe
attrition deterioration, reduction
atypical abnormal
au courant well informed
audacity boldness
audient listening, attentive
audition tryout
augment increase
augur predict
august noble
aura atmosphere, emanation
auspices patronage, protection
auspicious favorable
austere harsh, Spartan

authorize grant, sanction
automaton robot
autonomous self-governing
auxiliary secondary
avail assistance
avant garde vanguard
avarice greed
avatar incarnation
averse loath, reluctant
avert turn away
avian pertaining to birds
avid enthusiastic
avocation hobby
avouch attest, guarantee
avow declare
avuncular like an uncle
awry crooked
axiom self-evident truth
aye affirmative vote
azure sky blue

B

babbittry smugness

Quiz 2 (Matching)

Match each word in the first column with its definition in the second column.

1.	ANATHEMA	A.	hard
2.	ANNIHILATE	B.	curse
3.	ANOMALOUS	C.	gully
4.	APATHETIC	D.	suffocate
5.	ARCHAIC	E.	antiquated
6.	ARDUOUS	F.	destroy
7.	ARROYO	G.	abnormal
8.	ASPHYXIATE	H.	unconcerned
9.	ASTRINGENT	I.	make amends
10.	ATONE	J.	causing contraction

---

bacchanal orgy
badger pester
badinage banter
bagatelle nonentity, trifle
bailiwick area of concern or business
baleen whalebone
baleful hostile, malignant
balk hesitate
balky hesitant

ballad song
ballast counterbalance
ballistics study of projectiles
balm soothing ointment
banal trite
bandy exchange
bane poison, nuisance
barbarian savage
bard poet

baroque ornate
barrister lawyer
bask take pleasure in, sun
basso low male voice
bastion fort
bathos sentimentality
batten fasten, board up
battery physical attack
bauble trinket
beatify sanctify
beatitude state of bliss
beckon lure
becoming proper
bedlam uproar
befit to be suitable
beget produce, procreate
begrudge resent, envy
beguile deceive, seduce
behemoth monster
behest command
beholden in debt
belabor assail verbally
belated delayed, overdue
beleaguer besiege
belfry bell tower
belie misrepresent
belittle disparage
bellicose warlike
belligerent combative
bellow shout
bellwether leader, guide
bemoan lament
bemused bewildered
benchmark standard
benediction blessing
benefactor patron
benevolent kind
benign harmless
bent determined
bequeath will
bequest gift, endowment
berate scold
bereave rob
bereft deprived of
berserk crazed
beseech implore
beset harass, encircle
besiege beleaguer, surround

besmirch slander, sully
bespeak attest
bestial beast-like, brutal
bestow offer, grant
betrothed engaged
bevy group
bibliography list of sources of information
bicameral having two legislative branches
bicker quarrel
biennial occurring every two years
bilateral two-sided
bilious ill-tempered
bilk swindle
biodegradable naturally decaying
biopsy removing tissue for examination
biped two-footed animal
bistro tavern, cafe
bivouac encampment
blandish flatter, grovel
blasé bored with life
blasphemy insulting God
bleak cheerless
blight decay
bliss happiness
blithe joyous
bloated swollen
bode portend
bogus forged, false
bogy bugbear
boisterous noisy
bolt move quickly and suddenly
bombast pompous speech
bon vivant gourmet, epicure
bona fide made in good faith
bonanza a stroke of luck
boon payoff
boor vulgar person
bootless unavailing
booty loot
botch bungle
bourgeois middle class
bovine cow-like
boycott abstain in protest
bracing refreshing
brackish salty
brandish display menacingly
bravado feigned bravery
bravura technically difficult

brawn strength
brevity shortness of expression
brigand robber
brink edge
broach bring up a topic of conversation
bromide cliché
brook tolerate
browbeat to bully
brusque curt
bucolic rustic
buffet blow
buffoon fool
bulwark fortification
buncombe empty, showy talk
buoyant floatable
burgeon sprout
burlesque farce
burly husky
buttress support

C

cabal plot
cabaret night club
cache hiding place
cachet prestige
cacophony dissonance, harsh noise
cadaver corpse
cadaverous haggard
cadence rhythm
cadet a student of a military academy
cadge beg
cadre small group
cajole encourage, coax
calamity disaster
calculating scheming
caliber ability
callous insensitive
callow inexperienced
calumny slander
camaraderie fellowship
canaille rabble
canard hoax
candid frank, unrehearsed
candor frankness
canine pertaining to dogs
canon rule
cant insincere speech

cantankerous peevish
cantata musical composition
canvass survey
capacious spacious
capillary thin tube
capital most significant, pertaining to wealth
capitol legislative building
capitulate surrender
capricious fickle, impulsive
caption title
captious fond of finding fault in others
captivate engross, fascinate
carafe bottle
carbine rifle
carcinogenic causing cancer
carcinoma tumor
cardinal chief
cardiologist one who studies the heart
careen swerve
carrion decaying flesh
cartographer mapmaker
cascade waterfall
cashmere fine wool from Asia
Cassandra unheeded prophet
castigate criticize
castrate remove the testicles
casuistry specious reasoning
cataclysm catastrophe
catastrophic disastrous
categorical absolute, certain
cathartic purgative, purifying
catholic universal, worldly
caucus meeting
cause célèbre celebrated legal case
caustic scathing (of speech)
cauterize to sear
cavalier disdainful, nonchalant
caveat warning
caveat emptor buyer beware
cavil quibble
cavort frolic
cede transfer ownership
celestial heavenly
celibate abstaining from sex
cenotaph empty tomb
censorious condemning speech
censure condemn
ceramics pottery
cerebral pertaining to the brain

ACT Verbal Prep Course

Quiz 3 (Matching)

Match each word in the first column with its definition in the second column.

1.	BESMIRCH	A.	unheeded prophet
2.	BICAMERAL	B.	peevish
3.	BILATERAL	C.	pertaining to dogs
4.	BOOTLESS	D.	plot
5.	BRANDISH	E.	farce
6.	BURLESQUE	F.	display menacingly
7.	CABAL	G.	unavailing
8.	CANINE	H.	two-sided
9.	CANTANKEROUS	I.	having two legislative branches
10.	CASSANDRA	J.	sully

---

cessation a stoping
chafe abrade
chagrin embarrassment
chalice goblet
champion defend
chaperon escort
charade pantomime
charlatan quack
chartreuse greenish yellow
chary cautious
chaste pure, virgin
chasten castigate
chateau castle
cheeky brass, forward
cherub cupid
cherubic sweet, innocent
chicanery trickery
chide scold
chimerical imaginary, dreamlike
choleric easily angered
chortle laugh, snort
chronic continual
chronicle a history
chronology arrangement by time
churl a boor
chutzpah gall
Cimmerian dim, unlit
cipher zero
circa about
circuitous roundabout
circumcise remove the foreskin
circumlocution roundabout expression
circumspect cautious
circumvent evade

citadel fortress
citation summons to appear in court
clamor noise
clan extended family
clandestine secret
claustrophobia fear of enclosed places
cleave split
cleft split
clemency forgiveness
clique a small group
cloister refuge
clone duplicate
clout influence
cloven split
cloy glut
cloyed jaded
co-opt preempt, usurp
coagulate thicken
coalesce combine
coda concluding passage
coddle pamper
codicil supplement to a will
coercion force
coffer strong box
cogent well-put, convincing
cogitate ponder
cognate from the same source
cognizant aware
cognomen family name
cohabit live together
cohere stick together
cohort an associate
coiffure hairdo
collaborate work together

collar seize
collateral securities for a debt
colloquial informal speech
colloquy conference
collusion conspiracy
colonnade row of columns
comatose stupor
combine unite, blend
commandeer seize for military use
commemorate observe
commend praise
commensurate proportionate
commiserate empathize
commissary food store
commission authorization to perform a task
commodious spacious
commodity product
commodore naval officer
communion fellowship
commutation exchange, substitution
commute lessen punishment
compact covenant
compassion kindness
compatible well-matched, harmonious
compatriot countryman
compelling convincing
compendium summary
compensate make up for
compensatory redeeming
competence skillfulness
compile collect
complacent self-satisfied
compliant submissive
complicity guilt by association
comport to conduct oneself
composed cool, self-possessed
compound augment
comprehensive thorough
comprise consist of
compulsive obsessive
compulsory obligatory
compunction remorse
concatenate link
concave curving inward
concede yield, grant
concerted done together
conch spiral shell
conciliatory reconciling

concise brief
conclusive convincing, ending doubt
concoct devise
concomitant accompanying, concurrent
concord accord
concordat agreement
concourse throng
concubine mistress
concur agree
concurrent simultaneous
condescend patronize, talk down to
condiment seasoning
condolence commiseration
condone overlook wrong doing, pardon
conducive helping
conduit pipe
confabulate discuss
confection candy
confederacy alliance
confer bestow
conference meeting
confidant trusted friend
confide trust another (with secrets)
confiscate seize
conflagration large fire
confluence flowing together
confound bewilder
confront challenge
confuse perplex
confute disprove
congeal solidify
congenial friendly
congenital inborn, existing from birth
congeries pile
congruence conformity
coniferous bearing cones
conjecture hypothesis
conjugal pertaining to marriage
conjure summon
connive conspire
connoisseur an expert, gourmet
consanguineous related by blood
conscientious honorable, upright
conscription draft, enlistment
consecrate make holy
consecutive one after another
consensus general agreement
considered well thought out, contemplated

consign assign
consolation comfort
console comfort
consolidate unite, strengthen
consonant harmonious
consort spouse
consortium cartel
conspicuous obvious
conspire plot
constellation arrangement of stars
consternation anxiety, bewilderment
constrained confined
construe interpret
consummate perfect
contagion infectious agent
contemplate meditate
contempt disdain
contend struggle
contented satisfied
contentious argumentative
contiguous adjacent, abutting
continence self-control
contingent conditional

contort twist
contraband illicit goods
contraction shrinkage
contractual related to a contract
contrariety opposition
contrast difference, comparison
contravene oppose
contretemps unfortunate occurrence
contrite apologetic
contrive arrange, artificial
controversial subject to dispute
controvert dispute
contumacy disobedience
contusion bruise
conundrum puzzle, enigma
convene assemble (a group)
conventional customary, standard
converge come together
conversant familiar
converse opposite
convex curving outward
convey communicate
conviction strongly held belief

Quiz 4 (Matching)

Match each word in the first column with its definition in the second column.

1. COMMANDEER	A. seize for military use
2. COMMUNION	B. apologetic
3. COMPATRIOT	C. perfect
4. CONCERTED	D. accord
5. CONCORD	E. done together
6. CONFLUENCE	F. pile
7. CONGERIES	G. flowing together
8. CONSONANT	H. harmonious
9. CONSUMMATE	I. countryman
10. CONTRITE	J. fellowship

convivial sociable, festive
convocation gathering
convoke convene, summon
convoluted twisted, complicated
copious abundant
coquette a flirt
cordial friendly
cordon bond, chain
cornucopia cone-shaped horn filled with fruit
corollary consequence
coronation crowning of a sovereign

corporeal of the body
corps group of people
corpulent fat
corroborate confirm
cortege procession
coruscate sparkle
cosmopolitan worldly, sophisticated
cosset coddle
coterie small group
countenance facial expression
countermand overrule

counterstrike strike back
countervail counterbalance
coup master stroke
coup de grâce final stroke, a blow of mercy
court-martial military trial
courtesan prostitute
courtier member of the king's court
covenant agreement, pact
covert secret
covet desire
cower showing fear
crass crude
crave desire
craven cowardly
credence belief
credenza buffet
credulity gullibility
credulous believing
creed belief
crescendo becoming louder
crestfallen dejected
crevice crack
cringe cower
criterion a standard used in judging
critique examination, criticism
croon sing
cruet bottle
crux gist, key
cryptic mysterious
cubism a style of painting
cudgel club
culinary pertaining to cooking
cull pick out, select
culminate climax
culpable blameworthy
culprit offender
culvert drain
cumbersome unwieldy
cumulative accumulate
cupidity greed
curb restrain, block
curmudgeon boor
curriculum course of study
curry seek favor by flattery
cursory hasty
curt abrupt, rude
curtail shorten
cyclone storm

cynical scornful of the motives of others
cynosure celebrity
czar Russian emperor

D

dab touch lightly
dais platform
dally procrastinate
dank damp
dauntless courageous
de facto actual
de jure legally
de rigueur very formal
deadpan expressionless
dearth scarcity
debacle a rout, defeat
debase degrade
debauch corrupt
debauchery indulgence
debilitate weaken
debonair sophisticated, affable
debrief interrogate
debunk refute, expose
debutante a girl debuting into society
decadence decay (e.g. moral or cultural)
decant pour
decapitate kill by beheading
decathlon athletic contest
deceive trick
deciduous shedding leaves
decimate destroy
decipher decode
decline decrease in number
decommission take a ship out of service
decorous seemly
decorum protocol
decree official order
decrepitude enfeeblement
decry castigate
deduce conclude
deduct subtract
deem judge
deface mar, disfigure
defamation (noun) slander
defame (verb) slander
defeatist one who is resigned to defeat
defer postpone

deference courteously yielding to another
deficit shortage
defile pollute
definitive conclusive, final
deflect turn aside
deflower despoil
defraud swindle
defray pay
deft skillful
defunct extinct
degrade demean
dehydrate dry out
deign condescend
deity a god
delectable delicious
delegate authorize
delete remove
deleterious harmful
deliberate ponder
delineate draw a line around, describe
delinquent negligent, culpable
delirium mental confusion, ecstasy
delude deceive
deluge a flood
delve dig, explore (of ideas)
demagogue a politician who appeals to base instincts
demean degrade
demeanor behavior
demented deranged
demise death
demobilize disband
demography study of human populations
demoralize dishearten
demote lower in rank
demur take exception
demure sedate, reserved
denigrate defame
denizen dweller
denomination class, sect
denote signify, stand for
denouement resolution
denounce condemn
denude strip bare
depart leave
depict portray
deplete exhaust

deplore condemn
deploy arrange forces
deportment behavior
deposition testimony
depravity immorality
deprecate belittle
depredation preying on, plunder
deprive take away
deracinate uproot
derelict negligent
deride ridicule
derisive mocking
derogatory degrading
derrick crane
desecrate profane
desiccate dehydrate
designate appoint
desist stop
desolate forsaken
despicable contemptible
despise loathe
despondent depressed
despot tyrant
destitute poor
desuetude disuse
desultory without direction in life
detached emotionally removed
detain confine
détente truce
detention confinement
deter discourage, prevent
deterrent hindrance
detract lessen
detractor one who criticizes
detrimental harmful
detritus debris
devastate lay waste
deviate turn away from
devise plan
devoid empty
devotee enthusiast, follower
devout pious
diabolical devilish
dialectic pertaining to debate
diaphanous sheer, translucent
diatribe long denunciation

> **Quiz 5 (Matching)**
>
> Match each word in the first column with its definition in the second column.
>
> 1. DEBUNK   A. decode
> 2. DECIPHER   B. refute
> 3. DEDUCE   C. conclusive
> 4. DEFINITIVE   D. conclude
> 5. DEFUNCT   E. to draw a line around
> 6. DELINEATE   F. extinct
> 7. DENOMINATION   G. belittle
> 8. DEPRECATE   H. sect
> 9. DESOLATE   I. pertaining to debate
> 10. DIALECTIC   J. forsaken

dicey risky
dichotomy a division into two parts
dictate command
dictum saying
didactic instructional
diffident shy
digress ramble **dilapidated** neglected
dilate enlarge
dilatory procrastinating
dilemma a difficult choice
dilettante amateur, dabbler
diligent hard-working
diminution reduction
diocese district
dire dreadful
dirigible airship, blimp
disabuse correct
disaffect alienate
disarray disorder
disavow deny
disband disperse
disburse pay out
discernible visible
discerning observant
disclaim renounce
disconcert confuse
disconsolate inconsolable
discord lack of harmony
discourse conversation
discreet prudent
discrepancy difference
discrete separate
discretion prudence
discriminating able to see differences

discursive rambling
disdain contempt
disengage release, detach
disfigure mar, ruin
disgruntle disappointed
dishevel muss
disinclination unwillingness
disingenuous deceptive
disinter unearth
disinterested impartial
disjointed disconnected, incoherent
dismal gloomy
dismantle take apart
dismay dread
disparage belittle
disparate various
disparity difference
dispassionate impartial
dispatch send
dispel cause to banish
disperse scatter
dispirit discourage
disposition attitude
dispossess take away possessions
disputatious fond of arguing
dispute debate
disquietude anxiety
disquisition elaborate treatise
disrepute disgrace
dissemble pretend
disseminate distribute
dissent disagree
dissertation lecture
dissidence disagreement

dissipate scatter
dissolute profligate, immoral
dissolution disintegration
dissonance discord
dissuade deter
distend swell
distortion misinterpret, lie
distract divert
distrait preoccupied, absent-minded
distraught distressed
distrust suspect
dither move without purpose
diurnal daily
diva prima donna
diverge branch off
diverse varying
diversion pastime
diversity variety
divest strip, deprive
dividend distributed profits
divine foretell
divisive causing conflict
divulge disclose
docile domesticated, trained
dock curtail
doctrinaire dogmatic
document verify
dodder tremble
dogged persistent
doggerel poor verse
dogmatic certain, unchanging in opinion
dolce sweetly
doldrums dullness
doleful sorrowful
dolorous gloomy
domicile home
dominion authority
don assume, put on
donor contributor
dormant asleep
dossier file
dotage senility
doting attending
double-entendre having two meanings one of which is sexually suggestive
doughty resolute, unafraid
dour sullen
dowager widow

doyen dean of a group
draconian harsh
dregs residue, riffraff
drivel inane speech
droll amusing
drone speak in a monotonic voice
dubious doubtful
ductile stretchable
dudgeon resentment, indignant humor
duenna governess
duet twosome
dulcet melodious
dupe one who is easily trick, victim
duplicity deceit, treachery
duress coercion
dynamic energetic

E

ebb recede
ebullient exuberant
eccentric odd, weird
ecclesiastical churchly
echelon degree
éclat brilliance
eclectic from many sources
ectoderm top layer of skin
ecumenical universal
edict order
edifice building
edify instruct
editorialize express an opinion
educe draw forth, evoke
efface obliterate
effeminate unmanly
effervescence exuberance
effete worn out
efficacious effective
efficacy effectiveness
effigy likeness, mannequin
effloresce to bloom
effrontery insolence
effulgent brilliant
effusion pouring forth
egocentric self-centered
egregious grossly wrong
egress exit
ejaculate exclaim

eke to supplement with great effort, strain
elaboration detailed explanation
elate raise spirits
electorate voters
eleemosynary pertaining to charity
elegant refined, exquisite
elegiac sad
elephantine large
elicit provoke
elide omit
elite upper-class
ellipsis omission of words
eloquent well-spoken
elucidate make clear
elude evade
elusive evasive
emaciated underfed, gaunt
emancipate liberate
emasculate castrate, dispirit
embargo restriction
embellish exaggerate
embezzlement theft
emblazon imprint, brand
embody personify
embrace accept
embrangle embroil
embroil involve
embryonic rudimentary
emend correct
emergent appearing
emeritus retired, but retaining title
eminent distinguished, famous
emissary messenger
emote to display exaggerated emotion
empathy compassion, sympathy
employ use
empower enable, grant
emulate imitate
enact decree, ordain
enamored charmed, captivated
enate related on the mother's side
encapsulate condense
enchant charm
enclave area enclosed within another region
encomium praise
encompass contain, encircle
encore additional performance
encroach trespass

encumber burden
encyclopedic comprehensive
endear enamor
endeavor attempt, strive
endemic peculiar to a particular region
endocrinologist one who studies glands of internal secretion
endoderm within the skin
endorse approve
endowment property, gift
endure suffer
enervate weaken
enfranchise liberate
engaging enchanting, charming
engender generate
engrave carve into a material
engross captivate
engulf overwhelm
enhance improve
enigmatic puzzling
enjoin urge, order
enlighten inform
enlist join
enmity hostility, hatred
ennoble exalt
ennui boredom
enormity large, tragic
ensemble musical group
enshroud cover
ensnare trap
ensue follow immediately
entail involve, necessitate
enterprise undertaking
enthrall mesmerize
entice lure
entomology the study of insects
entourage assemblage
entreat plead
entrench fortify
entrepreneur businessman
enumerate count
enviable desirable
envision imagine
envoy messenger
eon long period of time
ephemeral short-lived
epic majestic
epicure gourmet

epidemic spreading rapidly
epidemiology study of the spread of disease
epigram saying
episode incident
epistemology the branch of philosophy dealing with knowledge

Quiz 6 (Matching)

Match each word in the first column with its definition in the second column.

1.	DORMANT	A.	exuberant
2.	DOUGHTY	B.	puzzling
3.	DUET	C.	comprehensive
4.	EBULLIENT	D.	asleep
5.	EFFEMINATE	E.	omission of words
6.	ELLIPSIS	F.	unmanly
7.	EMANCIPATE	G.	charm
8.	ENCHANT	H.	liberate
9.	ENCYCLOPEDIC	I.	twosome
10.	ENIGMATIC	J.	resolute

---

epithet name, appellation
epoch era
epoxy glue
equable even-tempered
equanimity composure
equine pertaining to horses
equitable fair
equivocate make intentionally ambiguous
era period of time
eradicate abolish
ergo therefore
erode wear away
err mistake, misjudge
errant wandering
erratic constantly changing
erroneous mistaken
ersatz artificial
erudite learned
erupt burst forth
escalate intensify
escapade adventure
escarpment a steep slope
eschew avoid
esoteric known by only a few
esplanade boardwalk
espouse advocate
esteem respect
esthetic artistic
estimable meritorious
estrange alienate
eternal endless
ethereal light, airy
ethical conforming to accepted standards of behavior
ethos beliefs of a group
etiquette manners
etymology study of words
euphemism genteel expression
euphoria elation
euthanasia mercy-killing
evade avoid
evanescent fleeting, very brief
evangelical proselytizing
evasive elusive
eventful momentous
eventual ultimate, coming
eventuate bring about
evidential pertaining to evidence
evince attest, demonstrate
eviscerate disembowel
evoke draw forth
evolution gradual change
ewe female sheep
ex officio by virtue of position
exacerbate worsen
exact use authority to force payment
exacting demanding, difficult
exalt glorify
exasperate irritate
excerpt selection, extract
excision removal
exclaim shout

exclude shut out
exclusive prohibitive
excommunicate expel
excruciate torture
execrable abominable
execute put into effect
exegesis interpretation
exemplary outstanding
exempt excuse
exhaustive thorough
exhibitionist one who draws attention to himself
exhort strongly urge
exhume uncover
exigency urgency
exiguous scanty
exile banish
exodus departure, migration
exonerate free from blame
exorbitant expensive
exorcise expel
expanse extent of land
expansive sweeping
expedient advantageous
expedite hasten
expel drive out
expertise knowledge, ability
expiate atone
expletive oath
expliate atone
explicate explain
explicit definite, clear
exploit utilize, milk
expose divulge
expostulate protest
expound explain
expropriate dispossess
expunge erase
exquisite beautifully made
extant existing
extemporize improvise
extent scope
extenuate mitigate
extirpate seek out and destroy
extol praise highly
extort extract, force
extract to pull out, exact
extradite deport, deliver
extraneous not essential

extrapolate infer
extremity farthest point
extricate disentangle
extroverted outgoing
extrude force out
exuberant joyous
exude emit
exult rejoice

F

fabrication a lie
facade mask
facet aspect
facetious joking, sarcastic
facile easy
facilitate make easier
facility skill
facsimile duplicate
faction clique, sect
factious causing disagreement
factitious artificial
factotum handyman
fallacious false
fallacy false belief
fallow unproductive, unplowed
falsetto high male voice
falter waver
fanaticism excessive zeal
fane temple
fanfare publicity
farcical absurd
farrago mixture
fascism totalitarianism
fastidious meticulous
fatal resulting in death
fathom understand
fatuity foolishness
fatuous inane, stupid
fauna animals
faux pas false step, mistake
fealty loyalty
feasible likely to succeed
feat deed
febrile feverish, delirious
feckless incompetent
fecund fertile
feign pretend

felicity happiness
felonious criminal
femme fatale a woman who leads men to their destruction
fend ward off
feral untamed, wild
ferment turmoil
ferret rummage through
fertile fruitful
fervor intensity
fester decay
festive joyous
festoon decorate
fete to honor
fetid stinking
fetters shackles
fey eccentric, whimsical
fiasco debacle
fiat decree
fickle always changing one's mind
fictitious invented, imaginary
fidelity loyalty
figment falsehood, fantasy
filch steal
filial son
filibuster long speech

fillip stimulus
finale conclusion
finesse skill
firebrand agitator
firmament sky
fiscal monetary
fitful irregular
fjord inlet
flabbergasted amazed, dumbfounded
flagellate whip
flagrant outrageous
flail whip
fledgling just beginning, struggling
flippant pert
florid ruddy
flout to show disregard for the law or rules
fluctuate waver, vary
foible weakness, minor fault
foil defeat
foist palm off a fake
foment instigate
font source, fountainhead, set of type
forage search for food
foray raid
forbear abstain
force majeure superior force

Quiz 7 (Matching)

Match each word in the first column with its definition in the second column.

1.	EXHORT	A.	free from blame
2.	EXONERATE	B.	strongly urge
3.	EXPOSTULATE	C.	agitator
4.	EXTRADITE	D.	untamed
5.	EXULT	E.	debacle
6.	FACTITIOUS	F.	inane
7.	FATUOUS	G.	artificial
8.	FERAL	H.	deport
9.	FIASCO	I.	rejoice
10.	FIREBRAND	J.	protest

---

foreclose exclude
forensic pertaining to debate
foresight ability to predict the future
forestall thwart
forgo relinquish
forsake abandon
forswear deny
forthright frank

forthwith immediately
fortify strengthen
fortitude patience, courage
fortuitous lucky
foster encourage
founder sink
fracas noisy fight
fragile easily broken

fragmented broken into fragments
fraternity brotherhood
fraught filled
frenetic harried, neurotic
fret worry
fritter squander
frivolity playfulness
frolic romp, play
frond bending tree
frugal thrifty
fruitful productive
fruition realization, completion
fruitless unprofitable, barren
fulminate denounce, menace
fulsome excessive, insincere
fuming angry
furlough leave of absence
furor commotion
furtive stealthy
fusillade bombardment
futile hopeless

G

gaffe embarrassing mistake
gainful profitable
gainsay contradict
galvanize excite to action
gambit plot
gamut range
gargantuan large
garner gather
garnish decorate
garrote stranglehold
garrulous talkative
gauche awkward
genealogy ancestry
generic general
genesis beginning
genetics study of heredity
genre kind, category
genteel elegant
genuflect kneel in reverence
genuine authentic
geriatrics pertaining to old age
germane relevant
ghastly horrible
gibe heckle

gingivitis inflammation of the gums
gist essence
glabrous without hair
glaucoma disorder of the eye
glean gather
glib insincere manner
glower stare angrily
glut surplus, excess
glutton one who eats too much
gnarl deform
gnome dwarf-like being
goad encourage
googol a very large number
gorge stuff, satiate
gorgon ugly person
gormandize eat voraciously
gory bloody
gossamer thin and flimsy
Gothic medieval
gouge overcharge
gracious kindness
gradient incline, rising by degrees
gradual by degrees
grandiose impressive, large
granular grainy
grapple struggle
gratis free
gratitude thankfulness
gratuitous unwarranted, uncalled for
gratuity tip
gravamen the essential part of an accusation
gravity seriousness
gregarious sociable
grievous tragic, heinous
grimace expression of disgust
grisly gruesome
grovel crawl, obey
grudging reluctant
guffaw laughter
guile deceit
gullible easily deceived
gusto great enjoyment
guttural throaty
gyrate whirl

H

habitat natural environment

habituate accustom
hackneyed trite
haggard gaunt
halcyon serene
hale healthy
hallucination delusion
hamper obstruct
hapless unlucky
harangue tirade
harass torment
harbinger forerunner
harbor give shelter, conceal
hardy healthy
harlequin clown
harp complain incessantly
harridan hag
harrowing distressing
harry harass
haughty arrogant
haven refuge
havoc destruction
hearsay gossip
hedonism the pursuit of pleasure in life
heed follow advice
heedless careless
hegemony authority, domination
hegira a journey to a more pleasant place
heinous vile
heliocentric having the sun as a center
helix a spiral
helots slaves
herald harbinger
herbivorous feeding on plants
Herculean powerful, large
hermetic airtight, sealed
hermit one who lives in solitude
herpetologist one who studies reptiles
heterodox departing form established doctrines
heuristic teaching device or method
hew cut
heyday glory days
hiatus interruption
hibernal wintry
hidalgo nobleman
hidebound prejudiced
hideous horrible
hie to hasten
highbrow intellectual

hirsute bearded
histrionic overly dramatic
holograph written entirely by hand
homage respect
homely plain
homily sermon
homogeneous uniform
homonym words that are identical in spelling and pronunciation
hone sharpen
horde group
hortatory inspiring good deeds
hospice shelter
hovel shanty, cabin
hoyden tomboy
hubris arrogance
hue color
humane compassionate
humanities languages and literature
humility humbleness
hummock knoll, mound
humus soil
husbandry management
hybrid crossbreed
hydrophobia fear of water
hygienic sanitary
hymeneal pertaining to marriage
hymn religious song
hyperactive overactive
hyperbole exaggeration
hypertension elevated blood pressure
hypocritical deceiving, two-faced
hypoglycemic low blood sugar
hypothermia low body temperature

I

ibidem in the same place
ichthyology study of fish
iconoclast one who rails against sacred institutions
idiosyncrasy peculiarity
idyllic natural, picturesque
ignoble dishonorable
ilk class, clan
illicit unlawful
illimitable limitless
illusory fleeting
illustrious famous

imbibe drink
imbue infuse
immaculate spotlessly clean

immaterial irrelevant
immense huge

Quiz 8 (Matching)

Match each word in the first column with its definition in the second column.

1. GRANDIOSE
2. GRIEVOUS
3. HALCYON
4. HARLEQUIN
5. HEDONISM
6. HEURISTIC
7. HIDEBOUND
8. HUBRIS
9. HYMENEAL
10. IMBIBE

A. drink
B. pertaining to marriage
C. arrogance
D. prejudiced
E. teaching device or method
F. the pursuit of pleasure in life
G. clown
H. serene
I. heinous
J. impressive

---

immerse bathe
imminent about to happen
immobile still
immolate sacrifice
immunity exemption from prosecution
immure build a wall around
immutable unchangeable
impair injure
impale pierce
impartial not biased
impasse deadlock
impassioned fiery, emotional
impassive calm
impeach accuse, charge
impeccable faultless
impecunious indigent
impede hinder
impediment obstacle
impel urge, force
impending approaching
imperative vital, pressing
imperceptible slight, intangible
imperialism colonialism
imperil endanger
imperious domineering
impertinent insolent
imperturbable calm
impervious impenetrable
impetuous impulsive
impetus stimulus, spark
impinge encroach, touch

implant instill
implausible unlikely
implement carry out, execute
implicate incriminate
implicit implied
implore entreat
implosion bursting inward
impolitic unwise
imponderable difficult to estimate
import meaning, significance
importune urgent request
imposing intimidating
imposition intrusion
impotent powerless
impound seize
imprecation curse, inculcate
impregnable invincible
impresario promoter
impressionable susceptible, easily influenced
impressionism a style of painting
imprimatur sanction
impromptu spontaneous
improvise invent
impudence insolence
impugn criticize
impulse inclination
impulsive to act suddenly
impunity exemption from harm
impute charge
in toto in full, entirely
inadvertent unintentional

inadvisable not recommended
inalienable that which cannot be taken away
inane vacuous, stupid
inanimate inorganic, lifeless
inaudible cannot be heard
inaugurate induct
inborn innate
incalculable immeasurable
incandescent brilliant
incantation chant
incapacitate disable
incarcerate imprison
incarnate embody, personify
incendiary inflammatory
incense enrage
incentive stimulus
incessant unceasing
incest sex among family members
inchoate just begun
incidental insignificant, minor
incinerate burn
incipient beginning
incision cut
incisive keen, penetrating
incite foment, provoke
incivility disdain
inclement harsh
inclusive comprehensive
incognito disguised
incommunicado unable to communicate with others
incomparable peerless
incompatibility inability to live in harmony
inconceivable unthinkable
incongruous out of place, absurd
inconsiderate thoughtless
inconspicuous not noticeable
incontrovertible indisputable
incorporate combine
incorrigible unreformable
incredulous skeptical
increment step, increase
incriminate accuse
incubus nightmare
inculcate instill, indoctrinate
inculpate accuse
incumbent obligatory
incursion raid

indecent offensive
indecorous unseemly
indelible permanent
indemnity insurance
indict charge
indifferent unconcerned
indigenous native
indigent poor
indignant resentment of injustice
indiscreet lacking sound judgment, rash
indiscriminate random
indispensable vital, essential
indistinct blurry, without clear features
indolent lazy
indomitable invincible
indubitable unquestionable
induce persuade
indulge succumb to desire
indurate harden
industrious hard-working
inebriate intoxicate
ineffable inexpressible
ineffectual futile
ineluctable inescapable
inept unfit
inert inactive
inestimable priceless
inevitable unavoidable, predestined
inexorable relentless
infallible unerring
infamous notorious
infamy shame
infantry foot soldiers
infatuate immature love
infer conclude
infernal hellish
infidel nonbeliever
infidelity disloyalty
infiltrate trespass
infinitesimal very small
infirmary clinic
infirmity ailment
inflammatory incendiary
influx inflow
infraction violation
infringe encroach
infuriate enrage
infuse inspire, instill

ingenious clever
ingrate ungrateful person
ingratiate pleasing, flattering, endearing
ingress entering
inherent innate, inborn
inhibit restrain
inimical adverse, hostile
inimitable peerless
iniquitous unjust, wicked
iniquity sin
initiate begin
initiation induction ceremony
injunction command
inkling hint
innate inborn
innervate invigorate
innocuous harmless
innovative new, useful idea
innuendo insinuation
inopportune untimely
inordinate excessive
inquest investigation
inquisition interrogation
inquisitive curious
insatiable gluttonous
inscribe engrave

inscrutable cannot be fully understood
insensate without feeling
insidious treacherous
insignia emblems
insinuate allude
insipid flat, dull
insolent insulting
insolvent bankrupt
insouciant nonchalant
installment portion
instant at once
instigate incite
insubordinate disobedient
insufferable unbearable
insular narrow-minded
insuperable insurmountable
insurgent rebellious
insurrection uprising
intangible not perceptible by touch
integral essential
integrate make whole
integration unification
integument a covering
intelligentsia the intellectual elite of society
intensive extreme
inter bury

Quiz 9 (Matching)

Match each word in the first column with its definition in the second column.

1.	INCONGRUOUS	A.	harden
2.	INCONSPICUOUS	B.	relentless
3.	INDECOROUS	C.	hostile
4.	INDIGNANT	D.	cannot be fully understood
5.	INDURATE	E.	out of place, absurd
6.	INEXORABLE	F.	not noticeable
7.	INIMICAL	G.	unseemly
8.	INSCRUTABLE	H.	resentment of injustice
9.	INSOUCIANT	I.	nonchalant
10.	INSUPERABLE	J.	insurmountable

intercede plead on behalf of another
intercept prevent
interdict prohibit
interject interrupt **interloper** intruder
interlude intermission
interminable unending
internecine mutually destructive
interpolate insert

interpose insert
interregnum interval between two successive reigns
interrogate question
intersperse scatter
interstate between states
intervene interfere, mediate
intestate leaving no will

intimate allude to
intractable unmanageable
intransigent unyielding
intrepid fearless
intricate complex
intrigue plot, mystery
intrinsic inherent
introspection self-analysis
inundate flood
inure accustom, habituate, harden
invalidate disprove
invective verbal insult
inveigh to rail against
inveigle lure
inventive cleaver, resourceful
inverse directly opposite
inveterate habitual, chronic
invidious incurring ill-will
invincible cannot be defeated
inviolate sacred
invocation calling on God
irascible irritable
irate angry
ironic oddly contrary to what is expected
irrational illogical
irrelevant unrelated, immaterial
irreparable cannot be repaired
irresolute hesitant, uncertain
irrevocable cannot be rescinded
isosceles having two equal sides
itinerant wandering
itinerary route

J

jabberwocky nonsense
jaded spent, bored with one's situation
jargon specialized vocabulary
jaundiced biased, embittered
jeer mock
jejune barren
jest joke
jilt reject
jingoistic nationalistic, warmongering
jocular humorous
jostle push, brush against
journeyman reliable worker
joust combat between knights on horses

jubilant in high spirits
judicious prudent
juggernaut unstoppable force
jugular throat
juncture pivotal point in time
junoesque stately beauty
junta small ruling group
jurisdiction domain
jurisprudence law
justify excuse, mitigate
juvenescent making young
juxtapose to place side by side

K

kaleidoscope series of changing events
keen of sharp mind
ken purview, range of comprehension
kindle arouse, inspire
kindred similar
kinetic pertaining to motion
kismet fate
kite bad check
kitsch trashy art
kleptomania impulse to steal
knave con man
knead massage
knell sound of a bell
Koran holy book of Islam
kowtow behave obsequiously
kudos acclaim

L

labyrinth maze
lacerate tear, cut
lachrymose tearful
lackey servant
laconic brief, terse
lactic derived from milk
lacuna a missing part, gap
laggard loafer
lagniappe bonus
laity laymen
lambent softly radiant
lament mourn
lamina layer
lampoon satirize

languish weaken
lanyard short rope
larceny theft
largess generous donation
lascivious lustful
lassitude lethargy
latent potential
laudatory commendable
laurels fame
lave wash
lavish extravagant
lax loose, careless
laxity carelessness
layman nonprofessional
lectern reading desk
leery cautious
legacy bequest
legerdemain trickery
legible readable
legislate make laws
legitimate lawful
lenient forgiving
lethargic drowsy, sluggish
levee embankment, dam
leviathan a monster
levity frivolity
liable responsible
liaison relationship, affair
libertarian one who believes in complete freedom
libertine roué, rake
libidinous lustful
licentious lewd, immoral
lien financial claim
lieutenant one who acts in place of another
ligature bond
ligneous woodlike
Lilliputian very small
limerick poem
limn portray, describe
limpid transparent, clearly understood
linchpin something that is indispensable
lineage ancestry
linguistics study of language
liquidate eliminate
lissome agile, supple
listless lacking spirit or interest
litany list
lithe supple
litigate contest
litotes two negative statements that cancel to make a positive statement
liturgy ceremony
livid enraged
loath reluctant
loathe abhor
lofty high
logistics means of supplying troops
logo symbol
logy sluggish
loquacious talkative
lothario rake, womanizer
lout goon
lucid clearly understood
lucrative profitable
lucre money, profit
ludicrous absurd
lugubrious sad
luminous bright
lupine wolf-like
lure entice
lurid ghastly
luster gloss
luxuriant lush
lynch hang without trial

M

macabre gruesome
Machiavellian politically crafty, cunning
machination plot
macrobiosis longevity
macroscopic visibly large
maelstrom whirlpool
magisterial arbitrary, dictatorial
magnanimous generous, kindhearted
magnate a powerful, successful person
magnitude size
magnum opus masterpiece
maim injure
maladjusted disturbed
maladroit clumsy
malady illness
malaise uneasiness, weariness
malapropism comical misuse of a word
malcontent one who is forever dissatisfied
malediction curse

malefactor evildoer
malevolence bad intent, malice
malfeasance wrong doing

malice spite
malign defame
malignant virulent, pernicious

Quiz 10 (Matching)

Match each word in the first column with its definition in the second column.

1. LACHRYMOSE
2. LAGGARD
3. LASCIVIOUS
4. LEGERDEMAIN
5. LIBERTINE
6. LILLIPUTIAN
7. LOQUACIOUS
8. MACHIAVELLIAN
9. MAGISTERIAL
10. MALAPROPISM

A. trickery
B. roué
C. very small
D. tearful
E. loafer
F. lustful
G. talkative
H. comical misuse of a word
I. arbitrary, dictatorial
J. politically crafty, cunning

---

malinger shirk
malleable moldable, tractable
malodorous fetid
mammoth huge
manacle shackle
mandate command
mandatory obligatory
mandrill baboon
mania madness
manifest obvious, evident
manifesto proclamation
manifold multiple, diverse
manslaughter killing someone without malice
manumit set free
manuscript unpublished book
mar damage
marauder plunderer
marginal insignificant
marionette puppet
maroon abandon
marshal array, mobilize
martial warlike
martinet disciplinarian
martyr sacrifice, symbol
masochist one who enjoys pain
masticate chew
mastiff large dog
mastodon extinct elephant
maternal motherly
maternity motherhood
matriarch matron

matriculate enroll
matrix array
matutinal early
maudlin weepy, sentimental
maul rough up
mausoleum tomb
maverick a rebel
mawkish sickeningly sentimental
mayhem mutilation
mea culpa my fault
meager scanty
meander roam, ramble
median middle
mediocre average
medley mixture
megalith ancient stone monument
melancholy reflective, gloomy
melee riot
mellifluous sweet sounding
melodious melodic
memento souvenir
memoir autobiography
memorabilia things worth remembering
memorandum note
menagerie zoo
mendacity untruth
mendicant beggar
menial humble, degrading
mentor teacher
mercantile commercial
mercenary calculating, venal

mercurial changeable, volatile
metamorphosis a change in form
mete distribute
meteoric swift
meteorology science of weather
methodical systematic, careful
meticulous extremely careful, precise
metier occupation
metonymy the substitution of a phrase for the name itself
mettle courage, capacity for bravery
miasma toxin
mien appearance, bearing
migrate travel
milieu environment
militant combative
militate work against
milk extract
millennium thousand-year period
minatory threatening
mince chop, moderate
minion subordinate
minstrel troubadour
minuscule small
minute very small
minutiae trivia
mirage illusion
mire marsh
mirth jollity
misanthrope hater of mankind
misappropriation use dishonestly
misbegotten illegitimate
miscarry abort
miscegenation intermarriage between races
miscellany mixture of items
misconstrue misinterpret
miscreant evildoer
misgiving doubt
misnomer wrongly named
misogyny hatred of women
misshapen deformed
missive letter
mitigate lessen the severity
mnemonics that which aids the memory
mobilize assemble for action
mobocracy rule by mob
modicum pittance
modish chic

module unit
mogul powerful person
molest bother
mollify appease
molten melted
momentous of great importance
monocle eyeglass
monolithic large and uniform
monologue long speech
monstrosity distorted, abnormal form
moot disputable
moral ethical
morale spirit, confidence
morass swamp, difficult situation
moratorium postponement
mordant biting, sarcastic
mores moral standards
moribund near death
morose sullen
morphine painkilling drug
morsel bite, piece
mortify humiliate
mosque temple
mote speck
motif theme
motive reason
motley diverse
mottled spotted
motto slogan, saying
mountebank charlatan
mousy drab, colorless
muckraker reformer
muffle stifle, quiet
mulct defraud
multifarious diverse, many-sided
multitude throng
mundane ordinary
munificent generous
murmur mutter, mumble
muse ponder
muster to gather one's forces
mutability able to change
mute silent
mutilate maim
mutiny rebellion
mutter murmur, grumble
muzzle restrain
myopic narrow-minded

myriad innumerable
myrmidons loyal followers
mystique mystery, aura
mythical fictitious

N

nadir lowest point
narcissism self-love
narrate tell, recount
nascent incipient
natal related to birth
nativity the process of birth
naturalize grant citizenship
ne'er-do-well loafer, idler
nebulous indistinct
necromancy sorcery
nefarious evil
negate cancel
negligible insignificant
nemesis implacable foe
neologism newly coined expression
neonatal newborn
neophyte beginner
nepotism favoritism
nervy brash

nether under
nettle irritate
neurotic disturbed
neutralize offset, nullify
nexus link
nicety euphemism
niche nook
niggardly stingy
nimble spry
nirvana bliss
noctambulism sleepwalking
nocturnal pertaining to night
nocturne serenade
noisome harmful
nomad wanderer
nomenclature terminology
nominal slight, in name only
nominate propose
nominee candidate
nonchalant casual
noncommittal neutral, circumspect
nondescript lacking distinctive features
nonentity person of no significance
nonesuch paragon, one in a thousand
nonpareil unequaled, peerless

Quiz 11 (Matching)

Match each word in the first column with its definition in the second column.

1.	MISCELLANY	A.	peerless
2.	MISSIVE	B.	to gather one's forces
3.	MOOT	C.	newly coined expression
4.	MOUNTEBANK	D.	self-love
5.	MULTIFARIOUS	E.	loyal followers
6.	MUSTER	F.	letter
7.	MYRMIDONS	G.	diverse
8.	NARCISSISM	H.	charlatan
9.	NEOLOGISM	I.	disputable
10.	NONPAREIL	J.	mixture of items

---

nonpartisan neutral, uncommitted
nonplus confound
notable remarkable, noteworthy
noted famous
notorious wicked, widely known
nouveau riche newly rich
nova bright star

novel new, unique
novice beginner
noxious toxic
nuance shade, subtlety
nub crux
nubile marriageable
nugatory useless, worthless

nuisance annoyance
nullify void
nullity nothingness
numismatics coin collecting
nurture nourish, foster
nymph goddess

O

oaf awkward person
obdurate unyielding
obeisance homage, deference
obelisk tall column, monument
obese fat
obfuscate bewilder, muddle
obituary eulogy
objective (adj.) unbiased
objective (noun) goal
objectivity impartiality
oblation offering, sacrifice
obligatory required
oblige compel
obliging accommodating, considerate
oblique indirect
obliquity perversity
obliterate destroy
oblong elliptical, oval
obloquy slander
obscure vague, unclear
obsequious fawning, servile
obsequy funeral ceremony
observant watchful
obsolete outdated
obstinate stubborn
obstreperous noisy, unruly
obtain gain possession
obtrusive forward, meddlesome
obtuse stupid
obviate make unnecessary
Occident the West
occlude block
occult mystical
octogenarian person in her eighties
ocular optic, visual
ode poem
odious despicable
odoriferous pleasant odor
odyssey journey

offal inedible parts of a butchered animal
offertory church collection
officiate supervise
officious forward, obtrusive
offset counterbalance
ogle flirt
ogre monster, demon
oleaginous oily
oligarchy aristocracy
olio medley
ominous threatening
omnibus collection, compilation
omnipotent all-powerful
omniscient all-knowing
onerous burdensome
onslaught attack
ontology the study of the nature of existence
onus burden
opaque nontransparent
operative working
operetta musical comedy
opiate narcotic
opine think
opportune well-timed
oppress persecute
oppressive burdensome
opprobrious abusive, scornful
opprobrium disgrace
oppugn assail
opt decide, choose
optimum best condition
optional elective
opulence wealth
opus literary work or musical composition
oracle prophet
oration speech
orator speaker
orb sphere
orchestrate organize
ordain appoint
orderly neat
ordinance law
ordnance artillery
orient align
orison prayer
ornate lavishly decorated
ornithology study of birds
orthodox conventional

oscillate waver
ossify harden
ostensible apparent, seeming
ostentatious pretentious
ostracize ban
otherworldly spiritual
otiose idle
ouster ejection
outmoded out-of-date
outré eccentric
outset beginning
ovation applause
overrule disallow
overture advance, proposal
overweening arrogant, forward
overwhelm overpower
overwrought overworked, high-strung
ovum egg, cell

P

pachyderm elephant
pacifist one who opposes all violence
pacify appease
pact agreement
paean a song of praise
pagan heathen, ungodly
page attendant
pageant exhibition, show
pains labor
painstaking taking great care
palatial grand, splendid
palaver babble, nonsense
Paleolithic stone age
paleontologist one who studies fossils
pall to become dull or weary
palliate assuage
pallid pale, sallow
palpable touchable
palpitate beat, throb
palsy paralysis
paltry scarce
pan criticize
panacea cure-all
panache flamboyance
pandemic universal
pandemonium din, commotion
pander cater to people's baser instincts

panegyric praise
pang pain
panoply full suit of armor
panorama vista
pant gasp, puff
pantomime mime
pantry storeroom
papyrus paper
parable allegory
paradigm a model
paragon standard of excellence
parameter limit
paramount chief, foremost
paramour lover
paranoid obsessively suspicious, demented
paranormal supernatural
parapet rampart, defense
paraphernalia equipment
paraphrase restatement
parcel package
parchment paper
pare peel
parenthetical in parentheses
pariah outcast
parish fold, church
parity equality
parlance local speech
parlay increase
parley conference
parochial provincial
parody imitation, ridicule
parole release
paroxysm outburst, convulsion
parrot mimic
parry avert, ward off
parsimonious stingy
parson clergyman
partake share, receive
partial incomplete
partiality bias
parting farewell, severance
partisan supporter
partition division
parvenu newcomer, social climber
pasquinade satire
passé outmoded
passim here and there
pastel pale

pasteurize disinfect
pastoral rustic
patent obvious

paternal fatherly
pathetic pitiful
pathogen agent causing disease

Quiz 12 (Matching)

Match each word in the first column with its definition in the second column.

1.	ORDNANCE	A.	a model
2.	ORTHODOX	B.	local speech
3.	OUTMODED	C.	convulsion
4.	PALAVER	D.	stingy
5.	PANEGYRIC	E.	agent causing disease
6.	PARADIGM	F.	artillery
7.	PARLANCE	G.	conventional
8.	PAROXYSM	H.	out-of-date
9.	PARSIMONIOUS	I.	babble
10.	PATHOGEN	J.	praise

---

pathogenic causing disease
pathos emotion
patrician aristocrat
patrimony inheritance
patronize condescend
patronymic a name formed form the name of a father
patter walk lightly
paucity scarcity
paunch stomach
pauper poor person
pavilion tent
pawn (noun) tool, stooge
pawn (verb) pledge
pax peace
peaked wan, pale, haggard
peal reverberation, outburst
peccadillo a minor fault
peculate embezzle
peculiar unusual
peculiarity characteristic
pedagogical pertaining to teaching
pedagogue dull, formal teacher
pedant pedagogue
pedantic bookish
peddle sell
pedestrian common
pedigree genealogy
peerage aristocracy
peevish cranky
pejorative insulting

pell-mell in a confused manner
pellucid transparent
pen write
penance atonement
penchant inclination
pend depend, hang
pending not decided
penitent repentant
pensive sad
penurious stingy
penury poverty
peon common worker
per se in itself
perceptive discerning
percolate ooze, permeate
perdition damnation
peregrination wandering
peremptory dictatorial
perennial enduring, lasting
perfectionist purist, precisionist
perfidious treacherous (of a person)
perforate puncture
perforce by necessity
perfunctory careless
perigee point nearest to the earth
perilous dangerous
peripatetic walking about
periphery outer boundary
perish die
perishable decomposable
perjury lying

permeate spread throughout
permutation reordering
pernicious destructive
peroration conclusion
perpendicular at right angles
perpetrate commit
perpetual continuous
perpetuate cause to continue
perpetuity eternity
perplex puzzle, bewilder
perquisite reward, bonus
persecute harass
persevere persist, endure
persona social facade
personable charming
personage official, dignitary
personify embody, exemplify
personnel employees
perspicacious keen
perspicacity discernment, keenness
persuasive convincing
pert flippant, bold
pertain to relate
pertinacious persevering
pertinent relevant
perturbation agitation
peruse read carefully
pervade permeate
pessimist cynic
pestilence disease
petite small
petition request
petrify calcify, shock
petrology study of rocks
pettifogger unscrupulous lawyer
petty trivial
petulant irritable, peevish
phantasm apparition
phenomena unusual natural events
philanthropic charitable
philanthropist altruist
philatelist stamp collector
philippic invective
Philistine barbarian
philosophical contemplative
phlegmatic sluggish
phobia fear
phoenix rebirth

physic laxative, cathartic
physique frame, musculature
picaresque roguish, adventurous
picayune trifling
piecemeal one at a time
pied mottled, brindled
piety devoutness
pilfer steal
pillage plunder
pillory punish by ridicule
pine languish
pinnacle highest point
pious devout, holy
piquant tart-tasting, spicy
pique sting, arouse interest
piscine pertaining to fish
piteous sorrowful, pathetic
pithy concise
pitiable miserable, wretched
pittance alms, driblet
pittance trifle
pivotal crucial
pixilated eccentric, possessed
placard poster
placate appease
placid serene
plagiarize pirate, counterfeit
plaintive expressing sorrow
platitude trite remark
platonic nonsexual
plaudit acclaim
pleasantry banter, persiflage
plebeian common, vulgar
plebiscite referendum
plenary full
plentiful abundant
pleonasm redundancy, verbosity
plethora overabundance
pliable flexible
pliant supple, flexible
plight sad situation
plucky courageous
plumb measure
plummet fall
plutocrat wealthy person
plutonium radioactive material
poach steal
podgy fat

podium stand, rostrum
pogrom massacre, mass murder
poignant pungent, sharp
polemic a controversy
polity methods of government
poltroon dastard
polychromatic many-colored
polygamist one who has many wives
ponder muse, reflect
ponderous heavy, bulky
pontiff bishop
pontificate to speak at length
pootroon coward
porcine pig-like
porous permeable, spongy
porridge stew
portend signify, augur
portent omen
portly large
portmanteau suitcase
posit stipulate
posterior rear, subsequent
posterity future generations
posthaste hastily
posthumous after death
postulate supposition, premise
potent powerful
potentate sovereign, king
potion brew
potpourri medley
potter aimlessly busy
pragmatic practical
prate babble
prattle chatter
preamble introduction
precarious dangerous, risky
precedent an act that serves as an example
precept principle, law
precinct neighborhood
precipice cliff
precipitate cause
precipitous steep
précis summary
precise accurate, detailed
preclude prevent
precocious advanced
preconception prejudgment, prejudice
precursor forerunner

predacious plundering
predecessor one who proceeds
predestine foreordain
predicament quandary
predicate base
predilection inclination
predisposed inclined
preeminent supreme
preempt commandeer
preen groom
prefabricated ready-built
prefect magistrate
preference choice
preferment promotion
prelate primate, bishop
preliminary introductory
prelude introduction
premeditate plan in advance
premonition warning
prenatal before birth
preponderance predominance
prepossessing appealing, charming
preposterous ridiculous
prerequisite requirement
prerogative right, privilege
presage omen
prescribe urge
presentable acceptable, well-mannered
preside direct, chair
pressing urgent
prestidigitator magicians
prestige reputation, renown
presume deduce
presumptuous assuming
presuppose assume
pretense affectation, excuse
pretentious affected, inflated
preternatural abnormal, supernatural
pretext excuse
prevail triumph
prevailing common, current
prevalent widespread
prevaricate lie
prick puncture
priggish pedantic, affected
prim formal, prudish
primal first, beginning
primate head, master

primogeniture first-born child
primp groom
princely regal, generous
prismatic many-colored, sparkling
pristine pure, unspoiled
privation hardship

privy aware of private matters
probe examine
probity integrity
problematic uncertain
proboscis snout
procedure method

Quiz 13 (Matching)

Match each word in the first column with its definition in the second column.

1. PHOENIX
2. PILLORY
3. PITTANCE
4. PLAUDIT
5. PLETHORA
6. POGROM
7. POSTHUMOUS
8. PRECIPICE
9. PREDILECTION
10. PREMONITION

A. cliff
B. inclination
C. warning
D. acclaim
E. overabundance
F. after death
G. massacre
H. rebirth
I. punish by ridicule
J. trifle

---

proceeds profit
proclaim announce
proclivity inclination
procreate beget
proctor supervise
procure acquire
procurer pander
prod urge
prodigal wasteful
prodigious marvelous, enormous
prodigy a person with extraordinary ability or talent
profane blasphemous
profess affirm
proffer bring forward
proficient skillful
profiteer extortionist
profligate licentious, prodigal
profound deep, knowledgeable
profusion overabundance
progenitor ancestor
progeny children
prognosis forecast
prognosticate foretell
progressive advancing, liberal
proletariat working class
proliferate increase rapidly
prolific fruitful, productive

prolix long-winded
prologue introduction
prolong lengthen in time
promenade stroll, parade
promethean inspirational
promiscuous sexually indiscreet
promontory headland, cape
prompt induce
prompter reminder
promulgate publish, disseminate
prone inclined, predisposed
propaganda publicity
propellant rocket fuel
propensity inclination
prophet prognosticator
prophylactic preventive
propinquity nearness
propitiate satisfy
propitious auspicious, favorable
proponent supporter, advocate
proportionate commensurate
proposition offer, proposal
propound propose
proprietor manager, owner
propriety decorum
prosaic uninspired, flat
proscenium platform, rostrum
proscribe prohibit

proselytize recruit, convert
prosody study of poetic structure
prospective expected, imminent
prospectus brochure
prostrate supine
protagonist main character in a story
protean changing readily
protégé ward, pupil
protocol code of diplomatic etiquette
proton particle
protract prolong
protuberance bulge
provender food
proverb maxim
proverbial well-known
providence foresight, divine protection
provident having foresight, thrifty
providential fortunate
province bailiwick, district
provincial intolerant, insular
provisional temporary
proviso stipulation
provisory conditional
provocation incitement
provocative titillating
provoke incite
prowess strength, expertise
proximity nearness
proxy substitute, agent
prude puritan
prudence discretion
prudent cautious
prudish puritanical
prurient lewd
pseudo false
pseudonym alias
psychic pertaining the psyche or mind
psychopath madman
psychotic demented
puberty adolescence
puckish impish, mischievous
puerile childish
pugilism boxing
pugnacious combative
puissant strong
pulchritude beauty
pulp paste, mush
pulpit platform, priesthood

pulsate throb
pulverize crush
pun wordplay
punctilious meticulous
pundit learned or politically astute person
pungent sharp smell or taste
punitive punishing
puny weak, small
purblind obtuse, stupid
purgative cathartic, cleansing
purgatory limbo, netherworld
purge cleanse, remove
puritanical prim
purlieus environs, surroundings
purloin steal
purport claim to be
purported rumored
purposeful determined
pursuant following, according
purvey deliver
purview range, understanding
pusillanimous cowardly
putative reputed
putrefy decay
putsch a sudden attempt to overthrow a government
pygmy dwarf
pyrotechnics fireworks
pyrrhic a battle won with unacceptable losses

Q

quack charlatan
quadrennial occurring every four years
quadrille square dance
quadruped four foot animal
quaff drink
quagmire difficult situation
quail shrink, cower
quaint old-fashioned
qualified limited
qualms misgivings
quandary dilemma
quantum quantity, particle
quarantine detention, confinement
quarry prey, game
quarter residence
quash put down, suppress

quasi seeming, almost
quaver tremble
quay wharf
queasy squeamish
queer odd
quell suppress, allay
quench extinguish, slake
querulous complaining
questionnaire interrogation
queue line
quibble bicker
quicken revive, hasten
quiddity essence
quiescent still, motionless
quietus a cessation of activity
quill feather, pen
quip joke
quirk eccentricity
quiver tremble
quixotic impractical, romantic
quizzical odd
quorum majority
quota a share or proportion
quotidian daily

R

rabble crowd
rabid mad, furious
racketeer gangster

raconteur story teller
radical revolutionary
raffish rowdy
rail rant, harangue
raiment clothing
rake womanizer
rally assemble
rambunctious boisterous
ramification consequence
rampage run amuck
rampant unbridled, raging
ramrod rod
rancid rotten
rancor resentment
randy vulgar
rankle cause bitterness, resentment
rant rage, scold
rapacious grasping, avaricious
rapidity speed
rapier sword
rapine plunder
rapport affinity, empathy
rapprochement reconciliation
rapture bliss
rash hasty, brash
rasp scrape
ratify approve
ration allowance, portion
rationale justification

Quiz 14 (Matching)

Match each word in the first column with its definition in the second column.

1. PROTEAN   A. bulge
2. PROTUBERANCE   B. changing readily
3. PROVISIONAL   C. steal
4. PUNDIT   D. majority
5. PURLOIN   E. temporary
6. PURPORT   F. a cessation of activity
7. QUAVER   G. line
8. QUEUE   H. tremble
9. QUIETUS   I. claim to be
10. QUORUM   J. politically astute person

---

ravage plunder
ravish captivate, charm

raze destroy
realm kingdom, domain

realpolitik cynical interpretation of politics
reap harvest
rebuff reject
rebuke criticize
rebus picture puzzle
rebuttal reply, counterargument
recalcitrant stubborn
recant retract
recapitulate restate, summarize
recede move back
receptacle container
receptive open to ideas
recidivism habitual criminal activity
recipient one who receives
reciprocal mutual, return in kind
recital performance
recitation recital, lesson
reclusive solitary
recoil flinch, retreat
recollect remember
recompense repay
reconcile adjust, balance
recondite mystical, profound
reconnaissance surveillance
reconnoiter to survey
recount recite
recoup recover
recourse appeal, resort
recreant cowardly
recrimination countercharge, retaliation
recruit draftee
rectify correct
recumbent reclining
recuperation recovery
recur repeat, revert
redeem buy back, justify
redeemer savior
redemption salvation
redolent fragrant
redoubt fort
redoubtable formidable, steadfast
redress restitution
redundant repetitious
reek smell
reel stagger
referendum vote
refined purified, cultured
reflux ebb

refraction bending, deflection
refractory obstinate
refrain abstain
refurbish remodel
refute disprove
regal royal
regale entertain
regalia emblems
regime a government
regiment infantry unit
regrettable lamentable
regurgitate vomit
rehash repeat
reign rule, influence
rein curb
reincarnation rebirth
reiterate repeat
rejoice celebrate
rejoinder answer, retort
rejuvenate make young again
relapse recurrence (of illness)
relegate assign to an inferior position
relent soften, yield
relentless unstoppable
relic antique
relinquish release
relish savor
remedial corrective
remiss negligent
remit forgive, send payment
remnant residue, fragment
remonstrance protest
remorse guilt
remuneration compensation
renaissance rebirth
renascent reborn
rend to tear apart
render deliver, provide
rendezvous a meeting
rendition version, interpretation
renege break a promise
renounce disown
renown fame
rent tear, rupture
reparation amends, atonement
repartee witty conversation
repatriate to send back to the native land
repellent causing aversion

repent atone for
repercussion consequence
repertoire stock of works
repine fret
replenish refill
replete complete
replica copy
replicate duplicate
repose rest
reprehensible blameworthy
repress suppress
reprieve temporary suspension
reprimand rebuke
reprisal retaliation
reprise repetition
reproach blame
reprobate miscreant
reprove rebuke
repudiate disavow
repugnant distasteful
repulse repel
repulsive repugnant
repute esteem
reputed supposed
requiem rest, a mass for the dead
requisite necessary
requisition order
requite to return in kind
rescind revoke
reserve self-control
reside dwell
residue remaining part
resigned accepting of a situation
resilience ability to recover from an illness
resolute determined
resolution determination
resolve determination
resonant reverberating
resort recourse
resound echo
resourceful inventive, skillful
respectively in order
respire breathe
respite rest
resplendent shining, splendid
restitution reparation, amends
restive nervous, uneasy
resurgence revival

resurrection rebirth
resuscitate revive
retain keep
retainer advance fee
retaliate revenge
retch vomit
reticent reserved
retiring modest, unassuming
retort quick reply
retrench cut back, economize
retribution reprisal
retrieve reclaim
retrograde regress
retrospective reminiscent
revamp recast
reveille bugle call
revel frolic, take joy in
revelry merrymaking
revenue income
revere honor
reverent respectful
reverie daydream
revert return
revile denounce, defame
revision new version
revive renew
revoke repeal
revulsion aversion
rhapsody ecstasy
rhetoric elocution, grandiloquence
rheumatism inflammation
ribald coarse, vulgar
rickety shaky, ramshackle
ricochet carom, rebound
rife widespread, abundant
riffraff dregs of society
rifle search through and steal
rift a split, an opening
righteous upright, moral
rigor harshness
rime crust
riposte counterthrust
risible laughable
risqué off-color, racy
rivet engross
robust vigorous
rogue scoundrel
roister bluster

romp frolic
roseate rosy, optimistic
roster list of people
rostrum podium
roué libertine
rouse awaken
rout vanquish

rubicund ruddy
ruck the common herd
rudiment beginning
rue regret
ruffian brutal person
ruminate ponder
rummage hunt

Quiz 15 (Matching)

Match each word in the first column with its definition in the second column.

1.	REGIME	A.	vulgar
2.	REJOINDER	B.	quick reply
3.	REMUNERATION	C.	uneasy
4.	RENDEZVOUS	D.	necessary
5.	RENT	E.	miscreant
6.	REPROBATE	F.	rupture
7.	REQUISITE	G.	a meeting
8.	RESTIVE	H.	compensation
9.	RETRIBUTION	I.	retort
10.	RIBALD	J.	a government

---

runel stream
ruse trick
rustic rural

S

Sabbath day of rest
sabbatical vacation
saber sword
sabotage treason, destruction
saccharine sugary, overly sweet tone
sacerdotal priestly
sack pillage
sacrament rite
sacred cow idol, taboo
sacrilege blasphemy
sacrosanct sacred
saddle encumber
sadist one who takes pleasure in hurting others
safari expedition
saga story
sagacious wise
sage wise person
salacious licentious
salient prominent
saline salty

sallow sickly complected
sally sortie, attack
salutary good, wholesome
salutation salute, greeting
salvation redemption
salve medicinal ointment
salvo volley, gunfire
sanctify consecrate
sanctimonious self-righteous
sanction approval
sanctuary refuge
sang-froid coolness under fire
sanguinary gory, murderous
sanguine cheerful
sans without
sapid interesting
sapient wise
sarcophagus stone coffin
sardonic scornful
sartorial pertaining to clothes
satanic pertaining to the Devil
satchel bag
sate satisfy fully
satiate satisfy fully
satire ridicule
saturate soak
saturnine gloomy

satyr demigod, goat-man
saunter stroll
savanna grassland
savant scholar
savoir-faire tact, polish
savor enjoy
savory appetizing
savvy perceptive
scabrous difficult
scant inadequate, meager
scapegoat one who takes blame for others
scarify criticize
scathe injure, denounce
scepter a rod, staff
scheme plot
schism rift
scintilla speck
scintillate sparkle
scion offspring
scoff jeer
scone biscuit
scorn disdain, reject
scoundrel unprincipled person
scour clean
scourge affliction
scruples misgivings
scrupulous principled, fastidious
scrutinize examine closely
scurf dandruff
scurrilous abusive, insulting
scurry move quickly
scuttle to sink (a ship)
scythe long, curved blade
sear burn
sebaceous like fat
secede withdraw
secluded remote, isolated
seclusion solitude
sectarian denominational
secular worldly, nonreligious
secure make safe
sedation state of calm
sedentary stationary, inactive
sedition treason
seduce lure
sedulous diligent
seedy rundown, ramshackle
seemly proper, attractive

seethe fume, resent
seismic pertaining to earthquakes
seismology study of earthquakes
self-effacing modest
semantics study of word meanings
semblance likeness
seminal fundamental
semper fidelis always loyal
senescence old age
senescent aging
seniority privilege due to length of service
sensational outstanding
sensible wise
sensory relating to the senses
sensualist epicure
sensuous appealing to the senses
sententious concise
sentient conscious
sentinel watchman
sepulcher tomb
sequacious dependent
sequel continuation, epilogue
sequester segregate
seraphic angelic
serendipity making fortunate discoveries
serene peaceful
serpentine winding
serried saw-toothed
serum vaccine
servile slavish
servitude forced labor
sessile permanently attached
session meeting
settee seat, sofa
sever cut in two
severance division
shallot onion
sham pretense
shambles disorder
shard fragment
sheen luster
sheepish shy
shibboleth password
shirk evade (work)
sliver fragment
shoal reef
shoring supporting
shortcomings deficiencies

shrew virago
shrewd clever
shrill high-pitched
shun avoid
shunt turn aside
shyster unethical lawyer
sibilant a hissing sound
sibling brother or sister
sickle semicircular blade
sidereal pertaining to the stars
sidle move sideways
siege blockade
sierra mountain range
sieve strainer
signatory signer
signet a seal
silhouette outline
silo storage tower
simian monkey
simile figure of speech
simper smile, smirk
simulacrum likeness
sinecure position with little responsibility
sinewy fibrous, stringy
singe burn just the surface of something
singly one by one
singular unique
sinister evil
sinistral left-handed
siphon extract
sire forefather, to beget

siren temptress
site location
skeptical doubtful
skinflint miser
skirmish a small battle
skittish excitable
skulk sneak about
skullduggery trickery
slake quench
slander defame
slate list of candidate
slaver drivel, fawn
slay kill
sleight dexterity
slew an abundance
slither slide
slogan motto
sloth laziness
slovenly sloppy
smattering superficial knowledge
smelt refine metal
smirk smug look
smite strike, afflict
smock apron
snare trap
snide sarcastic
snippet morsel
snivel whine
snub ignore
snuff extinguish
sobriety composed

Quiz 16 (Matching)

Match each word in the first column with its definition in the second column.

1.	SCRUPLES	A.	figure of speech
2.	SCYTHE	B.	proper, attractive
3.	SEEMLY	C.	long, curved blade
4.	SENTENTIOUS	D.	left-handed
5.	SERENDIPITY	E.	pertaining to the stars
6.	SHIBBOLETH	F.	signer
7.	SIDEREAL	G.	making fortunate discoveries
8.	SIGNATORY	H.	password
9.	SIMILE	I.	misgivings
10.	SINISTRAL	J.	concise

---

sobriquet nickname
socialite one who is prominent in society
sociology study of society

sodality companionship
sodden soaked
sojourn trip

solace consolation
solder fuse, weld
solecism ungrammatical construction
solemn serious, somber
solemnity seriousness
solicit request
solicitous considerate, concerned
soliloquy monologue
solstice furthest point
soluble dissolvable
solvent financially sound
somatic pertaining to the body
somber gloomy
somnambulist sleepwalker
somnolent sleepy
sonnet poem
sonorous resonant, majestic
sop morsel, compensation
sophistry specious reasoning
soporific sleep inducing
soprano high female voice
sordid foul, ignoble
sorority sisterhood
soubrette actress, ingenue
souse a drunk
sovereign monarch
spar fight
spasmodic intermittent
spate sudden outpouring
spawn produce
specimen sample
specious false but plausible
spectacle public display
spectral ghostly
spectrum range
speculate conjecture
speleologist one who studies caves
spew eject
spindle shaft
spindly tall and thin
spinster old maid
spire pinnacle
spirited lively
spirituous alcohol, intoxicating
spite malice, grudge
spittle spit
splay spread apart
spleen resentment, wrath

splenetic peevish
splurge indulge
spontaneous extemporaneous
sporadic occurring irregularly
sportive playful
spry nimble
spume foam
spurious false, counterfeit
spurn reject
squalid filthy
squall rain storm
squander waste
squelch crush, stifle
stagnant stale, motionless
staid demure, sedate
stalwart pillar, strong
stamina vigor, endurance
stanch loyal
stanchion prop
stanza division of a poem
stark desolate
startle surprise
stately impressive, noble
static inactive, immobile
statue regulation
staunch loyal
stave ward off
steadfast loyal
stealth secrecy, covertness
steeped soaked
stenography shorthand
stentorian loud
sterling high quality
stern strict
stevedore longshoreman
stifle suppress
stigma mark of disgrace
stiletto dagger
stilted formal, stiff
stimulate excite
stint limit, assignment
stipend payment
stipulate specify, arrange
stodgy stuffy, pompous
stoic indifferent to pain or pleasure
stoke prod, fuel
stole long scarf
stolid impassive

stout stocky
strait distress
stratagem trick
stratify form into layers
stratum layer
striate to stripe
stricture censure
strife conflict
striking impressive, attractive
stringent severe, strict
strive endeavor
studious diligent
stultify inhibit, enfeeble
stunted arrested development
stupefy deaden, dumfound
stupendous astounding
stupor lethargy
stylize formalize
stymie hinder, thwart
suave smooth
sub rosa in secret
subcutaneous beneath the skin
subdue conquer
subjugate suppress
sublet subcontract
sublimate to redirect forbidden impulses (usually sexual) into socially accepted activities
sublime lofty, excellent
sublunary earthly
submit yield
subordinate lower in rank
subsequent succeeding, following
subservient servile, submissive
subside diminish
subsidiary subordinate
subsidize financial assistance
substantiate verify
substantive substantial
subterfuge cunning, ruse
subterranean underground
subvert undermine
succor help, comfort
succulent juicy, delicious
succumb yield, submit
suffice adequate
suffrage vote
suffuse pervade, permeate
suggestive thought-provoking, risqué

sullen sulky, sour
sully stain
sultry sweltering
summon call for, arraign
sumptuous opulent, luscious
sunder split
sundry various
superb excellent
supercilious arrogant
supererogatory wanton, superfluous
superfluous overabundant
superimpose cover, place on top of
superintend supervise
superlative superior
supernumerary subordinate
supersede supplant
supervene ensue, follow
supervise oversee
supine lying on the back
supplant replace
supplication prayer
suppress subdue
surfeit overabundance
surly rude, crass
surmise to guess
surmount overcome
surname family name
surpass exceed, excel
surreal dreamlike
surreptitious secretive
surrogate substitute
surveillance close watch
susceptible vulnerable
suspend stop temporarily
sustenance food
susurrant whispering
suture surgical stitch
svelte slender
swank fashionable
swarthy dark (as in complexion)
swatch strip of fabric
sweltering hot
swivel a pivot
sybarite pleasure-seeker
sycophant flatterer, flunky
syllabicate divide into syllables
syllabus schedule
sylph a slim, graceful girl

sylvan rustic
symbiotic cooperative, working in close association
symmetry harmony, congruence
symposium panel (discussion)
symptomatic indicative

synagogue temple
syndicate cartel
syndrome set of symptoms
synod council
synopsis brief summary
synthesis combination

Quiz 17 (Matching)
Match each word in the first column with its definition in the second column.

1.	STAVE	A.	distress
2.	STEVEDORE	B.	diligent
3.	STRAIT	C.	ward off
4.	STUDIOUS	D.	longshoreman
5.	SUBJUGATE	E.	various
6.	SUBTERFUGE	F.	overabundant
7.	SUNDRY	G.	suppress
8.	SUPERFLUOUS	H.	cunning
9.	SUPINE	I.	dreamlike
10.	SURREAL	J.	lying on the back

systole heart contraction

T

tabernacle temple
table postpone
tableau scene, backdrop
taboo prohibition
tabulate arrange
tacit understood without being spoken
taciturn untalkative
tactful sensitive
tactics strategy
tactile tangible
taint pollute
talion punishment
tally count
talon claw
tandem two or more things together
tang strong taste
tangential peripheral
tangible touchable
tantalize tease
tantamount equivalent
taper candle
tariff tax on imported or exported goods
tarn small lake

tarnish taint
tarry linger
taurine bull-like
taut tight
tautological repetitious
tawdry gaudy
technology body of knowledge
tedious boring, tiring
teem swarm, abound
temerity boldness
temperate moderate
tempest storm
tempestuous agitated
tempo speed
temporal pertaining to time
tempt entice
tenable defensible, valid
tenacious persistent
tendentious biased
tenement decaying apartment building
tenet doctrine
tensile stretchable
tentative provisional
tenuous thin, insubstantial
tenure status given after a period of time
tepid lukewarm
terminal final
terminology nomenclature

ternary triple
terpsichorean related to dance
terrain the feature of land
terrapin turtle
terrestrial earthly
terse concise
testament covenant
testy petulant
tether tie down
theatrics histrionics
theologian one who studies religion
thesaurus book of synonyms
thesis proposition, topic
thespian actor
thews muscles
thorny difficult
thrall slave
threadbare tattered
thrive prosper
throes anguish
throng crowd
throttle choke

thwart to foil
tiara crown
tidings news, information
tiff fight
timbre tonal quality, resonance
timorous fearful, timid
tincture trace, vestige, tint
tinsel tawdriness
tirade scolding speech
titan accomplished person
titanic huge
titer laugh nervously
tithe donate one-tenth
titian auburn
titillate arouse
titular in name only, figurehead
toady fawner, sycophant
tocsin alarm bell, signal
toil drudgery
tome large book
tonal pertaining to sound
topography science of map making

Quiz 18 (Matching)

Match each word in the first column with its definition in the second column.

1. SWATCH   A. to foil
2. SYNOD   B. anguish
3. TACIT   C. concise
4. TALON   D. provisional
5. TAURINE   E. agitated
6. TEMPESTUOUS   F. bull-like
7. TENTATIVE   G. claw
8. TERSE   H. understood without being spoken
9. THROES   I. council
10. THWART   J. strip of fabric

torment harass
torpid lethargic, inactive
torrid scorching, passionate
torsion twisting
torus doughnut shaped object
totter stagger
touchstone standard
tousled disheveled
tout praise, brag
toxicologist one who studies poisons
tractable docile, manageable
traduce slander

tranquilize calm, anesthetize
transcribe write a copy
transfigure transform, exalt
transfix impale
transfuse insert, infuse
transgression trespass, offense
transient fleeting, temporary
transitory fleeting
translucent clear, lucid
transpire happen
transpose interchange
trauma injury

travail work, drudgery
traverse cross
travesty caricature, farce
treatise book, dissertation
trek journey
trenchant incisive, penetrating
trepidation fear
triad group of three
tribunal court
tributary river
trite commonplace, insincere
troglodyte cave dweller
trollop harlot
troublous disturbed
trounce thrash
troupe group of actors
truckle yield
truculent fierce, savage
trudge march, slog
truism self-evident truth
truncate shorten
truncheon club
tryst meeting, rendezvous
tumbler drinking glass
tumefy swell
tumult commotion
turbid muddy, clouded
turgid swollen
turpitude depravity
tussle fight
tussock cluster of glass
tutelage guardianship
twain two
twinge pain
tyrannical dictatorial
tyranny oppression
tyro beginner

U

ubiquitous omnipresent, pervasive
ulterior hidden, covert
ultimatum demand
ululate howl, wail
umbrage resentment
unabashed shameless, brazen
unabated ceaseless
unaffected natural, sincere
unanimity agreement
unassuming modest
unavailing useless, futile
unawares suddenly, unexpectedly
unbecoming unfitting
unbridled unrestrained
uncanny mysterious, inexplicable
unconscionable unscrupulous
uncouth uncultured, crude
unctuous insincere
undermine weaken
underpin support
underscore emphasize
understudy a stand-in
underworld criminal world
underwrite agree to finance, guarantee
undue unjust, excessive
undulate surge, fluctuate
unduly excessive
unequivocal unambiguous, categorical
unexceptionable beyond criticism
unfailing steadfast, unfaltering
unfathomable puzzling, incomprehensible
unflagging untiring, unrelenting
unflappable not easily upset
unfrock discharge
unfurl open up, spread out
ungainly awkward
uniformity sameness
unilateral action taken by only one party
unimpeachable exemplary
unison together
unkempt disheveled
unmitigated complete, harsh
unmoved firm, steadfast
unprecedented without previous occurrence
unremitting relentless
unsavory distasteful, offensive
unscathed unhurt
unseat displace
unseemly unbecoming, improper
unstinting generous
unsullied spotless
unsung neglected
untenable cannot be achieved
untoward perverse
unwarranted unjustified
unwieldy awkward

unwitting unintentional
upshot result
urbane refined, worldly
ursine bear-like
usurp seize, to appropriate
usury overcharge

utilitarian pragmatic
utopia paradise
utter complete
uxorious a doting husband

Quiz 19 (Matching)

Match each word in the first column with its definition in the second column.

1.	TIDINGS	A.	incisive
2.	TITER	B.	omnipresent
3.	TITULAR	C.	lethargic
4.	TORPID	D.	figurehead
5.	TRADUCE	E.	unrestrained
6.	TRENCHANT	F.	news
7.	UBIQUITOUS	G.	laugh nervously
8.	ULULATE	H.	ceaseless
9.	UNABATED	I.	wail
10.	UNBRIDLED	J.	slander

V

vacillate waver
vacuous inane
vagary whim
vain unsuccessful
vainglorious conceited
valediction farewell speech
valiant brave
validate affirm
valor bravery
vanguard leading position
vanquish conquer
vapid vacuous, insipid
variance discrepancy
vassal subject
vaunt brag
vehement adamant
venal mercenary, for the sake of money
vendetta grudge, feud
veneer false front, facade
venerable revered
venial excusable
venom poison, spite
venture risk, speculate
venturesome bold, risky
venue location

veracity truthfulness
veranda porch
verbatim word for word
verbose wordy
verdant green, lush
verdict decision
vernacular common speech
vertigo dizziness
vestige trace
veto reject
vex annoy
viable capable of surviving
viaduct waterway
viand food
vicious evil
vicissitude changing fortunes
victuals food
vie compete
vigil watch, sentry duty
vigilant on guard
vignette scene
vigor vitality
vilify defame
vindicate free from blame
vindictive revengeful
virile manly
virtuoso highly skilled artist
virulent deadly, poisonous

visage facial expression
viscid thick, gummy
visitation a formal visit
vital necessary
vitiate spoil, ruin
vitreous glassy

vitriolic scathing
vituperative abusive
vivacious lively
vivid lifelike, clear
vocation occupation

Quiz 20 (Matching)

Match each word in the first column with its definition in the second column.

1.	UNCOUTH	A.	disheveled
2.	UNDULY	B.	capable of surviving
3.	UNFLAGGING	C.	awkward
4.	UNKEMPT	D.	uncultured
5.	UNSTINTING	E.	truthfulness
6.	UNTENABLE	F.	whim
7.	UNWIELDY	G.	unrelenting
8.	VAGARY	H.	cannot be achieved
9.	VERACITY	I.	generous
10.	VIABLE	J.	excessive

vociferous adamant, clamoring
vogue fashion, chic
volant agile
volatile unstable
volition free will
voluble talkative
voluminous bulky, extensive
voracious hungry
votary fan, aficionado
vouchsafe confer, bestow
vulgarity obscenity
vulnerable susceptible
vulpine fox-like

W

wager bet
waggish playful
waive forego
wallow indulge
wan pale
wane dissipate, wither
want need, poverty
wanton lewd, abandoned
warrant justification
wary guarded
wastrel spendthrift

waylay ambush
wean remove from nursing, break a habit
weir dam
welter confusion, hodgepodge
wheedle coax
whet stimulate
whiffle vacillate
whimsical capricious
wield control
willful deliberate
wily shrewd
wince cringe
windfall bonus, boon
winnow separate
winsome charming
wistful yearning
wither shrivel
wizened shriveled
woe anguish
wont custom
woo court, seek favor
wraith ghost
wrath anger, fury
wreak inflict
wrest snatch
wretched miserable
writ summons
writhe contort

wry twisted

X

xenophillic attraction to strangers
xenophobia fear of foreigners
xylophone musical percussion instrument

Y

yarn story
yearn desire strongly

yen desire
yore long ago
young Turks reformers

Z

zeal earnestness, passion
zealot fanatic
zenith summit
zephyr gentle breeze

Answers to Quizzes

Quiz 1	Quiz 2	Quiz 3	Quiz 4	Quiz 5	Quiz 6	Quiz 7	Quiz 8	Quiz 9	Quiz 10
1. I	1. B	1. J	1. A	1. B	1. D	1. B	1. J	1. E	1. D
2. G	2. F	2. I	2. J	2. A	2. J	2. A	2. I	2. F	2. E
3. E	3. G	3. H	3. I	3. D	3. I	3. J	3. H	3. G	3. F
4. F	4. H	4. G	4. E	4. C	4. A	4. H	4. G	4. H	4. A
5. C	5. E	5. F	5. D	5. F	5. F	5. I	5. F	5. A	5. B
6. D	6. A	6. E	6. G	6. E	6. E	6. G	6. E	6. B	6. C
7. B	7. C	7. D	7. F	7. H	7. H	7. F	7. D	7. C	7. G
8. J	8. D	8. C	8. H	8. G	8. G	8. D	8. C	8. D	8. J
9. A	9. J	9. B	9. C	9. J	9. C	9. E	9. B	9. I	9. I
10. H	10. I	10. A	10. B	10. I	10. B	10. C	10. A	10. J	10. H

Quiz 11	Quiz 12	Quiz 13	Quiz 14	Quiz 15	Quiz 16	Quiz 17	Quiz 18	Quiz 19	Quiz 20
1. J	1. F	1. H	1. B	1. J	1. I	1. C	1. J	1. F	1. D
2. F	2. G	2. I	2. A	2. I	2. C	2. D	2. I	2. G	2. J
3. I	3. H	3. J	3. E	3. H	3. B	3. A	3. H	3. D	3. G
4. H	4. I	4. D	4. J	4. G	4. J	4. B	4. G	4. C	4. A
5. G	5. J	5. E	5. C	5. F	5. G	5. G	5. F	5. J	5. I
6. B	6. A	6. G	6. I	6. E	6. H	6. H	6. E	6. A	6. H
7. E	7. B	7. F	7. H	7. D	7. E	7. E	7. D	7. B	7. C
8. D	8. C	8. A	8. G	8. C	8. F	8. F	8. C	8. I	8. F
9. C	9. D	9. B	9. F	9. B	9. A	9. J	9. B	9. H	9. E
10. A	10. E	10. C	10. D	10. A	10. D	10. I	10. A	10. E	10. B

Practice Test

Time: 45 minutes for 75 questions.

Directions: Following are five passages with underlined portions. Alternate ways of stating the underlined portions come after the passages. Choose the best alternative; if the original is the best way of stating the underlined portion, choose NO CHANGE.

The test also has questions that refer to the passages or ask you to reorder the sentences within the passage. These questions are identified by a number in a box. Choose the best answer and shade in the corresponding oval on your answer sheet.

Passage 1:

Mind and Media: The Effects of Television, Video Games, and Computers - Patricia Marks Greenfield

[1]

If <u>dynamic visual graphics, sound effects, and, automatic scorekeeping</u> are the features that
₁
account for the popularity of video games (the <u>latter</u> being addictive in nature), why are parents
₂
so worried? <u>All seem quite innocent.</u> But another
₃
source of concern is that the games available in arcades have, almost without exception, themes of physical aggression. <u>There has long been</u> the
₄
belief that violent content may teach violent behavior. And yet again our society finds a new medium in which to present that <u>content, and yet</u>
₅
<u>again</u> the demand is nearly <u>insatiable could be</u>
₅   ₆
looked at as another instance where human history has repeated <u>it'self</u>. And there is evidence
₇
that violent video games breed violent behavior. [8]

[2]

The effects of video violence are less simple, however, than <u>it</u> at first appeared. The
₉
same group of researchers who found negative effects [from certain video games] <u>has more</u>
₁₀
<u>recently found</u> that two-player aggressive video
₁₀
games, whether cooperative or competitive, reduce the level of aggression in children's <u>play, that is surprising.</u>
₁₁

[3]

It may be that the most harmful aspect of the violent video games <u>are</u> that they are solitary
₁₂
in nature. A two-person aggressive game (video boxing, in this study) seems to provide <u>a cathartic</u>
₁₃
<u>or releasing effect</u> for aggression, while a solitary
₁₃
aggressive game (such as Space Invaders) may stimulate further aggression. <u>TV viewing typically</u>
₁₄
<u>involves little social interaction.</u> [15]
₁₄

1. A. NO CHANGE
   B. dynamic visual graphics, sound effects; and, automatic scorekeeping
   C. dynamic visual graphics, sound effects: and, automatic scorekeeping
   D. dynamic visual graphics, sound effects, and automatic scorekeeping

2. F. NO CHANGE
   G. last
   H. final
   J. latest

3. A. NO CHANGE
   B. All of these features seem quite innocent.
   C. All of those features seem quite innocent.
   D. All features seem quite innocent.

4. F. NO CHANGE
   G. There will long have been
   H. There could long have been
   J. There long is

5. A. NO CHANGE
   B. , and, yet again,
   C. and yet again
   D. , yet

6. F. NO CHANGE
   G. insatiable; could be
   H. insatiable, that could be
   J. insatiable, which could be

7. A. NO CHANGE
   B. itself
   C. it's self
   D. its self

8. Is it logical to omit the final sentence of paragraph one?
   F. Yes, because it restates information that has already been presented.
   G. Yes, because the conjunction *and* has been used to start too many sentence in the paragraph.
   H. No, because it sets up the topic for the next paragraph.
   J. No, because you should never delete anything from an essay, so that you never miss a point.

9. A. NO CHANGE
   B. he
   C. they
   D. them

10. F. NO CHANGE

    G. has, more recently found

    H. has been more recently finding

    J. have more recently found

11. A. NO CHANGE

    B. , which is surprising

    C. ; that is surprising

    D. . That is surprising.

12. F. NO CHANGE

    G. is

    H. will be

    J. OMIT UNDERLINED PORTION

13. A. NO CHANGE

    B. a cathartic, or releasing effect,

    C. a cathartic or releasing affect

    D. a cathartic, or releasing, effect

14. F. NO CHANGE

    G. TV viewing, typically, involves little social interaction.

    H. TV viewing involved little social interaction.

    J. OMIT UNDERLINED PORTION

15. According to the passage, which of the following would be likely to stimulate violent behavior in a child playing a video game?

    I. Watching the computer stage a battle between two opponents

    II. Controlling a character in battle against a computer

    III. Challenging another player to a battle in a non-cooperative two-person game

    A. II only

    B. III only

    C. I and II only

    D. II and III only

Passage 2:

The Technological Society - Jacques Ellul

[1]

The technical phenomenon, embracing all the separate techniques, forms a whole. Not only is it useless to look for differentiations (because they only exist secondarily), but it serves almost
<u>16</u>
no purpose. After the common features of the technical phenomenon are sharply drawn, then it
<u>17</u>
is easy to discern that which is the technical phenomenon and that which is not. And the common features draw themself. [19]
<u>18</u>

[2]

To analyze these common features is tricky, but it is simple to grasp them, just as there
<u>20</u>
are principles common to things as different as a wireless set and an internal-combustion engine, so to the organization of an office and the construction of an aircraft have certain identical features. That is the primary mark of that
<u>21</u>
thoroughgoing unity, it makes the technical
<u>22</u>
phenomenon a single essence despite the extreme diversity of its appearances. The
<u>23</u>
technical phenomenon is a single entity.
<u>23</u>

[3]

As a corollary, it is impossible to analyze this or that element out of it--a truth which is today
<u>24</u>
particularly misunderstood. The great tendency of
<u>25</u>
all persons who study techniques to make
<u>25</u>
distinctions. They distinguish between the
<u>25</u>
different elements of technique, maintaining some
<u>26</u>
and discarding others. They distinguish among
<u>26</u> <u>27</u>
technique and the use to which it is put. These distinctions are completely invalid and show only that he whose made them understood nothing of
<u>28</u>
the technical phenomenon. Its parts are ontologically tied together; being that, use is
<u>29</u>
inseparable from being. [30]

16. F. NO CHANGE
    G. , also it serves
    H. , but also it serves
    J. , but also looking serves

17. A. NO CHANGE
    B. ; it
    C. , it
    D. ; then,

18. F. NO CHANGE
    G. they
    H. themselves
    J. itself

19. The "technical phenomenon" referred to in the opening line can best be defined as

    A. all of the machinery in use today

    B. the abstract idea of the machine

    C. a way of thinking in modern society

    D. what all machines have in common

20. F. NO CHANGE

    G. them. Just

    H. them; just

    J. them just

21. A. NO CHANGE

    B. These distinctions are

    C. It is

    D. Which is

22. F. NO CHANGE

    G. unity that makes

    H. unity, which makes

    J. unity, so makes

23. A. NO CHANGE

    B. The technical phenomenon is not a single entity.

    C. The technical phenomenon is confusing.

    D. OMIT UNDERLINED PORTION

24. F. NO CHANGE

    G. it; a

    H. it, a truth

    J. it a truth

25. A. NO CHANGE

    B. The great tendency of all persons who study techniques is to make distinctions.

    C. The great tendency of all persons who study techniques are to make distinctions.

    D. OMIT UNDERLINED PORTION

26. F. NO CHANGE

    G. technique. Maintaining some and discarding others.

    H. technique...maintaining some and discarding others.

    J. technique; maintaining some and discarding others.

27. A. NO CHANGE

    B. over

    C. between

    D. against

28. F. NO CHANGE

    G. he who made those

    H. he whom had made them

    J. he who has made them

29. A. NO CHANGE
    B. in it,
    C. since,
    D. often,

30. The author wrote this essay for an assignment in which he had to describe a technical society. Did the author meet his assignment?

    F. Yes, because the technical phenomenon is about a technical society.
    G. Yes, because writing something with the word *technical* in it is better than writing nothing at all.
    H. No, because discussing the technical phenomenon does not describe the necessary elements of a technical society.
    J. No, because the essay makes no sense.

Passage 3:

A Shorter History of Science

- Sir William Cecil Dampier

[1]

As Xenophanes recognized as long ago as the sixth century before Christ, its certain that man makes gods in his. Being that the gods of Greek mythology first appear in the writings of Homer and Hesiod, and, from the character and actions of these picturesque and, for the most part, if you think about it, friendly beings, we get some idea of the men who made them and brought them to Greece. Homer is believed to have been a writer and poet.

[2]

But ritual is more fundamental than mythology, the reason because Greek ritual during recent years has shown that, beneath the belief or skepticism with which the Olympians were regarded, lie an older magic, with traditional rites for the promotion of fertility by the celebration of the annual cycle of life and death, and the propitiation of unfriendly ghosts, gods or a demon. Some such survivals were doubtless widespread, and, prolonged into classical times, probably made the substance of Eleusinian and Orphic mysteries, against this dark and dangerous background arose Olympic mythology on the one hand and early philosophy and science on the other.

[3]

In classical times the need of a creed higher than the Olympian was felt; therefore, Aeschylus, Sophocles and Plato evolved from the pleasant but crude polytheism the idea of a single, supreme and righteous Zeus. Having changed, the decay of Olympus led to a revival of old and the invasion of new magic cults among the people; while some philosophers were looking to a vision of the uniformity of nature under divine and universal law. Greece had been changed by the gods. [45]

31. A. NO CHANGE
    B. There is
    C. its'
    D. It is

32. F. NO CHANGE
    G. his own image
    H. their own image
    J. his own

33. A. NO CHANGE
    B. Since the gods
    C. The gods
    D. Because the gods

34. F. NO CHANGE
    G. if you thought about it,
    H. when you think about it,
    J. OMIT UNDERLINED PORTION

35. A. NO CHANGE
    B. Homer was believed to have been a writer and poet.
    C. Homer has been a writer and a poet.
    D. OMIT UNDERLINED PORTION

36. F. NO CHANGE
    G. mythology; the reason because Greek ritual
    H. mythology. Greek ritual
    J. mythology, the reason because, Greek ritual

37. A. NO CHANGE
    B. lay
    C. lies
    D. laid

38. F. NO CHANGE
    G. ghosts, gods, or a demon
    H. ghosts, a god or a demon
    J. ghosts, gods or demons

39. A. NO CHANGE
    B. mysteries: against
    C. mysteries. Against
    D. mysteries--against

40. F. NO CHANGE
    G. felt, therefore,
    H. felt. Therefore,
    J. OMIT UNDERLINED PORTION

41. A. NO CHANGE
    B. Being changed,
    C. To be changed,
    D. OMIT UNDERLINED PORTION

42. F. NO CHANGE
    G. people, while
    H. people: while
    J. people. While

43. A. NO CHANGE
    B. was looking
    C. are looking
    D. will be looking

44. F. NO CHANGE
    G. Greece will be changed by the gods.
    H. The gods changed Greece.
    J. The gods will be changed by Greece.

45. The main idea of the passage is that

   A. Olympic mythology evolved from ancient rituals and gave rise to early philosophy.

   B. early moves toward viewing nature as ordered by divine and universal law coincided with monotheistic impulses and the disintegration of classical mythology.

   C. early philosophy followed from classical mythology.

   D. the practice of science, i.e., empiricism, preceded scientific theory.

Passage 4:

Psychotherapy East and West - Alan W. Watts

[1]

The idea of stuff expresses no more than the experience of coming to a limit at which our senses or our instruments are not fine enough to make out the pattern. 46

[2]

Something of the same kind happens, when, the scientist investigates any unit or pattern
47
so distinct to the naked eye that it has been considered a separate entity. At that time then he
48
finds that the more carefully he observes and describes it, the more he is *also* describing the environment in which it moves and other patterns to which it seems inseparably related. As Teilhard de Chardin has so well expressed it; the isolation
49
of individual, atomic patterns "is merely an
50
intellectual dodge. 51
50

[3]

Although the ancient cultures of Asia never attained the rigorously exact physical
52
knowledge of the modern West, they grasped in principle many things which are only now occurring to us. There way of life, Hinduism and
53
Buddhism, are impossible to classify as religion,
54
philosophy, science, or even mythology, or again as an amalgamation of all four, because departmentalization is foreign to them even in so basic a form as the separation of the spiritual and the material, Buddhism is not a culture but a
55
critique of culture, an enduring nonviolent revolution, or "loyal opposition," to the culture with which it is involved. But this gives these ways of
56
liberation something, however, in common with
56
psychotherapy beyond the interest in changing states of consciousness. For the task of the psychotherapist is to bring about a reconciliation between individual feeling and social norms without sacrificing the integrity of the individual. He tries to help him to be himself and to go it
57
alone in the world (of social convention) but not of the world. And there lays the beauty of ancient
58
Asia. 59 60

46. Which sentence would make the topic idea of this paragraph clearer.

F. NO CHANGE

G. Stuff expresses the experience of coming to the limit at which our senses or instruments stop working.

H. The limit at which our senses or instruments become less effective is because of the idea of stuff.

J. The idea of stuff expresses the precipice at which our senses or instruments become inefficient at sensing a pattern.

47. A. NO CHANGE
    B. --when--
    C. . When,
    D. when

48. F. NO CHANGE
    G. At that time, then
    H. At that time; then
    J. OMIT UNDERLINED PORTION

49. A. NO CHANGE
    B. it, the
    C. it. The
    D. it, and the

50. F. NO CHANGE
    G. "'is merely an intellectual dodge.'"
    H. "is merely an intellectual dodge".
    J. 'is merely an intellectual dodge.'

51. For the sake of clarity, should the author provide a longer quote?
    A. Yes, because it is unclear whether the quote is about the isolation of an individual or atomic patterns.
    B. Yes, because only "is merely an intellectual dodge" is cutting the great Chardin short.
    C. No, because the quote is effective and concise as is.
    D. No, because long quotes are unnecessary.

52. F. NO CHANGE
    G. never attain
    H. never attains
    J. never attaining

53. A. NO CHANGE
    B. Their
    C. They're
    D. Theirs

54. F. NO CHANGE
    G. were
    H. to be
    J. is

55. A. NO CHANGE
    B. material; and Buddhism
    C. material. Buddhism
    D. material and Buddhism

56. F. NO CHANGE
    G. But this gives these ways of liberation something however
    H. But this gives these ways of liberation something
    J. But this however gives these ways of liberation something

57. A. NO CHANGE
    B. the individual
    C. her
    D. it

58. F. NO CHANGE
    G. have lain
    H. laid
    J. lies

59. For the sake of logic and coherence, where should the last sentence of the passage be placed?
    A. NO CHANGE
    B. paragraph 1, sentence 1
    C. paragraph 2, sentence 4
    D. paragraph 3, sentence 3

60. What does the passage suggest about the theme of the book from which it is excerpted?
    F. The book attempts to understand psychotherapy in the context of different and changing systems of thought.
    G. The book argues that psychotherapy unites elements of an exact science with elements of eastern philosophy.
    H. The book describes the origins of psychotherapy around the world.
    J. The book compares psychotherapy in the West and in the East.

Passage 5:

On Natural Death - Lewis Thomas

[1]

While an elm in our backyard caught the
<u>blight this summer and dropped stone dead,</u>
<u>leafless, almost overnight.</u> One weekend it was a
   61
normal-looking elm, <u>maybe a little bare in spots</u>
<u>but nothing alarming,</u> and the next weekend it
   62
was gone, passed over, departed, taken.

[2]

The dying of a field mouse, at the jaws of an amiable household cat, is a spectacle I have beheld many times. It used to make me wince. It wasn't <u>since</u> I thought about it that I was <u>lead</u> or
           63   64
came to believe that Nature was an abomination.

[3]

Recently I've done some thinking about that mouse<u>, however,</u> and I wonder if his dying is
                    65
necessarily all that different from the passing of our elm. The main difference, if there is one, would be in the matter of pain. <u>Pain hurts.</u> I do not
                                                        66
believe that an elm tree has pain receptors, and even so, the blight seems to me a relatively painless way to go. But the mouse dangling tail-down from the teeth of a gray cat is something else again, with pain beyond bearing, you'd think, all over his small body. There are now some plausible reasons for thinking it is not like that at all.

[4]

At the instant of being trapped and penetrated by teeth, peptide hormones are released by cells in the hypothalamus and the pituitary <u>gland; called endorphins, instantly these</u>
                      67
<u>substances are</u> attached to the surfaces of other
    67
cells responsible for pain perception; the <u>hormones has</u> the pharmacologic properties of
        68
opium; there is no pain. Thus <u>its</u> that the mouse
                                            69
seems always to dangle so languidly from the jaws, lies there so quietly when dropped, dies of his injuries without a struggle. If a mouse could shrug, he'd shrug....

[5]

<u>Affectively</u>, pain is useful for avoidance,
    70
for getting away when there's time to get <u>away,</u>
                                                            71
<u>when</u> it is end game, and no way back, pain is
    71
likely to be turned off, and the mechanisms for this are wonderfully precise and quick. If it were up to <u>Tom or I</u> to design an ecosystem in which
          72
creatures had to live off each other and in which dying was an indispensable part of living, I could not think of a better way to manage. 73

61. A. NO CHANGE
    B. Since an elm in our backyard caught the blight this summer and dropped stone dead, leafless, almost overnight.
    C. Until an elm in our backyard caught the blight this summer and dropped stone dead, leafless, almost overnight.
    D. An elm in our backyard caught the blight this summer and dropped stone dead, leafless, almost overnight.

62. F. NO CHANGE
    G. maybe a little bare in spots but nothing alarming.
    H. ; maybe a little bare in spots, but nothing alarming,
    J. OMIT UNDERLINED PORTION

63. A. NO CHANGE
    B. when
    C. until
    D. from

64. F. NO CHANGE
    G. led
    H. leads
    J. leading

65. A. NO CHANGE
    B. ; however,
    C. . However,
    D. however,

66. F. NO CHANGE
    G. Pain does not hurt.
    H. Pain hurts?
    J. OMIT UNDERLINED PORTION

67. A. NO CHANGE
    B. gland, called endorphins, instantly these substances are
    C. gland (called endorphins) instantly these substances are
    D. gland; instantly these substances, called endorphins, are

68. F. NO CHANGE
    G. hormones have
    H. hormone have
    J. hormones having

69. A. NO CHANGE
    B. its'
    C. it's
    D. OMIT UNDERLINED PORTION

70. F. NO CHANGE
    G. Being that
    H. In effect
    J. In affect

71. A. NO CHANGE
    B. away. When
    C. away, and when
    D. away, but

72. F. NO CHANGE
    G. I or Tom
    H. Tom and I
    J. Tom or me

73. Which one of the following would best characterize the author's attitude toward the relationship between pain and death?
    A. Dismay at the inherent cruelty of nature
    B. Amusement at the irony of the relationship between pain and death
    C. Admiration for the ways in which animal life functions in the ecosystem
    D. A desire to conduct experiments

Answers and Solutions

1. D	16. J	31. D	46. J	61. D
2. G	17. C	32. G	47. D	62. F
3. B	18. H	33. C	48. J	63. C
4. F	19. C	34. J	49. B	64. G
5. A	20. G	35. D	50. F	65. A
6. J	21. B	36. H	51. C	66. J
7. B	22. H	37. B	52. F	67. D
8. H	23. D	38. J	53. B	68. G
9. C	24. F	39. C	54. J	69. C
10. J	25. B	40. F	55. C	70. H
11. B	26. F	41. D	56. H	71. B
12. G	27. C	42. G	57. B	72. J
13. A	28. J	43. A	58. J	73. C
14. J	29. B	44. H	59. D	
15. C	30. H	45. B	60. F	

1. When separating a series of words, phrases, or verbs, placing a comma before the conjunction (*and, or, nor*) is optional; however, a comma should never be used after the conjunction. Choice (B) and (C) change the comma before the conjunction to a semi-colon and a colon, even though this is incorrect, but they do not remove the comma after the conjunction. The answer is (D).

2. The word *latter*, even though it appears in the middle of a parenthetic phrase, is referring to the series of nouns underlined in sentence one. And since it is referring to the last word in a series of three words, *latter* is incorrect. *Latter* distinguishes between two things; *last* refers to the final thing in a series of three or more. The answer is (G).

3. Although this sentence is not quite a fragment, the pronoun *all* makes it very unclear. What seems quite innocent? There's no way to know for sure, unless you reword the sentence. The passage is written in the present tense, so choice (C)'s past *those features* is incorrect. Choice (D) makes it unclear which features the sentence is referring to, so the answer is (B).

4. As mentioned earlier, the passage is written in the present tense, so the present perfect tense *there has long been* is correct. The answer is (F).

5. *Yet again* is a transitional word phrase, so this question is really about combining two independent clauses with a comma and the conjunction *and*. Choice (B) could technically be correct, but since the author chooses not to set off *yet again* with commas the first time he uses it, the latter part of the compound sentence should be parallel with the former. Choice (C) removes the punctuation and creates a run-on sentence, and choice (D) removes part of the meaning of the sentence. The underlined portion is correct as is. The answer is (A).

6. Here we have a dependent clause being joined to an independent clause without punctuation. Choice (G) is wrong because a dependent clause cannot be joined to an independent clause with only a semicolon. Choice (H)'s use of a comma and *that* creates a subordinating clause but with the wrong subordinating conjunction. Choice (J) correctly joins the dependent clause to the sentence with a comma and the word *which*, creating a correct subordinating clause. The answer is (J).

7. The underlined portion joins *it is* with *self* by adding an apostrophe, which is incorrect. The correct pronoun, used to restate the noun *history*, is *itself*. The answer is (B).

8. This question is one of those tricky rhetoric, or strategy, questions we talked about earlier. Before answering a question like this, always ask yourself, "What is the BEST answer." Many choices will seem correct, but only one will be the *right* answer. The sentence in question is talking about *evidence* of violent behavior; and, previously, the passage only spoke about the *belief* of violent behavior being connected with violent video games, so choice (F) is incorrect. While choice (G) is correct in a lot of ways, the sentence in question provides a smooth transition to the next paragraph. So a stylistic use of *and* at the beginning of a sentence should not be enough to cut the sentence entirely. Choice (J) is heresy, so the answer is (H).

9. Remember when we talked about pronouns? When we said that a pronoun must have the same number and gender of the noun or noun phrase it is replacing? The noun in this sentence is *effects*, and it is plural and neuter, so the pronoun must agree. *It* is singular, *he* is masculine, and *them* usually refers to the object

of a clause instead of the subject (and we're talking about the subject here). *They* is plural and properly refers to the plural subject *effects*. The answer is (C).

10. It doesn't matter whether the verb follows directly after the subject, comes before the subject, or is separated from its subject by an intervening phrase, the subject and verb must always agree in number and person. The subject is *researchers*, and the verb is *has found*. If we put the two together, *researchers has found,* they sound odd, don't they? We need a plural verb for the plural subject, and the only answer-choice that addresses this is (J). The answer is (J).

11. The underlined portion joins two independent clauses with a comma, which is called a comma splice - and it is incorrect. Choice (C) changes the comma to a semicolon, but that is also incorrect. Choice (D) might be right if it wasn't at the end of the paragraph, but leaving a sentence like that at the end of a paragraph is distracting and weird. The best thing to do here is to drop the relative pronoun *that*, which is causing all the problems, and add *which,* creating a subordinating clause. The answer is (B).

12. This question is another subject-verb agreement fiasco. Being right next to *games*, *are* sounds correct, but it is not in agreement with its actual subject *aspect*. Since *aspect* is singular, it requires a singular verb. The answer is (G).

13. If everything looks right with an underlined portion and, more importantly, sounds right, more often than not it is right and should not be changed. The majority of people taking the ACT speak English natively and, as such, should use their ears and their gut. Not everything is a trick question. The underlined portion is correct as is and should not be changed. The answer is (A).

14. The underlined portion has absolutely nothing to do with violent video games or anything that the passage is talking about. Choice (G) and (H) reword and re-punctuate the needless sentence, but it should just be removed. The answer is (J).

15. Item I, True: Stimulation would occur. This choice is qualitatively the same as passively watching violence on television. Item II, True: Stimulation would also occur. This is another example of solitary aggression (implied by the second sentence of the last paragraph). Item III, False: No stimulation would occur. Two-player aggressive games are "cathartic" (again the needed reference is the second sentence of the last paragraph). The answer is (C).

16. Earlier in this sentence we saw the notorious correlative conjunction *not only*, so the underlined portion is testing your parallel *not only ... but also* knowledge. Choice (G) replaces *but* with *also*, but that is incorrect; choice (H) correctly uses *but also*, but the sentence still reads a bit funny. Remember, you will always be looking for the BEST answer. Choice (J) correctly uses *not only ... but also* but also clarifies the pronoun *it* by restating what *it* is replacing: *looking*. The answer is (J).

17. Many questions, like the previous one, will not only be testing the underlined portion, but also the sentence as a whole. Since the word *after* appears at the beginning of this sentence, *then* is redundant and should be removed. And since the only answer-choice that correctly joins a dependent clause with an independent clause without the word *then* is (C), the answer is (C).

Practice Test Solutions

18. This sentence is awkward, and normally I would say that it should be deleted, but we are not given the option to delete it. *Features* is the subject, and it is plural, so it needs a plural pronoun to restate it later in the sentence. Choice (F) and (J) are singular, and choice (G) is in the subjunctive case and not the proper objective case. The answer is (H).

19. This question is pretty much a reading comprehension question, since the actual definition of the technical phenomenon is never stated in the passage. You must use all the information in the passage to choose the BEST answer. The answer is (C).

20. When reading certain underlined portions on the ACT, it is usually a good idea to read the sentence quietly out loud to yourself. Many readers are conditioned to ignore mistakes, even if they don't know it, and our brains like to subconsciously fix small mistakes without telling us. But what your eyes subconsciously skip over, your ears will almost always pick up. Remember, if it sounds wrong, it probably is. This question is a run-on sentence with a comma splice. Out of the answer-choices, choice (G) is the only one that correctly fixes the run-on by separating the two sentences with a period. The answer is (G).

21. Whenever you see the word *that* as the subject of a sentence, it should probably be replaced. Granted, sometimes sentences are so closely related that there is no doubt what *that* is referring to, but more often than not *that* is unclear. When sentences become unclear, complex, or just plain confusing, the best thing to do is to restate the subject. The answer is (B).

22. Here we have another run-on sentence. You can either separate the two independent clauses, or you can combine them. Choice (G) and (J) do not properly combine the two sentences, and since we are not given the option here to separate them, choice (H) is the only answer that properly combines both sentences with a comma and the subordinating conjunction *which*. The answer is (H).

23. In speech, many people restate a fact several times in succession, for fear that whoever is listening to them might have missed a point. In essay writing, however, this is taboo. The underlined portion is repeating, almost exactly, what was said in the previous sentence. This is redundant, and the sentence should be deleted. The answer is (D).

24. When faced with a question about a dash, it is often very difficult to know whether or not the mark was actually used correctly, because they are so commonly misused. In some writings, it would seem that the dash is the only mark of punctuation that the author knows, and in others, dashes are as alive and kicking as a T-rex. So all the dash confusion is understandable, but not on the ACT. In the context of this sentence, though, the dash is correct. And while a comma would have also been correct here, the use of a dash adds emphasis to the explanatory information that follows; thus, it is correct. The answer is (F).

25. Here is another example where reading quietly out loud could be helpful. While your eyes might fix the sentence fragment by adding the small verb it is missing, your ears would never let that happen, not without making you re-read the sentence. Choice (C) adds a verb, but it is plural when it should be singular. The answer is (B).

26. The underlined portion correctly separates the verbal phrase from the rest of the sentence. Choice (G) creates a sentence fragment, choice (H) misuses the ellipsis (although it has become, incorrectly, a one-size-fits-all mark of punctuation, judging from text messages and Facebook statuses), and choice (J) misuses the semi-colon. The answer is (F).

27. *Among* distinguishes between three or more things; *between* distinguishes between two. The answer is (C).

28. While you might think that this question is about the endless battle between *who* and *whom*, it is a trick question. *Whose* is simply being misused as *who's* or *who has*, so we need to replace it with the correct words. The answer is (J).

29. This question is a tough one. Anytime you see *being that* in a sentence, it is generally wrong. Choice (C) makes the following section a dependent clause, so it cannot be joined with a semi-colon. Choice (D) is not a proper transitional word, so it cannot be used as a conjunction. And since the underlined portion is incorrect, that leaves choice (B), which is also a funky transition, yet it is the best answer, after checking the other options. The answer is (B).

30. Because of question 19, we know that the technical phenomenon is a way of thinking in a modern society. The authors assignment was to describe a technical society; instead, he described the way of thinking in said society and not the society itself. So both "yes" answers, choice (F) and (G), are incorrect, and choice (J) doesn't address the question at all, so the answer is (H).

31. When you come across *its* or *it's* in a question, always check and make sure that it is being properly used. Here, *its* is meant to mean *it is*, so the answer is (D).

32. This is not only a case of an unclear pronoun, but also, according to the answer-choices, the object of the sentence has been completely left out. Choice (J) still begs the question, "His own what?," and choice (H) uses a plural pronoun for the singular subject *man*, so that leaves choice (G). The answer is (G).

33. As mentioned earlier, anytime you see the phrase *being that* in a sentence, it is probably wrong. In fact, it doesn't even make sense for the beginning of this sentence to be a modifier at all. Choice (B) and (D) cut *being that* but still make the first clause a modifier of nothing. This independent clause should stand on its own. The answer is (C).

34. This is a common mistake for essay writers because people so often talk this way, which means that a lot of people will see nothing wrong with the underlined portion. This section is direct input from the author in a historical essay about the Greek gods. First of all, if we were to keep the underlined portion, it should either be parenthetical or between dashes. But since this phrase is wordy and provides no useful information, it should be omitted. The answer is (J).

35. While this sentence is grammatically correct, it gives no new information and acts as a poor transitional sentence into the next paragraph. It should be omitted. The answer is (D).

36. *The reason because* is redundant and wordy. Choices (G) and (J) change the punctuation but not *the reason because*. When it comes down to it, sometimes it is better to start a new sentence than to try to connect several sentences together with redundant transitional phrases. The answer is (H).

37. The verb *lie* is in the present tense, but the sentence is talking about something in the past. Even the author is referring to the Olympians in the past tense. The past tense of *lie* is *lay*. The answer is (B).

38. When items in a series, that are similar in content or function, are listed together, all of the parts must share the same grammatical form. In other words, they must be parallel. This question is not about comma usage, so choice (G) and (H) are incorrect. The only answer-choice that fixes the parallelism between *ghosts*, *gods*, and *demons* is (J). The answer is (J).

39. This is another run-on sentence with another comma splice. The second clause is not a list, and it is not redefining the first clause, so the use of the colon in choice (B) is incorrect. The same goes for choice (D). Again, sometimes the best thing to do with run-on sentences is to separate them. The answer is (C).

40. This is the correct usage of a semi-colon and the transitional word *therefore*; therefore, the answer is (F).

41. If you're left wondering, "What changed?" after reading an introductory phrase declaring, "Having changed," this is probably a good sign that you have a misplaced modifier on your hands. Choices (B) and (C) rephrase the modifier, but they don't change the fact that it is in the wrong place. And since we don't have the option of moving it, it is best to omit it. The answer is (D).

42. The latter part of the underlined portion is a dependent clause because of the word *while*, so it cannot be joined to an independent clause with only a semi-colon. It is also not a list, nor does it redefine the former part of the underlined portion, so the use of the colon in choice (H) is incorrect. And since we are talking about a dependent clause, making it its own sentence, as in choice (J), is also incorrect. Remember, we connect dependent clauses to an independent clause with a comma. The answer is (G).

43. Just because a section is underlined on the ACT does not mean that it is incorrect. There are usually several NO CHANGE questions scattered throughout each passage. But beware of marking too many Fs or As. If your test is filled with those letters, chances are you've been tricked a few times into thinking something was correct when it was actually incorrect. This question, however, is correct as is. The answer is (A).

44. At first glance, there doesn't seem to be anything wrong with this underlined portion, but if you look at all the answer-choices, one by one, you should be able to notice a pattern. Although the wordings and meanings are all different, the underlined portion, choice (G), and choice (J) are all written in the passive voice. As we mentioned earlier - and as I'm sure your English teacher has mentioned a thousand times before as well - the passive voice should always be avoided. It's weak. Choice (H) is the only answer-choice that changes the construction of the sentence to the strong active voice. The answer is (H).

45. Most main idea questions are rather easy. This one is not—mainly, because the passage itself is not an easy read. To find the main idea of a passage, check the last sentence of the first paragraph; if it's not there, check the closing of the passage. Reviewing the last sentence of the first paragraph, we see that it hardly presents a statement, let alone the main idea. Turning to the line before the closing line of the passage, however, we find the key to this question. The passage describes a struggle for ascendancy amongst four opposing philosophies: magic and traditional rites vs. Olympic mythology vs. monotheism (Zeus) vs. early philosophy and science. The closing lines of the passage summarize this and add that Olympic mythology lost out to monotheism (Zeus), while magical cults enjoyed a revival and the germ of universal law was planted. The answer is (B).

46. It's not that the first paragraph is wrong, per se, only that the word choices, and the order of those words, makes the paragraph sound jumbled. Choices (G) and (H) do nothing to improve the clarity of the paragraph. Only choice (J) concisely and clearly explains the main idea of the paragraph. The answer is (J).

47. Since the word *when* is not an interjection or transitional word, it does not need to be set of by any punctuation marks. The answer is (D).

48. *At that time then* is redundant. A choice should be made between either *at that time* or *then*. But since we are not given the option to delete one or the other, it is best to omit the phrase all together. The answer is (J).

49. This is another case of joining a dependent clause to an independent clause with only a semi-colon. By this point in the test, we should know how to fix that. The answer is (B).

50. The underlined portion uses quotation marks correctly. All the other answer-choices misuse them. The answer is (F).

51. This might be a tricky question for you or it might not be, depending on the way you write essays. *Individual* and *atomic* are adjectives describing the noun *patterns*. And for a quote to be about an adjective is ridiculous; thus, choice (A) is incorrect. Also, the reader thinking that there isn't enough Chardin, which probably means that the reader is a big fan, should not affect whether or not the quote needs to be longer, so choice (B) is incorrect. Choice (C) is correct because choice (D) makes a nonsensical claim. The answer is (C).

52. *Never attained* is the correct verb tense. The answer is (F).

53. There, their, or they're. The *there* that is used here refers to a location and not people, so it is incorrect. Choice (C) means *there are,* and choice (D) is in the wrong tense. The answer is (B).

54. Subject-verb agreement should never be affected by intervening clauses like *Hinduism and Buddhism*. *Way of life* is the subject, and it is singular, so it needs a singular verb. The answer is (J).

55. This is a run-on sentence with a comma splice. We know how to fix those now, right? The best way to fix a run-on, especially if both sentences are long and have a lot of punctuation, is to separate them. The answer is (C).

56. *But* and *however* mean the same thing, so the underlined portion is redundant. We need to get rid of *but* or *however*, and the only answer-choice that does this is (H). The answer is (H).

57. This pronoun is very unclear. Is *he* trying to help *himself* be *himself*, or someone else be *himself*? *He* and *him* are more than likely replacing the subject and object from the previous sentence, *He* being the psychotherapist and *him* being *the individual*. The best answer-choice here is the one that restates the object from the previous sentence, for greater clarity. The answer is (B).

58. This is a question about the conjugation of *lay*, which is *lay, lie,* and *have lain. Laid* has no place here, so choice (H) is incorrect, and choice (F) and (G) are in the wrong tense. The answer is (J).

59. Where the sentence is placed now, it doesn't really make much sense. The best thing to do would be to look back over the passage and place the sentence where ancient Asia is being discussed. Since paragraph three is the only paragraph to talk about Asia, logic tells us that choice (D) is correct. The answer is (D).

60. (F): Yes, this is the most accurate inference from the passage. The passage discusses how the more carefully a scientist views and describes something the more he describes the environment in which it moves, and the passage traces similarities between psychotherapy and Eastern systems of (evolving) thought. (G): No, this is too narrow an interpretation of what the whole book would be doing. (H): No, too vague; the passage is too philosophical to be merely a history. (J): No, also too vague, meant to entrap those of you who relied on the title without thinking through the passage. The answer is (F).

61. Since the word *while* starts this sentence, making it a dependent clause, and since this dependent clause is not joined to an independent clause, this sentence is a fragment. Choices (B) and (C), with the words *since* and *until* starting them off, are also sentence fragments. Choice (D) fixes the problem by removing the subordinating conjunctions and prepositions. The answer is (D).

62. The underlined portion is a nonrestrictive phrase and is correctly set off with commas. The answer is (F).

63. *Since* is the wrong subordinating conjunction here and changes the meaning of the sentence. The only answer-choice that makes sense in the context of this sentence is (C). The answer is (C).

64. The *lead* being used here - pronounced LEED - is not the metal. It is the present tense of *led* and is commonly misused. *Lead* sounds right here only because many pronounce it like lead, the metal. The answer is (G).

65. *However* is a transitional word here, and it is correctly set off with commas. The answer is (A).

66. The realization, here, that pain hurts is something that everyone who is human knows very well. This small sentence serves as a distraction and ruins the flow of the essay. It should be omitted. The answer is (J).

67. *Called endorphins* is a nonrestrictive clause and not a transitional phrase or a conjunction, so as it follows directly after the semi-colon, it is a misplaced modifier. The only answer-choice that fixes the misplaced modifier's position is (D), so the answer is (D).

68. Here we have a plural subject and a singular verb. For subject-verb agreement, the verb must also be plural. Choice (H) makes the subject singular but the verb plural, and choice (J) creates a sentence fragment by adding the beginning of a verbal phrase. Choice (G) has both a plural subject and a plural verb. The answer is (G).

69. The *its* that is used here is the possessive form; what is needed is the contraction *it's,* meaning *it is.* Choice (C) has this. The answer is (C).

70. *Affectively* is an adverb and not a transitional word, and it also means influenced by or resulting from emotions, which I'm sure is not what the author is trying to mean here. *Being that* is almost always incorrect, so choice (G) is incorrect. And the prepositional phrase *in affect* does not exist, so the answer is (H).

71. Here we have yet another run-on sentence, joined by a comma splice, and the best thing to do is separate the two independent clauses. The answer is (B).

72. Tom and I, me and you, you and I - the proper way to say a compound subject mixed with a pronoun can get confusing. But, when trying to decide whether to use *me* or *I*, the best thing to do is drop the other part of the compound subject and see which pronoun works. If we were to drop *Tom* here, *I* makes no sense, so the answer is (J).

73. The author's attitude toward the relationship between pain and death evolves through three stages. First, he expresses revulsion at the relationship. This is indicated in the second paragraph by the words *wince* and *abomination*. Then in the third paragraph, he adopts a more analytical attitude and questions his previous judgment. This is indicated by the clause, *I wonder if his dying is necessarily all that different from the passing of our elm*. And in closing the paragraph, he seems resigned to the fact that the relationship is not all that bad. This is indicated by the sentence, *If a mouse could shrug, he'd shrug*. Finally, in the last paragraph, he comes to express admiration for the relationship between pain and death. This is indicated by the phrase *wonderfully precise and quick*, and it is made definite by the closing line, *If I had to design an ecosystem . . . in which dying was an indispensable part of living, I could not think of a better way to manage*. Thus, the answer is (C).

www.ingramcontent.com/pod-product-compliance
Lightning Source LLC
Chambersburg PA
CBHW080726230426
43665CB00020B/2632